An eminent philosopher here offers ranging essay on the roles of chance, choice, purpose, and necessity in human events. He traces the many changes these concepts have undergone, from the analyses of Hobbes and Spinoza, through the eighteenth, nineteenth, and early twentieth centuries.

Maurice Mandelbaum examines two contrary tendencies in the history of social theories. Some, he shows, have explained the character of institutions in terms of their individual purposes, whereas others have stressed relationships of necessity among a society's institutions. Mandelbaum discusses chance, choice, and necessity at length and reaches some provocative conclusions about the ways in which they are interwoven in human affairs.

"A substantial and pertinent treatment of a problem, or rather set of problems, that remains a constant in almost all social science and philosophy." — Robert Nisbet, American Enterprise Institute

# Purpose & Necessity in Social Theory

**By the same author**

*The Problem of Historical Knowledge: An Answer to Relativism*
*Philosophy, Science, and Sense Perception: Historical and Critical Studies*
*The Phenomenology of Moral Experience*
*History, Man, and Reason: A Study in Nineteenth-Century Thought*
*The Anatomy of Historical Knowledge*
*Philosophy, History, and the Sciences: Selected Critical Essays*

# Purpose

## AND

# Necessity

## IN

# Social Theory

Maurice Mandelbaum

THE JOHNS HOPKINS UNIVERSITY PRESS
Baltimore and London

The Johns Hopkins University Press
701 West 40th Street,
Baltimore, Maryland 21211
The Johns Hopkins Press Ltd., London

The paper used in this publication meets the minimum requirements of
American National Standard for Information Sciences—Permanence of
Paper for Printed Library Materials, ANSI Z39.48-1984.

Library of Congress Cataloging-in-Publication Data
Mandelbaum, Maurice, 1908–
    Purpose and necessity in social theory.
    Bibliography: p.
    Includes index.
    1. Social sciences—Philosophy.   2. Necessity
(Philosophy)   3. Chance.   4. Social choice.   5. Social
change. I. Title.
H61.M4227   1987        300′.1        86-46283
ISBN 0-8018-3470-8 (alk. paper)

**TO L.B.M.**
with love and gratitude

# Contents

# Preface

Originally, this book was intended to be more historically oriented than it has turned out to be. I had also intended to discuss more of the categories used in the social sciences than those with which I have here been directly concerned. I found, however, that in order to do so I would have had to forego critical discussions of how these categories have in fact been used, and it seemed to me more important to evaluate some of their uses than to introduce other topics or provide further examples.

Many of the controversies with which I have here dealt reappear in new guises in much recent social theorizing, but given the range and variety of these theories I could not deal fairly with them were I to refer to them merely in passing; I have therefore not extended my survey beyond the first decades of this century. I hope, nevertheless, that the reader will see the applicability of my discussions to more recent theoretical writings, and that this book may succeed in disentangling a few misapprehensions concerning the place of necessity, choice, and chance in history.

During my tenure as a Mellon Senior Fellow at the National Humanities Center in 1986 I was able to complete the text of this book, and I am grateful to the Center for its support. Owing to illness, I then had to rely on others for editorial help; Marjorie Close and the entire reference staff of the Baker Library of Dartmouth College provided essential help, as did Professor Michael Ermarth and my copy editor, Carolyn Moser. I am happy to acknowledge my great debt to each of them.

# PART ⇨ ONE

# Introduction

# 1 ⇨ The Analysis of Social Theories

For the purposes of this study, the term *social thought* is construed in a broad sense, but one that is by no means all-inclusive. It is limited by the fact that I am exclusively concerned with Western thought, and within Western thought I deal only with the modern period, which I arbitrarily assume to have been inaugurated by Hobbes. Even so, the materials relevant for such a study would seem to exceed manageable bounds. They include not only the writings of political philosophers and philosophers of history but also the works of those who laid the foundations for all of the specialties which we now classify among the social sciences. To analyze this range of materials in detail would, of course, be a hopeless task.

On the other hand, one can often quite clearly see that theories which arise in different fields of social inquiry may be based on common presuppositions, and even opposed theories within a given field may have some presuppositions in common. The task of analyzing social thought, as I conceive it, involves uncovering the presuppositions that are present in the approach which all social theorists, whatever their fields, bring to bear on the concrete materials with which they work. Thus, it is with the analysis of those presuppositions common to a wide variety of social theories, and not with the analyses of these theories themselves, that I am concerned.

It may, I think, be taken for granted that however restricted the scope of a social theorist's investigations may be, the task he originally sets himself and the methods he follows will reveal certain basic *theoretical* presuppositions. It is with them that I am concerned. To be sure, it has sometimes been claimed that the *normative* presuppositions which a thinker brings to his work are no less important for understanding that work than are his theoretical presuppositions. While I do not deny that this is often true, I doubt that such a claim is universally applicable. Furthermore, even when true, no matter how strongly a theorist may be motivated by normative beliefs, his theoretical presuppositions will constitute a significant aspect of his work. Of course, the work of every social theorist will be affected not only by his basic theoretical and normative presuppositions but also by a host of personal factors, such as his training, his relations to both his contemporaries and his predecessors, and the social or political experiences which he has undergone. I shall not be concerned with these more specific differences among different social theories, but only with some very basic presuppositions with respect to which these theories agree or disagree. Such presuppositions tend to fall into pairs of polar opposites. For the sake of convenience, I shall speak of such pairs as *categories. Purpose* and *necessity* are the categories with which this book as a whole is concerned. In the present chapter, however, I wish to single out another pair of categories which has special importance in all social theorizing and is also directly relevant to some of the problems we shall later encounter with respect to the roles played by purpose and by necessity in social change.

Currently, this first pair of categories is most often referred to in terms of an opposition between "methodological individualism" and "holism." This formulation, as I have elsewhere argued, is somewhat misleading, since not all who reject "methodological individualism" accept what is labeled as "holism."[1] A more accurate characterization of this pair of approaches would be to contrast those social theories which are based on *individualistic* presuppositions with those which adopt an *institutional* approach. This is the terminology I shall use. To be sure, any social theory has to include reference both to individuals and to institutions, and to the relations between them; nevertheless, some theories have attempted to understand social institutions in terms of the basic character and needs of individuals, whereas others have rejected this approach, attempting to understand the nature of a society through a direct examination of its institutions and their relationships to one another.

The opposition between individualistic and institutional approaches has been reflected in social thought in many indirect ways. For example, debates concerning the invariance or variability of standards of value have often been affected by it: those accepting an individualistic approach have usually tended to hold that at least some basic values are universal and invariant, whereas those emphasizing institutional approaches have usually held that all values are historically conditioned and vary over time. The contrast between individualistic and institutional approaches is also sometimes reflected in other ways—for example, in arguments concerning the roles of "nature" and "nurture" in forming the character of individuals. Important as such contrasting views have been in the history of social thought, there is a significant difference between them and the categories of individualism and institutionalism with which I am presently concerned. This difference lies in the fact that the opposition between individualism and institutionalism is a methodological issue, whatever its further implications may be; on the other hand, questions concerning nature versus nurture and questions concerning the variability of values are primarily substantive; as such, views concerning them have been subject to radical change as new information or beliefs have affected the debate.

When we later come to examine the opposition between the categories of purpose and necessity, we shall see that they, too, have involved substantive issues, rather than being primarily methodological; we shall therefore be forced to trace how their uses have varied. In this connection we shall see that in some of their forms purposiveness and necessity were not regarded as being in all ways opposed, and in such cases we shall have to disentangle their actual relationships. On the other hand, even though individualism and institutionalism have been interpreted in different ways at different times, the contrast between theories which are built on a conception of the nature of individuals and those which approach society in institutional terms has been a remarkably persistent phenomenon in the history of social thought. In fact, one might say that there has been a tendency for the balance between these approaches to shift first toward one side and then the other in pendulum-like fashion. This I regard as unfortunate, since neither approach, taken by itself, is adequate to deal with all of the types of problems with which any general social theory must be concerned.

I

At the beginning of the modern period the individualistic approach was dominant, and the manner in which it was applied to phenomena reflected the analytic method of the new science of mechanics. Complex social phenomena were assumed to be the results of the constant action of a set of simple underlying forces which governed the behavior of individuals. Late in the eighteenth century, when the balance shifted, it was held that social life could not be understood through postulates concerning a set of unchanging factors regarding the motivation of individuals, but must be approached in historical terms. That which was "historical" was identified with that which was concrete and actual in social life, varying according to time and place, with each society having its own characteristic nature and value. What was held to give each society its unique character, binding the lives of individuals into an organic whole, were the history and traditions of that society.[2]

The most characteristic and striking examples of a conflict between analytic models of explanation based on individualistic assumptions and an institutional emphasis on historical wholes is to be found in the development of modern political theory. In the seventeenth century, and through much of the eighteenth, no claim was made that analyses of the nature and basis of the state had any direct reference to actual, well-authenticated historical events. In fact, those who used the analytical approach attempted to look beyond the differences between societies, seeking to reveal characteristics which were both constant and universal. On the other hand, in the late eighteenth century, there was a self-conscious rebellion against this approach, and in its place there arose an institutional approach, claiming to be historical, which emphasized diversity in the character of different societies.

Those who had followed a nonhistorical approach, attempting to uncover the common features underlying all societies, might have proceeded in a number of different ways, but one obvious way—one that has had a persisting influence on all forms of social thought—was based on the presupposition that societies are to be regarded as aggregates of individual human beings who, knowingly or unknowingly, weave the fabric of social life through each individual's pursuit of his own good. Consequently, in such theories one finds that the explanations of social phenomena are formulated in psychological terms.

The political philosophy of Hobbes provides an unusually clear example of four basic presuppositions characteristic of such an approach. First, he believed that wholes are aggregates of self-existing parts, and that the behavior of a whole is determined by the behavior of its parts. Second, he applied this doctrine to society, viewing a society as composed of individuals whose natures were what they were independently of the society to which they belonged. Third, he regarded human nature as both uniform and constant, not varying from individual to individual, nor according to time or place. Fourth, he assumed that this common human nature was ultimately simple, with every action of every individual derived from a single basic motive, or from some few such motives, each of which was universally shared. These presuppositions were not peculiar to Hobbes, but were characteristic of the thought of most of the major political theorists during the succeeding hundred years; the same presuppositions provided the foundation upon which classical eighteenth-century economic theory rested. They came to be challenged in the late eighteenth and nineteenth centuries by various thinkers, such as Herder and Hegel, as well as Burke and de Maistre, who differed on many issues but each of whom rejected the previous view. Each denied that wholes are to be understood as aggregates of self-existing parts, that the character of individuals is independent of the societies to which they belong, and that all motivation can be reduced to a single universal principle, such as utility.

The rejection of a Hobbesian approach was part of a widespread rebellion against analytic modes of thought in all fields, and against the mechanical view of nature with which those modes of thought were associated. Analogies drawn from mechanics no longer furnished models for understanding how societies function; instead, social phenomena were more often described in terms of biological metaphors. This involved a radical transformation in social thought. The new view was diametrically opposed to a Hobbesian approach in claiming that within any genuine whole, such as a living organism, every part is what it is, and functions as it does, only because of the nature of the whole to which it belongs. When applied to social life this view undermined the conviction that an adequate social theory must have at its foundation an understanding of the individual; instead, it was held that individuals can be understood only when reference is made to the culture of the societies to which they belong and in whose life they share. Furthermore, each culture came to be viewed as if it itself were a living form, distinct from other cultures and variable over time; there could therefore be no constant and universal set of motives which would lead all individuals, everywhere, to pursue identical goals. In addition, a new view of the dominant forces in history became prominent. Instead of regarding cultural and social change as being due primarily to the initiative of particular individuals, or to advancing individual enlightenment, these theories viewed the spirit of a people, formed through a common language and customs and molded by a common historical tradition, as defining the strength of a culture and determining that which it achieved or failed to achieve.

Later, owing to intellectual changes taking place in a variety of fields, the contrast between individualistic and institutional approaches came to be formulated in other terms, and I shall shortly examine some of these later developments. First, however, I wish to show that both the individualistic and the institutional models, as originally formulated, were extremely vulnerable to criticism. I shall start with the difficulties to be found in the form of analysis which, for brevity's sake, I have identified with a Hobbesian approach.

In opposition to a Hobbesian approach, I shall contend that whatever may be true of other wholes, the elements which together form a society are not parts which are separable, even in principle. This is a point easily overlooked, since the existence of a society presupposes the existence and activities of the individuals living in that society, and since the life of an individual, once he or she has been born and has survived infancy, will in most cases continue independently of the life of any other specific individual. It is therefore tempting to treat these individuals as isolable units and to analyze the ways in which societies function by appealing to the ways in which individuals, taken singly, are expected to behave. Consequently, it has been widely assumed—and not only by Hobbes—that social phenomena are to be explained in terms of whatever psychological principles govern the actions of individuals. This type of position has a distinct appeal to what passes for a realistic, "commonsense" approach, since in explaining the nature and functioning of societies it does not postulate the existence of any such shadowy entities as the spirit of a people, nor treat institutions as entities as real as, or *more* real than, individuals.

There are, however, strong reasons for rejecting such a view, as I have elsewhere attempted to demonstrate.[3] In the present context I shall confine my formulation of this criticism to one point to which I have not previously called attention. It is simply this. To conceive of a society as a group of individuals would be misleading if one did not take into account the specific ways in which this group of individuals interact. Therefore, in identifying a society with the behavior of individuals, one should—at a minimum—hold that the society is characterized by the nature of the *interactions* among individuals in that society; one should not equate it with these individuals themselves. Yet, even this manner of speaking would be misleading if it were taken to mean that *all* of the interactions among individuals who live in a society constitute features which are to be attributed to that society. The error in doing so becomes evident as soon as one realizes that only certain shared patterns of interaction among individuals serve to define the features of a society, distinguishing it from other societies; many other interactions among individuals are simply the ways in which these particular individuals, given their individual temperaments, their personal histories, and the situations in which they find themselves, happen to respond to one another. In short, the characteristics on the basis of which societies are to be identified are various patterns of learned behavior to which persons occupying different positions in a society, and playing different roles in its activities, are expected to conform. It is these normative patterns themselves, and not the individuals who behave in accordance with them, that must be taken into account when one wishes to describe the nature of a society and what constitute its essential parts. However, those who have searched for what have been called "rock-bottom" explanation in the social sciences have held that it is only in terms of individual behavior that the nature and functioning of a society can be understood. In short, they mistakenly treat social organization as a by-product of individual behavior, not as a major determinant of it.

This introduces a second misleading aspect of a Hobbesian type of approach. It has been widely assumed, and not only by Hobbes (the name of Bentham springs to mind), that if social phenomena are to be explained in terms of individual behavior, the basis for such explanations is to be found in one or more universal and unchanging characteristics of human nature. That assumption has most often been challenged on the ground that there are no such characteristics, but my objections to it lie elsewhere. I reject it because any explanation of the nature and functioning of an actually existing society cannot be concerned solely with whatever characteristics may be common to all persons. Of themselves, such characteristics could not explain the very different forms of behavior expected of individuals living in different societies. Consider, for example, the problem of male and female roles. Although every society draws some distinction regarding the sorts of behavior that are to be expected of males and of females in different types of situation, just what forms of behavior are appropriate for each varies greatly from society to society. Given this variability, the existence of distinctions between male roles and female roles cannot be explained in terms of whatever particular traits might be common to all males or to all females; *a fortiori*, such distinctions could not be explained in terms of traits possessed by all human beings. Similarly, in every society different roles are assigned to the young and to their elders, but these roles vary from society to society, and no traits of either the young or the old can serve to define their roles in different societies. In short, because individual behavior is always influenced by the social structure in which it takes place, the actual behavior of individuals in different societies cannot be explained solely by a theory that appeals to what is universal in human nature. It is only on the basis of historical explanations, rather than relying on what is universal in human nature, that such differences can be explained. In this respect a historical approach is superior to the purely analytic approach with which we have so far been concerned.

To be sure, it is possible for a social theory to combine a historical with a psychological approach, as one can see in the case of several political theories which developed out of, or in connection with, eighteenth-century associationist psychologies. Hume, for example, criticized the ahistorical character of social contract theories; nevertheless, there were two respects in which his own explanation of the origin and basis of civil societies resembled the individualistic approach of such exponents of a purely analytic method as Hobbes and Spinoza. In the first place, like them, Hume appealed to psychological principles which he held to be universal and constant. In the second place, he—like his fellow associationists Hartley and Adam Smith—believed that the basic conditions of human existence were at all times fundamentally similar, and that the universal principles of human nature therefore always tended to produce similar social consequences. Thus, in spite of his rejection of the theory of a social contract, Hume did not abandon the prevailing assumption that all societies resemble one another with respect to their fundamental principles of organization.

Other associationists, however, broke that tradition, emphasizing the extent to which societies differ because of differences that had developed in their institutions. Helvétius was one primary source for this emphasis on historical diversity; he, like John Stuart Mill and the reformers Godwin and Owen, held that through the association of ideas, human nature itself was capable of taking on new characteristics: that it had done so in the past and could be made to do so in the future. Yet, this did not involve the rejection of an individualistic approach to social theory: associationists continued to insist that social phenomena are in all cases to be explained in terms of the underlying principles of individual psychology. Furthermore, even though they recognized that there is no one pattern of institutional organization to which all societies conform, they did not abandon the belief that there is a single normative standard, derived from what is universal in human nature, in terms of which all social goals are to be measured. Thus, even when they introduced a historical dimension into their theories, none of the associationist school broke with the main individualistic presuppositions of those who had previously followed an analytic approah.

In this respect, as in many others, Rousseau was a harbinger of change. Symptomatic of the shift that was about to take place was the contrast between his position and that to which Hume had subscribed. With respect to history Hume had confidently held that

> mankind are so much the same, in all times and places, that history informs us of nothing new or strange in this particular. Its chief use is only to discover the constant and universal principles of human nature by showing men in all varieties of circumstances and situations.[4]

Rousseau, on the other hand, had said that

> there is, from people to people, a prodigious diversity of morals, manners, temperaments, and characters. Man is one; I admit it! But man modified by religions, governments, laws, customs, prejudices, and climates becomes so different from himself that one ought not to seek among us for what is good for men in general, but only what is good for them in this time or that country.[5]

In spite of a challenge such as this to the ideal of normative constancy, and in spite of his doctrine's rejection of much of the individualism of earlier theories, Rousseau's approach in his *Social Contract* was not in the least historical. It was only after metaphors of growth and development, drawn from the organic world, began to dominate philosophic and social thought that all traces of the analytic approach were abandoned.

Because of the stress which came to be laid on organic analogies, each nation and period came to be viewed as a living whole, all aspects of which shared a common life. While Rousseau's vision of an ideal semipastoral society had this characteristic, he denied its presence in all other forms of social life. For Herder and Hegel, on the other hand, each nation or people had its own essential unity, which developed out of an indwelling principle and was capable of being understood only if one turned away from abstractions regarding what was true of all men and approached each culture in terms of its own traditions and values. This was not only the position of Herder and Hegel, but was equally true of the views of Burke and de Maistre.

While there was no unanimity among these late-eighteenth- and early-nineteenth-century thinkers with respect to the specific principles of interpretation to which they appealed, there was at least one element they had in common: their emphasis on the spirit of a people or of an age. This aspect of their thought was also shared by subsequent thinkers such as Savigny and Ranke, whose works had an even greater direct influence on political and social thought.

Although historical studies were enlarged by this new approach, and in general benefited from it, serious difficulties arose whenever the notion of the spirit of a people, or of an age, was used as a means of explaining the character of specific institutions. Even when it was interpreted in a merely descriptive manner, it was often misleading, since those who used it tended to assume that all the activities and institutions which effectively shape political and social life are informed by, and dominated by, a single principle or spirit. At the time, such a view was attractive because it was widely held that intellectual analysis threatens the destruction of all that is unique and valuable in human life. Nevertheless, some forms of analysis must be employed if a historian is to offer concrete descriptions of the society or period with which he is concerned. One cannot deal with the spirit of a people or of an age except through understanding the various activities, institutions, and works of art through which that spirit manifests itself. This descent into historical detail cannot be carried out by a simple act of intuition; it demands that what is taken as representative of the spirit be separated out from that which is less truly representative of it, and from that which has been left over from the past. Thus, even those who suppose that there is a dominant unity of spirit in a people, or in an age, cannot treat a culture as if it were a single indivisible whole.

Furthermore, anyone who holds that each people, or each great age, manifests its own unique spirit must be in a position to compare various cultures, showing in what ways their specific institutions and laws, their works of art, their philosophies and religions, differ, for it is in these forms of life that the so-called spirit of a people or of an age is expressed. In order to be in a position to make such comparisons, a historian must focus attention on first one and then another facet of the life of the societies with which he is concerned: it is not through a single, simple, intuitive act that the spirit of a people or of an age can be grasped and compared with the characters of other peoples and ages. Only an exaggerated rhetoric, brought about by a reaction against preceding modes of thought, had led these late-eighteenth- and nineteenth-century social theorists to suppose that every form of analysis must be avoided if an understanding of what is essential in history is to be attained.

Turning to Comte and Marx, we find that they were as anti-individualistic in their views of society as were Herder or Hegel, Burke or de Maistre. Furthermore, they too emphasized the underlying unity to be found in each society. However, what they attempted to do was to analyze societies in institutional terms, establishing universally applicable laws concerning the structure of societies and the causes of social change. In this, they differed completely from those who had held that the unity of social life springs from a common spirit which animates a people or an age.[6]

One reason why this difference has been overlooked has been that the most basic law to which Comte appealed was his law of three stages: namely, that all sciences and all societies undergo a necessary transition from a theological stage through a metaphysical stage, to emerge at a positive, scientific stage. Because of his emphasis on there being a law of development, Comte's position seemed to resemble Hegel's philosophy of history, according to which history unfolded in a necessary linear pattern, with each stage representing a higher and more self-conscious form of freedom in its inner life. Marx can also be interpreted in a similar manner, though he need not be. When so interpreted, what is emphasized is his summation of history as revealing a pattern of development in which a primitive form of communism is transformed in Asiatic society, passes through slave societies to feudal society, and then gives way to capitalism, which, in its advanced stages, will eventually be replaced by a free communist society. Whenever this aspect of Marx's views is emphasized, it would seem that the law through which he sought to explain society was a law of development: that he regarded the history of human society as a single whole which exemplified a pattern of necessary change. Yet it is possible to interpret Marx's theory in a fundamentally different way. According to that interpretation, what is basic in any society are the productive forces (roughly, the land, labor, and technology) underlying its total economic system, and its economic system provides a substructure that determines the nature of all other institutional factors present within the society. On this interpretation, Marx does not hold that history is to be viewed as unfolding according to a necessary law of development; on the contrary, he would be claiming that the great periods of human history developed as they did because of the operation of the particular economic forces which his analyses of economic processes had revealed. As to

Comte, while his general theory had placed primary emphasis on the law of three stages, he also analyzed the interrelationships among the institutions which were simultaneously present in a society: thus, he was by no means exclusively occupied with interpreting societies in terms of a single, unanalyzable law of directional change.

Basic to their attempts to establish a science of society, was both Comte's and Marx's assumption that what had occurred in the history of social life had occurred necessarily. Although, as we have noted, Hegel's position was radically different from theirs, he too viewed the historical process as governed by necessity. Because of this, critics have sometimes tended to underestimate the differences in their views, attributing to each of them the same doctrine of historical inevitability. However, the concept of necessity can be applied in different ways, and since it was also central in the thought of other nineteenth-century social theorists, such as Buckle, Taine, and Spencer, it will be important for what follows that we untangle some of the main ways in which that concept was used.

In this connection there are two distinctions which are crucial, and the first of them was already implicit in what has been said concerning the alternative interpretations which might be offered regarding Marx's view of history. On the first interpretation Marx held that there is a necessary law of development that defines the stages through which human history inevitably passes. Interpreting Marx in this way, one would say that he believed there to be an ultimate law of development concerning the stages of social change. Whether or not this is the most adequate way of interpreting Marx, it is assuredly the usual and most obvious way of interpreting Comte's historical sociology, and it is the way in which one must indubitably interpret Hegel's philosophy of history. On the other hand, according to the second interpretation of Marx, the element of necessity is present in history only because there are necessary connections among certain factors present in any social system: if the productive forces in society never changed, the society itself would not change in any of its important structural characteristics; or if changes in the productive forces occurred but did not occur in a uniform manner, the pattern of change in other institutions would also be non-uniform. It should then be obvious that the concept of "necessity," as used by Marx, would have different applications according to which of these two interpretations of his theory one adopts. On the first interpretation, the necessity obtains with respect to a sequence of stages through which the history of societies passes: it is a developmental necessity. On the second interpretation, what is regarded as necessary are the interrelationships among specific factors within a society: the changes in direction which the society as a whole undergoes will depend upon changes in the most fundamental of these causal factors. In that case, unlike the first case, the flow of social history would not inevitably move in any particular direction. Thus, it is possible to claim that there may be necessary connections in history without embracing a doctrine of historical inevitability. I shall return to this distinction, and its importance, in a later chapter.

The second point at which different applications of the concept of necessity has caused confusion in discussions of social theory relates to the problem of whether the actions of individuals are free or determined. I shall also discuss this problem in a subsequent chapter; at present I am concerned only to show that it has no direct relevance to the question of whether an individualistic or an institutional approach should be adopted in social theory. To be sure, it may at first glance seem that if one could attribute free will to individuals, this would undermine an institutional approach, and that is an argument that has sometimes been used. It is, however, an argument without merit, since even though it may be true that most institutionalists have been determinists insofar as the individual is concerned, there is nothing in an institutional approach which necessarily commits them to that position. This follows from the fact that if social organization and change are not to be explained in terms of the actions of individuals, it will be irrelevant whether those actions were freely chosen or determined. This fact is especially apparent in the thought of those institutionalists who emphasize historical inevitability. In Hegel, for example, it is "the cunning of Reason" which leads to the fact that men's passions achieve goals other than those which the individual envisions; this being the case, the outcome of an individual's actions would be the same regardless of what is responsible for his pursuit of whatever ends he in fact pursues. The same lack of linkage between these problems is evident in the thought of those who adopt an individualist position. While such a position would clearly be compatible with a belief in free will, one must recall that Hobbes, Spinoza, and Hume (all of whom were individualists in their social theory) were determinists with respect to the actions of individuals. Furthermore, one may note that an individualist who accepts determinism with respect to individual action, as did Hume, need not regard the historical process as determined. Bearing all these facts in mind, it is unfortunate that questions concerning necessity and freedom should so often have intruded into discussions as to whether an individualistic or an institutional approach should be adopted in the realm of social theory.

In most of the nineteenth century the dominant approach to social theory was institutional; only the utilitarians, continuing the associationist tradition, attempted to explain the characteristics of organized social life on the basis of psychology. While two new movements in the latter part of the century did much to revive an individualistic approach, they did so independently of, and largely in opposition to, the fundamental principles of the associationists. One of these movements seized upon the Darwinian theory and emphasized the instinctivist basis of human behavior, whereas the other represented the revival of an idealist conception of the nature of individuals. While these latter forms of individualism in social theory were in most respects antagonistic, their combined influence eventually helped to undermine the necessitarian forms of institutionalism which were then dominant.

Their success in doing so was by no means immediate. For example, Buckle in England and Taine in France had considerable influence through their attempts to analyze the causes which underlay the differences between societies. Furthermore, independently of evolutionary theory in biology, interest came to be focused on the evolution of social institutions. While such an approach had its roots in some earlier doctrines of progress, the attempt to trace evolutionary change in specific institutions, rather than to offer a general philosophy of history, was initiated by legal historians such as Maine, Bachofen, and McLennan, and was expanded in the theories of cultural evolution propounded by Tylor and Morgan, as well as in Spencer's sociology. Unlike Darwin, their contemporary, these men were not concerned to establish that there was a continuity between animal and human life with respect to bodily form and mental traits; rather, they directed their primary attention to the evolutionary development of such specifically human features of social life as religion, law, and systems of marriage and descent. While there was a tendency among them to look on social evolution as following a regular path of development, only Spencer attempted to explain this development in terms of a definite law governing all forms of change. The others— and most of their contemporaries—did not view human history as following a course defined by an underlying law of change; rather, they regarded it as expressive of the tendency of the human race to progress through growth in man's material culture, his skills, and his knowledge. Even though they stressed this growth in human accomplishments as the basis for what they regarded as the general course of history, these theories adopted an institutional rather than an individualistic approach, for it was on the basis of the cultural heritage of the race, and not in terms of the character and actions of individuals, that they explained social organization and change.

On the other hand, Darwin's approach to social theory was distinctly individualistic, not institutional. His view of animal behavior, with its emphasis on the role of instincts, deeply affected the way in which he interpreted human behavior: in *The Descent of Man* his account of social behavior was based on instincts which were present in both animals and men. With reference to this theory, it is to be noted that even though he often mentioned an instinct of self-preservation, the instincts to which he turned when explaining the basis of social life were what he termed "the social instincts." While he did not offer a list of such instincts, in the fourth chapter of the *Descent of Man* one finds mention of "parental and filial affection" and "love and sympathy for one's fellows," and even a tendency in man "to be a faithful to his comrades and obedient to the leader of his tribe." Darwin held that these social instincts were also present to some degree in animals, and accounted for their social behavior. But this by no means exhausts the characteristics, such as intelligence, tool-making ability, and the ability to communicate, which Darwin believed men had in common with animals: and these, too, were obviously relevant to the development of social life. What is important to note is that both these special abilities and the social instincts themselves were independent of the instinct of self-preservation in the individual. In fact, under some conditions, the social instincts which Darwin mentions may work against the preservation of the life of the individual. Unfortunately, Darwin himself did not face this fact, often listing the instinct of self-preservation along with other, more specialized instincts, and this helps explain why his account of social behavior could on the one hand lead to "social Darwinism," where self-preservation in the struggle for survival played a dominant role, and could at the same time lead Huxley and others to infer that the correct implication to be drawn from evolutionary theory was the need for cooperative social endeavors. Darwin's own view emphasized the utility of group cooperation for the survival of the species, and he was by no means a social Darwinist. In fact, it was the cruelty of the struggle for existence in nature that was one of the important reasons leading him to abandon his original theistic convictions.[7] Yet, regardless of whether his theory was applied in the form of social

Darwinism, or whether cooperation was stressed, its appeal to an instinctivist basis was no less clear an example of the individualistic approach to social theory than associationism had been. Where it differed from associationism was in abandoning hedonism as its basic explanatory concept, stressing instead the hormic side of human nature.

The psychologist who later developed the most explicit and comprehensive approach to social theory on the basis of instincts was William McDougall, whose *Introduction to Social Psychology*, published in 1908, rapidly went through many editions, the sixteenth being published in 1923. It was his intention to lay the foundation for a theory of social institutions in terms of a psychology that took the inherited instincts of the individual as the basis on which these institutions developed. In a less explicit and systematized manner Freud, too, appealed to the concept of instincts and biologically based needs in his explanation of individual behavior, and he, too, used this individualistic approach in an attempt to account for social phenomena. What was stressed in his theory, however, was the way in which human instincts are inhibited, diverted, distorted, and controlled under the circumstances surrounding the individual's development. When he later used his theory as a way of accounting for the manner in which civilization and religion developed, what he tended to stress was the effects they had on the individual's psyche. Comparing the theories of McDougall and Freud, one is struck by the fact that in spite of the very great differences between their accounts of the factors responsible for social life, they are similar in one important respect: neither directly addressed questions concerning the differences between different societies nor attempted to account for such differences. To be sure, McDougall did suggest (but only in passing) that there might be differences between different races with respect to the relative strengths of the same innate tendencies, and that these innate factors might also be favored or checked—though not altered—by the social circumstances obtaining at different stages of human culture. However, neither theory recognized that institutions are not based solely on how individuals naturally tend to behave, but are in large measure formed through circumstances and through heritages from the past.

In contradistinction to the orientation of these instinctivist types of social theorizing, another form of individualistic theory arose in the late nineteenth century. It had its roots in German idealism, and its position was developed in deliberate opposition to both associationism and a biologically based instinctivist psychology. Its view of the individual stressed the fact that man is a self-developing and self-transforming being, and that the conditions necessary for his development are his social relations with his fellows. It was because of such needs that human societies develop, and it is only through society that the purposes of the individual can be fulfilled. Later, we shall deal in some detail with this purposive theory; what is here important to note is the stress which it placed on the harmony between the individual and society. This was an important influence on the development of both social psychology and sociology in the ensuing period, and in that development any apparent opposition between individualistic and institutional approaches to social theory was presumably overcome.

At the same time there came to be growing interest in cultural anthropology as a special discipline and, through the influence of Franz Boas and others, attempts to explain society and culture in terms of inherited characteristics were severely challenged by establishing that the variations in culture could not be accounted for in terms of biological inheritance. Among other factors, Boas investigated changes in physical characteristics, particularly the cephalic index, of individual members of a family when that family moved from one cultural environment to another, and these studies—along with others concerned with so-called racial differences—had a considerable influence in undermining the emphasis which had been placed on the role of inherited traits in accounting for cultural differences. It was at approximately the same time that behaviorism challenged the existence of most supposed cases of instinctive behavior; instead, the concept of conditioning became a widely accepted way of explaining what previously had been held to be the inborn tendency for animals and for men to act in specific ways. The concept of conditioning, which had originally had a precise meaning, soon came to be used in a loose, extended sense, and "social conditioning" became a common way of accounting for a wide variety of forms of individual behavior. Thus, different patterns of action in different societies tended to be attributed to "social conditioning," and there the question of explanation frequently stopped. In fact, it soon became fairly common to reject the assumption that some characteristics of individuals were innate, whereas others were acquired. At this point, the hyphenated phrase "personality-and-culture" came to be widely used as a way of suggesting that psychological processes could not be considered apart from cultural phenomena, and that culture could not be considered except in terms of the behavior of individuals. This tendency to conflate individual and institutional phenomena was symbolized in, and greatly encouraged by, those who had coined a new collective term, "the behavioral sciences," which was to include all that had formerly been classified under psychology as well as what had been included in the social sciences. As of now, there seems to be no important tendency to reject the assumptions on which this movement rests: thus it might seem as if the controversy between individualism and institutionalism has been laid to rest.

## II

While it may be true that when we look at these positions as they have developed historically, there was no necessary reason for the controversy to have developed, yet it is by no means clear that we should be satisfied with hyphenating these approaches. In fact, it is always doubtful whether one can solve complex problems through applying only one set of concepts: in order to cut through a problem one needs more than a sharp blade—there is also needed something that will provide resistance to the blade. Therefore, in what follows I shall argue that while it is unsatisfactory to adopt either a purely individualistic or a purely institutional approach, it is equally unsatisfactory to break down the distinction between what can be explained in terms of psychological concepts and what must be explained with reference to the societal context in which individuals act. Instead of attempting to obliterate that distinction, I shall argue that it must be maintained whenever one attempts to explain what occurs in organized social life.

This is not to say that when one is attempting to explain the behavior of an *individual,* one should draw what might appear to be an analogous distinction, attempting to isolate what belongs to the individual because of his or her biological inheritance from whatever effects the culture of his society has had upon him. There can be no doubt that the genetic constitution of each individual does play an important role in what he can or cannot become, but his actual development is not to be explained through inherited factors alone. Throughout the course of any individual's development, what is inherited and what derives from the culture in which he lives are inextricably fused. This has been established in our society even with respect to the physical effects of socioeconomic factors insofar as they affect prenatal development. Furthermore, regardless of the society into which a child is born, as the process of enculturation proceeds it becomes more and more impossible to isolate any aspects of behavior which are wholly attributable to inherited factors, or to find traits which have developed independently of potentialities which have been inherited. Yet, this interpenetration of what is inherited and what is socially acquired should not be assumed to hold when what one is to explain does not refer to the behavior of specific individuals, but concerns the question of how one is to account for that which occurs in organized social life.

Of course, societies exist only when individuals exist, and what occurs in a society would not occur except for the activities of individuals who, at any time, participate in its life. Consequently, one could not explain what occurs in a society without reference to the activities of individuals. However, from what has been said concerning the interpenetration of inherited and socially acquired factors in an individual's life, the individuals to whom one must make reference when dealing with social institutions are individuals who have already been shaped by society: they are not to be considered as if they had been stripped of all the characteristics which they had acquired through the social life in which they have shared. Unfortunately, those individualistic social theorists who had been influenced by the model of analytic mechanics did not recognize this fact, but built their theories directly on traits which they assumed to be the fundamental, common characteristics of all people.

The holistic theorists who reacted against this individualistic approach did not for a moment deny that the existence of societies depends upon the existence and activities of individuals. What they stressed was the extent to which individuals depend upon the accumulation of culture in order for them to be what they in fact are: truly human beings. Yet, they tended to press the importance of cultural inheritance even further, holding that it represented a force of such power that no individual could successfully resist it or alter its course. Consequently, when explaining what occurred in history, they did not appeal to the goals and efforts of individuals, but to what continued to be vital in the traditions of a people and to what changes occurred in the institutions which were fundamental in a society's life. While this was the extreme toward which anti-individualistic theories tended to move, it was not entailed by the fact that individuals are dependent upon their societies. Consequently, there is no reason why it should not be possible to account for social organization and social change through a joint appeal to individual and institutional factors, and that is what I contend one must do.

There is one objection to such a claim that must immediately be

faced, for it has been raised in various forms by many different the-
oreticians of the social sciences. It consists in denying that institutions can be made to serve an explanatory function because they are
not "real" in the same sense as individuals are real. The crudest form
of this claim has stressed the fact that institutions, unlike individuals, cannot be pointed to, touched, or otherwise made manifest
to the senses, nor can instruments indicate their presence and measure their effects; therefore, they cannot be a subject for scientific
investigation.[8] Whatever may be the merits of a behavioristic approach to animal behavior, or even to some psychological investigations concerning humans, such an approach is irrelevant to the explanation of human actions in social situations. The explanation of
social action cannot avoid taking meanings and intentions into account, and neither meanings nor intentions are factors which are
directly manifest to the senses. In fact, strictly speaking, when we
encounter our neighbors, or our employers, what is "manifest to the
senses" does not reveal them as our neighbors or employers, and
therefore has no direct relation to why it is that we behave differently
toward them than we do to any chance passerby.

Not all social theorists who object to speaking of institutions as
"real" would subscribe to an unmitigated behaviorism. For example,
Melville Herskovits adopted a more moderate position when he held
that the notion of an institution was simply a heuristic concept,
permitting the investigator to refer in summary fashion to the ways
in which individuals who belong to a certain society behave toward
one another under particular circumstances.[9] Thus, while admitting
that "culture *can* be studied without taking human beings into account," and that "it is essential that the structure of a culture" be
understood first of all, if the reasons why a people behave as they do
are to be grasped,"[10] he nevertheless insisted that "when culture is
closely analyzed, we find but a series of patterned reactions that
characterize the behavior of *individuals* who constitute a given
group."[11] Consequently, although granting the usefulness, for the
purposes of study, of reifying such patterned reactions *as if* they had
objective existence, Herskovits insisted that in actuality they were
simply "the discrete experiences of individuals in a group at a certain
time."[12]

There are aspects of social life in which a position such as this
seems to be unexceptionable. For example, it probably presents no
difficulties with respect to a cultural phenomenon such as language:
one must understand a given language before understanding the utterances of a given speaker, yet the language itself is not an entity

different from the ways in which it is used by those speaking or writing it. Furthermore, noting the ways in which languages change, it is reasonable to think of a language as a phenomenon depending on a continuous chain whereby influences spread in a series of acts of communication and in which, therefore, only individuals are ultimately involved.[13] Nevertheless, as Herskovits would admit, although language—like all other aspects of culture—can be studied as a phenomenon produced by the action of individuals, it is not to be identified with the individuals upon whom its existence depends. The language an individual speaks, or the types of tools he uses, may be produced by him, but they are not literally parts of him; and the changes he undergoes and the changes they undergo do not follow parallel lines. The need to distinguish between individuals and such aspects of culture as language and tools is so obvious that it is not apt to be challenged; rather, it is apt to be overlooked. Nonetheless, it is important to focus attention on it in order to understand what falls within the purview of the social sciences and what does not. This, as I now wish to show, is relevant to understanding the place of psychology among other disciplines.

Psychology is often classed as one of the social sciences, but insofar as it is actually cross-cultural, seeking to explain various aspects of individual behavior which do not depend upon the society to which an individual belongs, its concern is with the individual, not with the culture which the activities of individuals produce. Nevertheless, since culture does depend upon the activities of individuals, whatever is relevant to explaining individual behavior has possible relevance for understanding culture. In some areas this connection is especially intimate; in others it is relatively remote. For example, psycholinguistics is a branch of psychology which is intimately connected with other areas of language study, and it is therefore easy to see why, when one chooses such an example, psychology should be regarded as if it were one of the social or behavioral sciences. On the other hand, if one considers the history of technology one finds that psychology has relatively little to contribute to understanding it, even though technological inventions and their uses depend upon the activities of individuals. The same is of course true with respect to the arts. Thus, we may say that psychology may sometimes make very important contributions to the study of culture, but sometimes it has relatively meager contributions to make. In neither case, however, should it be regarded as a social science, since its attention is always focused on individual behavior, whether that behavior is social or not.

On the other hand, insofar as a social scientist studies individual behavior, he or she does so not in order to explain that behavior itself, but in order to understand how it affects some feature or features of human societies. These features fall into two broad classes, which I find it important to distinguish, but which are not always distinguished.[14] On the one hand, there are features, such as language, which are most properly designated as belonging to the *culture* of a people; on the other hand, there are the *institutions* which structure a society, and which thereby serve to define the status and roles of different individuals within the society. That which belongs to culture is transmitted from person to person through processes such as imitation or example, and includes not only language and technology but also customary habits and systems of belief. In contrast to these and other features of the culture of a people, any society has an institutional organization which defines the specific relations in which various individuals stand with respect to one another. For example, every society has a kinship system, some form of organized economic life according to which what is produced is distributed, rules governing marriage, and an organization of authority regulating various aspects of communal life. These interlocking systems serve to define property relations, the roles of male and female, and the status of the young and their elders, and they also control the distribution of actual power in various spheres of communal life. These are merely some of the most obvious factors in the complex structure which is present in any society and which, unlike the elements of its culture, serve to limit and define the status which particular individuals come to occupy in that society. Obviously, some of the cultural aspects of a particular society will affect its institutions as well as being affected by them: for example, technology affects and is affected by economic activities, just as systems of belief affect and are affected by the locus of what is recognized as authority. The difference lies in the fact that the position of an individual in his society is defined in institutional and not cultural terms. For example, when a person's form of speech serves to identify him as belonging to a certain group within a society—for example, an ethnic or racial minority—it is not the language he has acquired but the place of that group in society that leads to granting or denying him particular privileges or powers. Similarly, dress and manners may identify persons as belonging to a certain class within a society, but it is not these aspects of culture but the status of that class within the institutional structure of the society that tends to bestow or deny privileges. As these illustrations suggest, not all cultural elements need be diffused in identical form throughout a particular society. At the same time, one must also note that many cultural elements—such as a language, a particular form of technology, or a system of beliefs—may spread beyond the boundaries of any one society, in some cases changing as they spread, yet in other cases—such as science and technology—remaining substantially unaltered. Thus, culture and society not only differ in character but are also not to be regarded as coterminous.

When this is recognized, it becomes clear that the nature of a society cannot be adequately analyzed, as Herskovits claimed, into a series of patterned reactions. What is missing in such a definition is the extent to which societies *regulate* individual behavior through institutions which prescribe the obligations, rights, and privileges of individuals who occupy different statuses and play different roles within the organized social group. In fact, when Herskovits turned his attention to "Social Organization: The Structure of Society," he spoke of institutions as determining the position of men and women in society, as "dictating the relationships between the sexes and providing for the continuation of the group," as well as providing "the mechanisms for regulating conduct" without which "the integration of the individual into society would not be possible."[15] Thus, institutions are not merely a series of patterned reactions which individuals have somehow acquired; rather, they play an active role in creating the groups whose behavior evince such patterns.

As Herskovits pointed out, earlier anthropologists had frequently interpreted institutions in this manner, that is, as entities which they treated as being "objectively real."[16] He, on the contrary, held that every aspect of a society's culture (including its institutional structures) "is a construct which describes the similar modes of conduct of those who make up a given society. . . . In the final analysis, behavior is always the behavior of individuals however it may lend itself to summary in generalized terms."[17] There are, however, several difficulties in this view, one of which I regard as insuperable. As is clear from the preceding quotation, Herskovits assumed that one knows what constitutes "a given society": he does not speak as if he regarded the notion of "*a* society" as a construct. Yet, as we have seen, cultural phenomena such as language, technology, and systems of belief need not be coterminus with a particular society, and if institutions exist only as patterns of individual behavior which are brought under a general concept by an anthropologist for his own heuristic purposes, they will not provide a basis for distinguishing one society from another. In short, there must be a system of authority regulating the behavior of a group of individuals if one is to speak of a society as one particular entity. If all social phenomena were simply the thought and actions of individuals, "a society" would be as much a construct on the part of the anthropologist as institutions are claimed to be.

Unlike Herskovits and many other recent anthropologists, even those sociologists who had been influenced by behaviorism, and by the views of science associated with the behavioristic movement in psychology, did not equate the structural aspects of society with the ways in which individuals actually behave. Instead of attending to what was directly descriptive of individual behavior, they focused attention on the general *patterning* of interpersonal relationships. This approach differed from the views of earlier sociologists, such as Comte and Durkheim, in being individualistic, regarding institutions as by-products of interpersonal relations; it differed also in not being concerned with the historical contexts in which particular forms of institutions develop. The task of sociology, as they conceived it, was to discover basic principles regarding the relational aspects of group activities. For example, by using broad concepts such as cooperation and conflict, or leadership, they believed it possible to generalize concerning group organization, regardless of whether such groups were small and informal, whether they were crowds, political parties, or religious institutions. A formal sociology of this type, based on analyses of interpersonal action, had first been advocated by Georg Simmel, using a Kantian distinction between form and content, but was later adapted to a positivistic philosophy of science by Leopold von Wiese in Germany and by George Lundberg and others in the United States. It involved abandoning the view of most earlier sociologists that sociology was to be concerned with concrete analyses of different types of society, and with the specific factors which promoted stability or change in them. Instead, they argued that every science abstracts some particular feature of the environing world as its own particular subject of inquiry, and they held that the province of sociology should be a concern with the general forms of relationship which occur in all human societies regardless of all the differences they may exhibit in other respects.

While the attempt to construct a general sociology on this purely formal basis did not have a profound or lasting effect on either theoretical or empirical sociology, there was a steady growth of interest in studying more restricted similarities and differences in the structural properties of specific types of organization. Weber's analysis of the three types of authority—the traditional, the charismatic, and the rational-bureaucratic—had wide influence, as did Robert Michels' studies of oligarchical organization in political parties and in labor unions. These and other structural studies were not based on any general theory regarding formal relationships characterizing the whole society, nor were they merely descriptive of particular instances: they sought to abstract generalizations from concrete cases, and their generalizations were subsequently refined and developed by others, leading to the formulation of similar, historically testable generalizations in successive areas of concern.

Other sociologists, following the lead of Durkheim, took another turn, being primarily concerned with establishing the structural unity of social systems and with understanding the dysfunctions which might develop within these systems. Like Durkheim, they were frequently concerned with the effects which such unity, or lack of unity, had on individual behavior. While Durkheim dealt with this more or less systematically, and in general terms, a great deal of interest within applied sociology dealt with the same type of problem in terms of specific factors such as "social lag" or with respect to the nature of specific situations in which dysfunctions developed. The classic work of Thomas and Znaniecki, *The Polish Peasant*, belongs in this general category. In such studies the emphasis lay on how the structural features of a society influence individual behavior, but the same type of question was taken up from the point of view of social psychology, instead of sociology, by Kurt Lewin and those influenced by him. Instead of dealing with the institutional structure of a society, they studied how the structure of specific social situations affected the performance and attitudes of those exposed to them. For example, a whole series of studies dealt with the differing effects on children of authoritarian and nonauthoritarian classroom situations. Once such studies became common, it seemed equally reasonable to proceed in the opposite direction: instead of explaining the effects of structure on personality, there were attempts to explain differences in social institutions by means of the personality traits that a particular society tended to foster in its members. For example, under the influence of Freudian theory, it became fairly common among a few political scientists and among some influential anthropologists to offer explanations of the fundamental nature of different social systems in terms of child-rearing practices.

As a consequence of the prevalence of a wide variety of such studies, focusing on the ways in which various social situations affect individual behavior and on how individual behavior reflects important features of societal life, a conviction developed that there was no reason to distinguish between psychology and the social sciences. It was in this context that, as we have seen, the concept of the "behavioral sciences" was born.[18] The most ambitious attempt to establish a general framework for a unified theory that would include all facets of social life was Talcott Parsons' use of the concept of social action.[19] Without entering into a critical discussion of that system, nor of various attempts to make psychology the foundation of all social science, I shall argue for the essentially pluralistic nature of the social sciences, in contrast to the now fashionable rubric the "behavioral sciences." In this connection, I shall first consider reasons for denying that psychology—and even social psychology—is to be considered a social science.

As I have already suggested, even though every individual is deeply affected by the nature of his cultural background and by the character of his society, the task of psychology is to formulate concepts and establish generalizations which can be applied to all individuals, regardless of differences in their backgrounds. It might be thought that to pursue such a goal is to pursue a chimaera, since individuals who have been reared under different social conditions will exhibit very different traits. Yet, such differences do not preclude the possibility of offering generalizations which apply to all individuals. That such is the case with regard to physiological functions is, I suppose, universally recognized; that it is also the case with respect to many psychological functions—such as vision and audition, or memory and learning—is not likely to be denied.[20] It seems to me to be no less true with respect to many traits of great importance in interpersonal relations, but I shall illustrate this with respect to only one such trait: that which was once commonly referred to as "self-esteem."

It is, I submit, a useful hypothesis—though one not amenable to experimental test—that self-esteem is an important need in all individuals, regardless of the societies to which they belong. To be sure, the types of action capable of satisfying a need for self-esteem will vary from society to society, yet there are many aspects of individual behavior which cannot be explained unless the value of self-esteem is taken into account. This is a fact that pertains to psychology, but is also a fact which it is important for such social scientists as political scientists, economists, and sociologists to understand. Conversely, a psychologist is in need of help from historians, anthropologists, and sociologists to explain why in one society self-esteem is fostered by a particular form of behavior, whereas in other societies the same form of behavior would lead to a sense of degradation and shame. That difference can be said to be due to the "meaning" that attaches to the same form of behavior in different societies, but such a difference in meaning can be explained only by the histories and the structures of these societies, not by the investigations of psychologists. Thus, even in cases where the most intimate cooperation between psychologists and social scientists is called for, the contribution which each can make to a common understanding remains separate and distinct.

To this it might be objected that even if such were the case when one is dealing with differences in what fosters self-esteem in different societies, it would not apply to those cases in which two individuals raised in the same society—and even two siblings—might pursue entirely different paths to enhance their self-esteem. In such cases, it might be argued, the explanation would be wholly psychological: one sibling, for example, might have identified with the values of his or her parents whereas the other might have revolted against them and their values. Could it not then be the case that the differences between the two siblings depended solely upon the psychological relationships which had developed within this particular family, rather than reflecting what was present within the society at large? Unfortunately for such an argument, whatever relations exist between child and parent in the nuclear family are not isolated from the norms for parental-child relationships which are current in society. For a psychologist to understand what led each sibling to pursue a different path toward self-esteem, he must not only be aware of the psychological forces which led one sibling to rebel against his or her parents, and the other to identify with them, but must also be aware of the norms of behavior within that society, or he will be unable to explain why each sibling sought the sort of goals which he or she actually sought. Thus, even in these cases the explanation of different ways of satisfying a need for self-esteem will not be purely psychological, but will involve an understanding of the norms inherent in the social structure to which the individuals belong.

What holds as between psychology and the social sciences generally can also be said to hold among the various social sciences themselves: each is distinct from the others, though each can contribute to the understanding which the others seek. This is commonly acknowledged, but scant attention has been paid to what makes them distinct as well as related. To clarify this question it is necessary to distinguish between the descriptive elements present in every science and the attempt by every science to formulate generalizations or laws.

As is now almost universally recognized, every explanation of a concrete occurrence or of specific types of occurrences must appeal to some generalization or generalizations as to what can be expected to occur under particular circumstances. Such generalizations, however, cannot in and of themselves explain any specific occurrence unless the conditions obtaining with respect to that occurrence are specified. Specification of the initial and boundary conditions that permit one either to predict or to explain particular occurrences constitutes the necessary descriptive element in any scientific explanation, but description without at least a tacit use of generalizations provides no answer to any question as to why a particular object behaves as it does, or why a particular event has occurred. This is as true in the social sciences as it is in the natural sciences, though in the most advanced natural sciences, such as physics, the descriptive element occupies a relatively minor place, whereas in the social sciences descriptions have been easier to formulate than have adequate generalizations or laws. All descriptions in the social sciences concern institutional structures which order social life, but each concentrates attention on one rather than another facet of the overall structure of society. Since all are facets of one and the same society, it is not surprising that at many points any social science must draw upon the descriptive elements dealt with in the other social sciences. If it failed to do so, concentrating only on describing conditions with respect to the institutions with which it is primarily concerned, it would have insufficient data concerning the initial conditions and (especially) the boundary conditions to which its generalizations were to be applied.

The need for one social science to take account of the descriptive materials which lie within the special province of another social science should not, however, lead us to suppose that the laws or lawlike generalizations to be found in any particular social science have a special relationship to the laws of any other social science. Thus, while an economist may have to know what occurred in the sphere of government or international relations in order to explain a particular economic crisis, he need not use any generalizations drawn from political science in order to explain the relationships among the economic factors with which he deals. In short, no social science has a monopoly on any particular set of data, but the generalizations each attempts to formulate are limited in scope: each deals with a different aspect of the societies with which all are presumably concerned.[21]

If it is true, as I have argued, that every science, including the social sciences, involves both description and generalization, the question arises as to how history as a special discipline is related to the social sciences. When one considers that question historically, it is clear that the writing of history had long been a part of Western culture before there were many concerted attempts to establish general principles concerning politics, and certainly before there had been serious attempts to do so concerning such other factors of social organization as those which govern economic life. To be sure, both Aristotle and Herodotus approximated the types of generalizations which we currently regard as falling within the range of the social sciences, and there had also been a long tradition of normative social theory in which ideals of political and social organization were formulated and discussed; however, nothing like a systematic study of matters of fact concerning these topics developed until the eighteenth century, which saw the appearance of relevant works by Montesquieu, Quesnay, Smith, and others. Until then, historical writings were looked upon as the most important source of whatever understanding could be gained concerning the causes and consequence of political actions, and the advantages and disadvantages of different forms of political, economic, and social organization.

On the other hand, while those who were bent on establishing basic principles regarding political, economic, and social life did not wholly neglect past history, they relied more heavily on abstract analysis than on data drawn from the past. In fact, even the founders of sociology, such as Ferguson, Comte, and Spencer, who were historically minded, regarded conventional historical writing with contempt instead of viewing it as a possible source of data and—even more importantly—as a means of corroborating or correcting the generalizations which they attempted to establish through their own interpretations of the past. To be sure, there was some justification for their unwillingness to use traditional historical writing as a basis for their generalizations concerning society, since such writings were mainly cast as narratives of politics and statecraft and did not deal comprehensively with most other aspects of the organization of social life. Unfortunately, although historians at the time were increasing the range of materials they considered germane to their tasks and were also becoming more critical of their sources, they tended not to consider what they might gain from contemporary investigations of the economic factors operative in society and of other factors which influenced the organization of social life. While Buckle's work signaled a change in this respect, both the range of his data and his success were limited. With the possible exception of John Millar, only Marx fully appreciated the necessity of linking abstract social analysis with a careful study of historical fact, and unfortunately his polemical purposes and his desire to inspire revolutionary action sometimes interfered with his success in achieving the fusion of theoretical adequacy and historical accuracy which it was his aim to effect.

The prevalent split between historical description and the generalizations of the nascent social sciences was regarded by some as a necessary and important feature in the economy of knowledge. This split was characterized in a rectoral address by Wilhelm Windelband in 1894 as the difference between the "ideographic" interests of historians and the "nomothetic" approach of the sciences. It had also been signalized by Dilthey in his distinction between the activity of understanding (*verstehen*) and that of explaining (*erklären*). While such a distinction, as we shall see, is relevant to some aspects of historical understanding, the contrast which it drew between history and the sciences was in most respects misleading. In the first place, it overlooked the element of description, which is an aspect of all natural sciences, not only with respect to the events which they wish to explain but also with respect to the conditions—whether natural or experimental—under which those events occur and with respect to the description of the effects which follow from those events. To be sure, all such description is undertaken in the interest of arriving at an explanation of a particular type of phenomenon, and is not an end in itself. This being the case, one might argue that the basic distinction between an ideographic and a nomothetic approach to phenomena remains a valid though perhaps overdrawn distinction. However, when the issue is approached from the other direction, it is clear that such is not the case. Ideographic description is not free of nomothetic elements: it always presupposes some framework of generalizations in terms of which it is to be viewed. For example, a historian can attempt to reconstruct the past from documents, monuments, and other signs of past activities only by assuming that there are similarities in human nature such that he can interpret past actions in terms of analogies drawn from how he himself and his contemporaries behave. Furthermore, in attempting to grasp the rudiments of past social structures he must appeal to his knowledge of the social structure in which he himself lives and to the structures of other present societies with which he has become directly or indirectly acquainted. Thus, every description of another society presupposes generalizations concerning both human behavior and the ways in which societies tend to be organized. Unless such generalizations draw upon a broad range of data, they are not likely to provide an adequate framework for the description of societies remote in time or place from the historian's own. Consequently, the discipline of history must, at almost every point, make use of low-level generalizations, even though the historian's aim is not that of establishing laws concerning human behavior or concerning social structure and social change. Thus, it is a mistake to assume, as Windelband, Rickert, and others had assumed, that history deals with that which is unique and unrepeatable and that it does so by dispensing with generalizations of the sort at which the sciences aim.

Many factors serve to explain how this false notion arose. Among them were misconceptions regarding the sciences: not only was their descriptive component overlooked, but it was assumed that the essence of science lay in its ability to predict. (It was not recognized that prediction depends both on a knowledge of laws and on the possibility of knowing the initial and the boundary conditions which obtain with respect to that which one is to predict.) If science is to be identified with "prevision," as Comte claimed, history was not, and could not be, a science. On the other hand, not only history but all humanistic disciplines had disciplinary standards and were entitled to a place in the total economy of human knowledge. Given the prestige which the natural sciences enjoyed, it was natural for humanists to claim that their studies had a method distinct from that of the natural sciences, and one which was no less worthy of respect. That this was the case would best be justified by a contrast between two methods: the methods of the *Kulturwissenschaften* and those of the *Naturwissenschaften*, an ideographic and a nomothetic method, the first being a method aimed at interpretation and understanding, the second aimed at explaining.

Insofar as that dichotomy had plausibility, it depended on the fact that Dilthey and those who followed him were more interested in the history of *culture*—of philosophy, literature, the arts, and value systems— than in the *institutions* which structured the political, economic, and social life of societies. An adequate description of the various facets of culture almost always involves interpreting and understanding them prior to attempting to offer any explanations of the conditions which may serve to account for them. This is far less true with respect to events which concern the institutional structures of a society, such as the rise of a political party or the incidence of an economic depression. To be sure, such events must also be described, but their description is not isolable from the conditions out of which they arose nor from their relations to what occurred in other aspects of the same society at the same time.[22] Thus, there are differences between those types of methodology which are most appropriate for cultural historians on the one hand and for those concerned with institutional histories on the others. These differences are reflected in the situation which presently exists in history as an academic discipline: some of its concerns bring it very close to the domain of the social sciences, providing social scientists with materials for analytic and systematic studies, whereas others remain close to the sphere of humanistic studies, providing a background for interpreting and evaluating the various elements which constitute a given society's cultural heritage. Each type of historian must use some of the work of those who are primarily concerned with areas outside his or her own primary areas of concern, since various elements in a culture may affect the institutional structure of a society, and institutional changes often have a profound effect on cultural change.

Thus, no sharp line can be drawn between cultural and institutional historians. Yet, neither aspect of historiography is solely concerned with individuals or solely concerned with cultural and institutional phenomena. As we shall see, every explanation of facts concerning societies and their cultures will, at some points, have to take account of the contributions of individuals, though the focus of interest will not be on these individuals themselves; instead, it will be on their place in a cultural and institutional setting, and on whatever contributions in these areas may be attributable to them. On the other hand, we shall also see that the efficacy of an individual's actions is always relative to the cultural and institutional situation in which he acts. Because of these constraints on the actions of individuals, some social theorists have been led to stress the concept of necessity in explaining what occurs in social life.

In the chapters that follow, we shall have to disentangle the changes which the concepts of "purpose" and "necessity" have undergone in the course of modern social theory, attempting to state in what senses each has a role to play in understanding social life. To this end, the next chapter will consider how each of these concepts has been used by those who have adopted the methodology of individualism in thir social theories, while the third chapter will show how the same concepts have functioned among those adopting an institutional approach. The final section of the book will then be able to draw together the strands of these arguments and, after analyzing the concepts of chance and choice, will then reach some conclusions as to the roles of purpose and necessity in social life.

# PART TWO

# Individualistic & Institutional Theories

# 2 ⇨ Individualistic Theories of Purpose & Necessity

## ON PURPOSE IN INDIVIDUALISTIC THEORIES

There have been many attempts in the history of social thought to find some one characteristic which, apart from the bodily form of human beings and apart from their capacity to reproduce their own kind, serves to identify humans as human. In this connection one may recall the Aristotelian definition of man as a *rational* animal, Descartes's claim that only humans possess a mind and consciousness, Hobbes' view that man alone is capable of laughter, or Marx's characterization of man as an animal that produces the means of its own subsistence. Others have identified the distinctively human with some specific intellectual capacity, such as the possession of a power for abstract thought or the ability to communicate symbolically through language; still others have identified the human with specific modes of consciousness, such as the consciousness of self, or with the capacity to transcend the immediate present through foresight and through memory. Even when it is recognized—as it now should be—that there is no absolute distinction to be drawn between the capacities of humans and those of other species, distinctions in the degree to which such capacities are possessed must be recognized.

In general, these attempts to locate some distinctively human attributes have not been formulated solely for classificatory purposes: they have been motivated by a desire to identify some impor-

tant feature of human life. Consequently, there have also been attempts at defining that which is distinctively human in terms of
some feature common to the lives of human groups, rather than in
terms of the attributes of individuals. For example, Aristotle characterized man as a political as well as a rational animal. In the same
vein more recent theorists, such as Kroeber, have claimed that the
most essential difference between the human and the nonhuman is
that only in the case of humans does behavior depend not merely
upon biological inheritance but also on the cumulative growth of a
cultural inheritance.

Regardless of whether one is inclined to identify that which is
distinctively human in terms of the characteristics of individuals or
in terms of the forms of life which human beings everywhere develop,
human social life must be based upon the capacities of individuals; at
the same time, these forms of social life must be such as to satisfy
most of the basic needs of individuals. Given this reciprocal relationship between the characteristics of individuals and the structures of social life, it is not surprising that the concept of purpose has
often been regarded as the explanatory category best suited to serve as
the basis for any social theory. Individuals obviously have the capacity to act purposely for remote ends, and since social institutions
provide a common matrix within which different individuals pursue
their ends, it is natural to look to human purposes when one attempts to explain how these institutions originally developed, why
they persist, and why they have been subject to change.

One typical way in which the concept of purpose has served as a
link between individual behavior and the existence of social institutions is represented by social contract theories of the state. In analyses of this type, as we saw in the preceding chapter, societies were
treated as aggregates of individuals, and social institutions were explained as resulting from the interactions of these individuals when
each pursued his own good. While this was the most prevalent form
in which individual purposes were used to explain the foundations of
organized social life, it was not the only form which such theories
took. As the much-discussed view of Mandeville serves to remind us,
there was a theory as old as that of Thrasymachus that political
organization arose out of the will of a powerful coterie of the few in
order to establish dominance over the actions of others. On that
theory, too, calculations of self-interest lay at the basis of the state.
Others, however, denied that calculations of individual self-interest
constituted the dominant motive in human action; instead, they
conceived of man's basic motivation in terms of a purposive striving

toward self-realization and wholeness. It was on this basis that they sought to explain social organization and social change. As we shall see, these schools differed with respect to the roles of foresight, deliberation, and choice in purposive behavior, but both made use of the concept of purpose in explaining and in justifying social institutions. I shall criticize each in turn.

## Purposive Theories Based on Foresight, Deliberation, and Choice

In the preceding chapter we saw that contract theories came to be criticized by eighteenth-century social theorists, such as Hume, not only because they could not effectively explain the origin of the state, but also because the psychological premises on which they were based were false, involving an overestimation of the roles which self-interest and the rational calculation of benefits play in human affairs. While I, too, would argue that self-interest is not the sole motive of people, in what immediately follows I shall be concerned only with the other psychological presupposition of contract theories: that is, the role they assign to the rational calculation of benefits in explaining social organization and social change. Appeals to that factor are not confined to social contract theorists; they have had widespread influence in the history of social thought, and they are commonly assumed to be true in everyday discussions of politics and history. It is therefore appropriate that we show them to be mistaken insofar as they suggest that we can best understand social organization and change in terms of foresight, deliberation, and choice.

No one will deny that a capacity for foresight, deliberation, and choice is a characteristic of all whom we regard as normal adult human beings. It must also be admitted that this capacity, however one chooses to characterize it, is evidenced in many types of situation and on many occasions. Nevertheless, I wish to show that one should not look to its exercise in attempting to explain the basis of social organization. To be sure, some features of social life can be explained in this way: in our society, individuals often act purposively, after deliberation, to form associations designed to achieve limited ends; for example, they found schools and hospitals, enter into business partnerships, form clubs, and establish political organizations. In doing so they are acting in concert, having definite goals in mind, and the existence of these particular associations would not be explicable if one were to omit all reference to the purposes of the individuals who initiated them. Nevertheless, such associations can be formed only within boundaries set by already established institutions, and it is these already established institutions that serve to define the rules according to which any such associations are allowed to function. To assume that there ever was, or that there ever could have been, an aggregate of individuals who lived in close proximity to one another and originally lived according to no rules, and under no accepted institutions, until they had deliberately established them, would be to indulge in fantasy. To be sure, even the most dedicated exponents of the social contract theory have not usually supposed that their doctrine referred to some actual point in human history when all organized social life first came into being. However, the difficulties in those accounts of social organization that stress the conscious aims of individuals are not confined to the problem of how social life first arose. It is equally implausible to suppose that men in the earliest times, living under the most primitive conditions, would have had the capacity to envision the advantages which might gradually accrue to them if they were to develop new forms of social organization. Furthermore, even if one were to postulate that they had some dim apprehension of the possible advantages to be gained, it would be implausible to suppose that they could have had sufficient self-restraint to pursue the relatively remote goal of establishing a changed social order under which each might at a later time obtain a measure of welfare greater than that which he had previously enjoyed. In short, as Hume made clear in his essays on the social contract and the origin of the state, one simply cannot accept the psychological assumptions which underlie the view that people deliberately create the basic forms of their social life.

There is a second main reason why any attempt to explain the basis of social life in terms of individual deliberation and choice is bound to fail. Every human choice between alternatives is hemmed in by the situation under which such a choice is to be made, and when our choices concern possible changes in the structure of society, we find that we are inescapably constrained by much that has been inherited from the past. Unlike Socrates in the sixth book of *The Republic* (501), one cannot assume that there is any chance of making a completely fresh start, wiping the slate clean of all traces of the institutions under which we and others had formerly lived. Therefore, even if social institutions are assumed to reflect the purposes of individuals, what they reflect are simply whatever choices these individuals were in a position to make when they were faced by a limited set of alternatives: their actual choices cannot be assumed to reflect what they might have chosen had they been free to choose whatever they willed. At best, then, their choices represent the options which appeared most desirable, or least undesirable, among those from among which they could choose. Furthermore, there are no societies in which the choices of all individuals carry equal weight. Consequently, it is not surprising that among the individuals whose activities support a given institution or set of institutions, many will do so reluctantly, begrudgingly, or even resentfully. Therefore, it cannot be claimed that the structure of a society is to be explained in terms of what the individuals within that society actually will it to be.

*Purpose as the Impulse to Individual Self-Realization*

To be sure, among those who interpret social institutions in terms of purpose, some would reject the foregoing arguments, since in them it was assumed that the purposive element underlying organized social life necessarily involves foresight, deliberation, and conscious choice. Against this it might be urged that the category of purpose applies to many aspects of individual behavior other than those in which individuals act with full awareness of the ends they actually pursue. On this view, goal-directed striving is present in all human behavior, although it is only on certain occasions that the goals toward which that behavior implicitly tends are explicitly envisioned and become a matter of deliberate choice.

While this form of self-realizationist theory had been deeply rooted in the thought of Aristotle and of Aquinas, it came to be revived in new forms in the late eighteenth and early nineteenth century, and persisted among self-realizationists of diverse schools well into the twentieth century. For example, not only was the doctrine characteristic of the thought of Herder, Fichte, and Hegel, and of later British and American Hegelians; it was also an important element in the ethical theories of some who, like Green and Paulson, had been profoundly influenced by Kant. The same underlying self-realizationism was later prominent in the social sciences in America, dominating the sociology of Cooley and providing the foundation for Dewey's views regarding the relations between the individual and society. In none of these theories was there any longer a trace of the view that societies had been instituted by contract or design; instead, social institutions were regarded as having grown naturally out of common needs and interests, and were thus the concrete embodiments of many individual wills. Accordingly, any ultimate dualism or irreconcilable opposition between the individual and society was presumably overcome.[1]

Underlying the emphasis that came to be placed on the harmony between the individual and society was a rejection of those seventeenth- and eighteenth-century views of man which treated each person as an independent entity, having a basic character unaffected by the social relationships into which he entered. In opposition to that view, the social nature of the individual came to be stressed.

In speaking of the social nature of the individual one might have different things in mind. Among them would be the fact that people do not, and cannot, live in total independence of one another. They cannot do so, since if any individual were to be wholly deprived of the support accruing to him from the activities of others, he would not be able even to survive. Nor are people naturally inclined to live in isolation: they are gregarious and need affection, they are interested in their fellows, and they seek attention, competing for the regard of those with whom they associate. In short, humans are by nature social beings. Yet even these social traits, whose presence in human beings is now almost universally acknowledged, do not suffice to show that there is an essential harmony between the individual and his society; what they indicate is that human beings are naturally disposed to live among their fellows, but this propensity need not—and does not—preclude the possibility that there will be basic conflicts between the needs and desires of individuals and the rules structuring life in the social groups to which they belong.

Nor can one exclude the possibility of there being disharmonies between individuals and their society simply by showing that if one is to understand almost any characteristic of an individual, one must take his or her social environment into account. In explaining human behavior, almost all twentieth-century anthropologists, psychologists, and sociologists have stressed various aspects of the individual's social environment, rather than his biological inheritance. As major factors in that environment some have emphasized the individual's cultural inheritance, derived from the society or the social group in which he was brought up; others have focused on his family relationships; all have in one way or another stressed the successive influences brought to bear by others upon the individual during the formative years of his life. While the emphasis placed on each of these factors has varied, there has been general agreement that an individual's social experiences become part of him: that they permeate, alter, and develop his original potentialities, imparting to them whatever shape these potentialities ultimately assume. Yet, even this acknowledgement falls short of establishing a harmony between the individual and his society. Actually, the extent to which there may be a lack of harmony between the individuals and the societies in which they live has rarely if ever received greater emphasis than in the last decades, even though it is now almost universally claimed that the social environment is mainly responsible for an individual's nature.

Bearing this in mind, if one is to show that there can be no ultimate disharmony between individuals and their society, one must interpret the "social nature of the individual" as meaning more than that men cannot live in total independence with respect to one another, and more, too, than that there is no core of the self which remains uninfluenced by the social environment. To maintain that a harmony between the individual and society exists, and exists necessarily, one would have to hold that the values any individual embraces derive from the dominant values in his society, rather than being rooted in the individual's biological inheritance and his own specific experiences. Only then would his values and those of his society coincide; only then would it be the case that whatever might be his lot, he would feel himself to be at one with the group to which he belongs. So far as I can see, there is no other way in which the "social nature of the individual" can be interpreted and yet yield as its consequence a belief that there can be no ultimate conflict between the individual and his society.

There are various ways in which one might criticize the assumption that the values of an individual are identical with the values of the group to which he belongs. The most basic objection to such a view would be if one could show that the only source of an individual's values does not lie in the culture to which he has been exposed. I shall not attempt to establish that position, though what I shall say concerning values in the final chapter of this book will suggest that it is true. Rather, my criticism will be confined to a single point: that no society is a monolithic entity, possessing a single uniform set of values that all individuals, regardless of their status, equally share. To be sure, some values may be widely shared in any society, and some among them may even be shared by all members of that society; nevertheless, even under these circumstances, there are apt to be differences between different groups with respect to the specific rank-order they assign to whatever values they share. Furthermore, in any large-scale society there are apt to be important differences in the values of different groups, reflecting regional or occupational differences, or differences in class. Even within any such subgroup, not all values will be shared, since individuals do not live lives whose content is wholly determined by the nature and activities of the groups to which they belong. Consequently, the values which an individual holds particularly dear are not always—and perhaps not usually—determined by his occupying one or another particular position in his society. On the contrary, such values always bear some marks of the uniqueness of the individual's experience, and when one recognizes that the experience of siblings will vary greatly, even if they are close in age and of the same sex, one cannot assume that the values of individuals within any group will be uniform. Therefore, whatever the phrase "the social nature of the individual" can legitimately be taken to mean, one should not assume that the values of an individual will be a reflection of whatever values are dominant in his society, or dominant in the social group to which he most obviously belongs. Consequently, it is not to be assumed that harmony necessarily exists between the goals which individuals pursue and the structure of the societies to which they belong.

Social philosophers such as Bosanquet, who represent the tradition of objective idealism, would object to this conclusion on the ground that it rests on a failure to distinguish between the individual's real will and his actual will. What an individual from time to time actually wills may be inconsistent and self-defeating; what he *really* wills is a form of life which, if he could attain it, would be wholly satisfactory to him. Such a form of life, the objective idealist would claim, involves not only a harmonization of the specific interests of an individual but also the establishment of harmony between his interests and those of others, since it is only in conjunction with the work of others that he could attain the ends he wills for himself. Thus, once an individual comes to understand the difference between his fragmentary and changing personal goals and what it is that he really wills, he will be bound to acknowledge that whenever it appears that his interests are in conflict with the constraints society puts upon him, he has been mistaken as to where his real interests lie.

This thesis rests on Bosanquet's interpretation of social institutions as being embodiments of the underlying purposes of individuals. W. E. Hocking developed a similar view. For him, the state and other institutions represented what he termed "will-circuits." Will-circuits come into being when individuals share common paths to achieve their individual ends. Once these circuits have become entrenched in the joint activities of a group of individuals, they take on a life of their own, and the vital purposes they achieve for the group as a whole are not to be identified with the separate purposes of the individuals who comprise the group. Thus, while insisting that institutions exist only as embodiments of the purposive actions of individuals, Hocking (like Bosanquet) distinguished between the particular personal aims of individuals and the general human purposes which are served because these institutions exist.[2]

Hocking's way of putting the matter had the advantage of not having to rely on a contrast between an individual's "real" will and what that individual actually wills, yet it preserved the essence of that position. Furthermore, taken simply in itself it is not objectionable, since social institutions do in fact serve general human purposes without being identical with the purposes of the individuals who participate in them. Nevertheless, the view fails in its aim. It sought to demonstrate that there is no real disharmony between the will of the individual and the actual social structures within which his life is lived. Nevertheless, all that it actually serves to justify is the existence of social life *in general*; it merely shows that, if life is of any value, it is better for an individual to live in a society than to try to be free of all social bonds. What it fails to provide is any justification for whatever institutions actually characterize the society in which a particular individual happens to live. Thus, even though an individual could not survive if he were to be isolated from his fellows and deprived of the various skills which human beings have acquired in the course of their social existence, this does not establish harmony between what individuals desire and their own societies. No individual chooses the society into which he happens to have been born, and since it is rarely possible for anyone to leave his own society and establish himself in another, it is thoroughly misleading to speak as if the nature of a set of social institutions reflects what the individuals living in that society have chosen for themselves. While one might perhaps wish that a society's institutions would represent purposes which all of its members share, it is not plausible to account in this way for the origins of institutions nor for the nature of the specific institutions which exist in any actual society.

## THREE TYPES OF NECESSITARIAN EXPLANATION

Both types of theories discussed in the preceding section involved the assumption that the forms of social life are to be explained in terms of the purposes of individuals. In the one case, such purposes were assumed to be connected with the foresight, deliberation, and choices of individuals, whereas in the other they were seen as gradually developing out of needs that could be fulfilled only through social cooperation and mutual support. We have noted some of the difficulties which arise in connection with theories of both types, but have stressed those difficulties which arose because the category of purpose was taken to be fundamental in social thought. It must now be shown that other forms of individualism which stress necessity, rather than purpose, are equally subject to criticism. This is all the more important since, throughout the modern period, social theories have generally been modeled on whatever methodological beliefs dominated the natural sciences; and in the early modern period, following the scientific revolution, the concept of necessity supplanted that of purpose as the basic category for all explanation. Even social contract theory, which had a quite different origin, took on a necessitarian coloration.

*Necessity*, however, can be interpreted in various ways. At first it was taken in the sense of that which is *rationally* necessary. At the time, what was viewed as rationally necessary was by no means confined to the merely logical relations which Hume later identified as "relations among our ideas"; instead, the rationally necessary was interpreted in terms of relations of necessity which obtained between matters of fact. It was claimed that these relations were *necessary* in the sense that they were fixed, and could not be otherwise; furthermore, their necessity was held to be *evident:* reason was capable of directly grasping the ineluctable fact of their necessity. Nowhere is the difference between the seventeenth-century conception of necessity and more recent views more obvious than in the way in which the rationalists used the concept of cause. For them, the relation of cause and effect was a logical relation: the cause was the ground of the effect, and through understanding the cause one could see that the effect would necessarily follow. The "following" involved was not, however, sequential: what followed was a logical consequence, not a later occurrent. That the logical relation of ground and consequence, rather than temporal succession, was held to be fundamental to explanation can be seen in the role which the relation of substance and mode played in the great rationalist systems, as well as in the arguments which they offered in proof of God's existence. Nor was this emphasis on rational necessity wholly confined to the metaphysical systems of the rationalists; it was, at the time, a familiar view regarding the nature of adequate knowledge. It was widely assumed that if knowledge were to be adequate, it had to be susceptible of *proof,* and it was recognized that inferences based on observation could not meet this test. This, for example, is evident in Locke. Even though he was primarily an empiricist, Locke distinguished science from probable knowledge, and held that nothing was to be denominated as "science" unless it achieved the status of demonstrative knowledge. One may also note that Galileo's proof for the basic principles of motion had rested on his geometrical demonstrations, rather than being dependent upon experimental observation. All of this was drastically changed when the "new experimental method" of the Royal Society, which soon became identified with the methodological views of Newton, came to dominate scientific thought. There followed a series of attempts to apply an analogous method in social theory, which replaced former rationalistic constructions, at the same time greatly expanding the range of issues with which social thought was concerned. Thus, two successive forms of necessitarian doctrine, each of which was based on individualistic assumptions, are to be distinguished in the early history of modern social theory. Later, toward the end of the eighteenth century, some of the assumptions of the Newtonian method were abandoned, and necessitarian doctrines began to stress the effects of experience on the nature of individuals. This constituted a third form of individualistic necessitarianism, which can best be identified with the views of Helvétius, its first and perhaps most influential exponent.

In what follows I shall deal in turn with these three relatively distinct types of positions, designating them as (1) the method of rational deduction, (2) the Newtonian methods, and (3) the method of Helvétius.

*The Method of Rational Deduction*

When the method of rational deduction was taken to be the ideal form of explanation in both philosophy and the sciences, its establishment brought about a fundamental alteration in the previously dominant modes of social thought. The political philosophies of Hobbes and of Spinoza provide the boldest and most striking examples of this change, but the change was also evident in the field of jurisprudence. In Grotius, for example, the doctrine of a law of nature was at least partially freed from its theological underpinnings and was held to be adequately established by "right reason."[3] As Grotius said, "I have made it my concern to refer the proofs of things touching the law of nature to certain fundamental conceptions which are beyond question, so that no one can deny them without doing violence to himself. For the principles of that law, if only you pay strict heed to them, are in themselves manifest and clear, almost as evident are those things which we perceive by the external senses."[4] To be sure, the actual development of his theory failed to conform to this rationalistic ideal of proof, but one finds a similar view developed by Pufendorf, whose *De jure naturae et gentium* attempted to start from a few fundamental propositions from which a theory of the state and a whole system of law was to be developed. In opposition to Aristotle, Pufendorf claimed that it was possible to gain demonstrative knowledge in the moral sciences, as well as in mathematics, if one proceeded, as he proposed to do, "to deduce by a syllogism for things proposed for certain conclusion that must necessarily be accepted from particular principles taken as their causes."[5] Though Pufendorf's system of jurisprudence was in general conformity with this ideal, the fundamental propositions on which it was based were less clear than they needed to be, and the materials with which he was forced to deal were too complex to allow of rigid deduction from those premises. Thus, he had to rely throughout on modes of argumentation which lent some plausibility to his views but fell far short of demonstration.

In the political philosophies of Hobbes and Spinoza, on the other hand, the model of an adequate rational deduction was closely approximated. Of course, such a deduction had to rest upon some fundamental axioms, the most basic of which was that no normative theory concerning the good of an individual or of a state could be derived from anything but the most basic premises concerning man's actual nature. As Spinoza said, "My object in applying my mind to politics is not to make any new or unheard of suggestions, but to establish by sound and conclusive reasoning, and to deduce from the real nature of man, nothing save the principles and institutions which accord best with practice."[6] Coupled with this naturalistic starting point, both Hobbes and Spinoza accepted two further axioms: first, that for purposes of analysis, one must start from the nature of individuals and explain the existence of the state in terms of what follows from their nature; and, second, that the fundamental nature of each individual is an inherent drive to preserve his own being and achieve his own good. In short, their political philosophies started from an individualistic, not an institutional, base and depended throughout upon the acceptance of a hormic form of egoism. It was on the basis of these premises, without in any way appealing to matters of historical fact, that each sought to explain and to justify the nature and existence of the state and to establish the grounds of the state's authority.

While there had been other important issues with which classical and mediaeval political philosophy had been concerned, the rational deductive approach of Hobbes and Spinoza led them to think of society as identical with the state, that is, with the source of political authority. Although they were both deeply concerned with the relations between religious authority and civil life, the relations of the state to the family and to other aspects of communal organization were neglected, as were questions concerning the production and distribution of wealth. When contrasted with the social thought of Aristotle or Aquinas, this represented a drastic narrowing of the scope of social theory. To be sure, one can in part account for this limitation in terms of the rise of nation-states and the political struggles over the authority of the sovereign: for Hobbes and Spinoza the latter question was the dominant political issue of the times, and each was deeply concerned to defend his personal convictions with respect to it.[7] In addition, however, the ahistorical character of the method of rational deduction did much to determine their tendency to focus exclusive attention on the state, treating it as identical with society. In seeking a *reason* for the necessary existence of the state, they found it in the need to control the harm which egoistic individuals would inflict on one another were there no force superior to the individual's own will. No such explanation could be given for the existence of the family as a social unit, since family life is not to be explained in terms of the single motive of self-preservation. Furthermore, to explain other types of communal organization—such as caste or class systems, guilds and the various other institutions of economic life—one must look to their actual historical development: neither their existence nor the wide variety of forms to be found among them could be deduced from any set of basic axioms.[8] It was only later that social thought regained the scope it had possessed for Aristotle and for Aquinas, and economics, religion, the family, and education became no less important elements than forms of government in understanding the similarities and differences to be found among different societies. In this respect, as in many others, Locke was a transitional figure.[9]

## The Newtonian Method

In his political philosophy, no less than in his theory of knowledge, Locke combined—though he rarely completely harmonized—assumptions he had drawn from the rationalistic tradition and the approach characteristic of those of his fellow members of the Royal Society who favored the new experimental method. The heritage of rationalism was evident in his early *Essays on the Law of Nature*, where he held a position similar to that of Grotius, according to which all men are endowed with certain natural rights; he later maintained the same position in his *Second Treatise on Government*. In the opening chapters of the *Second Treatise*, when depicting the state of nature, Locke held that it was a law of nature that men "were equal and independent," and that "no one ought to harm another in his life, health, liberty, or possessions" (ch. 2, sec. 6). Although each individual had the right to protect himself and his property, and to punish any aggressor, Locke did not hold that this would result in a state of constant war. Not only did he regard men as being inherently sociable, but he also believed that since they were rational, they would acknowledge that it was a law of nature that they should not deprive others of their lives, health, liberty, or possessions. Civil authority arose only because there was need for "settled, standing rules, indifferent and the same to all parties," with a judicature capable of enforcing those rules in the name of the community (ch. 7, sec. 87). Prior to the establishment of such a civil authority, men had indeed lived social lives: their labor had given rise to the notion of property, with the family and property relations antedating the existence of the state.10 Thus, unlike Hobbes' and Spinoza's analysis, Locke's treatment of the state of nature was not a mere analytic device, but showed an interest in the historical issue of the probable origins of the state's authority. In this respect his political theory was analogous to his attempt in the *Essay Concerning the Human Understanding* to trace all knowledge back to its origins in experience. In each case, however, Locke's interest in the question of origins remained subservient to his interest in estimating the authority attaching to that which arose out of these origins. In short, strictly speaking, his method was not primarily a historical or genetic method: in politics he sought to provide a foundation for his assessment of views regarding the basis and limits of political authority, just as in his epistemology his "historical, plain method" provided the basis for his estimate of the "certainty and extent of human knowledge" (*Essay*, intro., sec. 2). Questions of the basis and limits of political authority were, of course, the dominant issues in the social thought of the time, so it is not surprising that Locke did not further develop the sociological point of view which characterized his discussion of man's social life in the so-called state of nature. Yet, when one considers his interest in cultural diversity, as shown in book 1 of the *Essay* as well as in his extensive catalogue of books concerned with voyages and travels to exotic regions, one might have expected him to deal with civil society in a less abstract and general manner and to have taken into account the wide range of differences in the ways in which authority was exercised in different societies. His neglect of such problems is at least partially explained by the fact that each of his political writings was focused on normative issues, not on analyses of matters of fact. Thus, it was left to a succeeding generation to inaugurate modern attempts to isolate the factors responsible for the varying structures which different societies display and to account for the degrees of success which, because of these factors, different forms of society were able to attain.[11]

Montesquieu's *Spirit of the Laws* exhibits this interest and also represents the extent to which the thought of the period was dominated by the conception that social phenomena are governed by laws comparable to the laws governing the course of natural events. The success of the new experimental method was seen as having culminated in the laws of Newtonian mechanics, and many then turned their attention to discovering comparable laws in the social realm. According to the interpretations of Newtonian science then current, nature was governed by fixed and universally applicable laws; whatever happened in any particular case depended upon the fact that nature always conformed to these laws. Although Newtonians rejected the rationalist view of necessity, according to which what occurred in nature was *logically* necessary and could not have been otherwise, they did not view the laws they discovered as being nothing more than descriptions of observed regularities. Rather, they regarded them as principles actually ingrained in nature and as directly responsible for whatever occurred. Montesquieu shared this conception. He attempted to discover laws which could explain the nature of different forms of government and would account for the strength and weaknesses of each. Even though he strongly believed in the freedom of individual human beings, he held that the character of different peoples was determined by "general causes" and that these causes were responsible for the basic nature of the various types of government under which they lived. That belief, found throughout *The Spirit of the Laws*, is especially evident in its preface and in book 1. In fact, book 1 opens with the statement that "laws, in the broadest sense of the term, are necessary relations arising from the nature of things, and in this sense all types of things have their laws."[12] Earlier, Montesquieu had expressed the same view in his *Considerations on the Cause of the Romans' Greatness and Decline* when he said: "It is not fortune that rules the world. . . . There are general causes, whether moral or physical, which act upon every monarchy, which advance, maintain, or ruin it. All accidents are subject to these causes. If the chance loss of a battle, that is, a particular cause, ruins a state, there is a general cause that created the situations whereby this state could perish by the loss of a single battle."[13]

In its emphasis on the causal factors affecting the forms of the state, Montesquieu's *Spirit of the Laws* differed significantly from earlier political theories. Not only were normative problems less prominent in his treatment and the historical dimension of his discussions greatly expanded, but his analyses also attempted to relate the state to the other institutions in a society. For example, he was interested in the economic aspects of national life to a far greater degree than Locke had been, devoting books 20–23 to the roles of commerce, colonies, money, population, and other economic factors in relation to different forms of past governments. He also related the character of a people and its institutions to the physical environment, and in particular to differences in climate. In addition, he placed great emphasis on the importance of manners, customs, and religion in determining the nature of a society. In short, in large segments of the *Spirit of the Laws* his interest can be said to have been concentrated on general sociological questions even though his more familiar and influential discussions concerned the structure of governments.

With respect to his sociological view, he stressed the interconnections of the various aspects of a society, emphasizing the presence of a dominant spirit in them. Yet, unlike Burke and Hegel, he did not interpret that spirit as being, in itself, a causal, controlling factor in a society. Instead, he explained the existence of such a spirit in terms of a variety of different factors, each of which was to some degree independent of the others.[14] Among the factors he listed were the climate, religion, legal and governmental structures, customs and manners, and the effects of examples drawn from the nation's past (bk. 19, ch. 4). Montesquieu held that the relative strengths of these factors varied from one people to the next, and it was in terms of such differences that he accounted for some of the striking differences among the nations of the past.[15] Had his interests been primarily normative, such variations would have created great difficulties for him, but he in fact tended to hold that laws and customs are to be accepted insofar as they are adapted to the circumstances under which a people lives. Only tyranny was completely rejected by him. Given this position one might suppose that apart from this one exception, Montesquieu's views were completely relativistic, but there is an important sense in which they were not. While granting the acceptability of great diversity among institutions, he distinguished between those conditions under which a particular form of government had vitality and health, and those when it did not. A position of this sort, in which some normative conclusions are held to follow from an analysis of how nature's laws operate, is a position which—though it is now frequently challenged—has often been, and still is, widely shared.

What Montesquieu held with respect to laws governing the characteristics of different forms of governance was paralleled by attempts to discover the laws governing the economy of nations. In that endeavor Quesnay was one of the leaders, and his views regarding the types of laws which govern economic processes in some ways resembled the ways in which Montesquieu sought to account for the structures of political life. For example, just as Montesquieu often stressed the effects of climate on the capacities of individuals in different parts of the world, and in this way explained some of the differences in the institutions of government, so Quesnay, a physician who had written a treatise on physiology in relation to medicine, viewed economic systems as controlled by principles resembling the principles responsible for an organism's health. He regarded the circulation of wealth as providing a parallel to the manner in which the circulation of the blood maintains the processes necessary for a body's continuing life, and he held that the circulation of wealth follows fixed laws. It was on this basis that he explained the relationships among the three economic classes which he regarded as basic in every society. It was from those fixed laws that he also derived a standard against which to measure what was advantageous and what was disadvantageous in the social realm, and in this respect, too, his position resembled that of Montesquieu. It was characteristic of the thought of both, as well as of others in the period, that the concept of a "law of nature" retained the same normative connotations that it had possessed in earlier theories; in their discussions, however, another element was added—these laws were not *simply* normative but were identified with the underlying causes which control the course of events.

It must be recognized, however, that neither Montesquieu's institutional emphasis nor Quesnay's physiological orientation, both of which stressed societies as wholes, succeeded in dominating social thought at the time. Rather, the social sciences in the eighteenth century were primarily associated with attempts to emulate Newtonian principles by explaining all large-scale social phenomena in terms of the actions of individual "particles," that is, in terms of psychological laws. Furthermore, in contradistinction to the immediately preceding period, these laws were formulated in mentalistic terms, independently of all physiological considerations. Descartes, for example, had attempted to find a physiological basis for the various passions, and in Hobbes and Spinoza the passions were correlated with the basic principles of motion according to which all bodies behave. To be sure, the tradition which sought to link psychology with physiology was not wholly extinguished: it was revived in the views of Diderot and Cabanis, of Saint-Simon and Comte. Nevertheless, associationism was the dominant psychology of the eighteenth century, and even though Hartley had believed that vibrations in the nervous system underlay the association of ideas, his speculations along this line did not persist in the associationist movement. In fact, apart from Priestley, the psychology of the time was by and large unabashedly mentalistic. That this was the case is evident in the emphasis placed on motives such as benevolence and pride, which bear no relation to the principles governing the behavior of bodies, but depend on the ideas which men hold regarding themselves and others. Furthermore, even though self-interest was commonly regarded as one of the fundamental motives of men (and sometimes, indeed, as the only such motive), it was identified with feelings of pleasure and the avoidance of pain, treated as affections of the mind; they were not viewed as correlated with states of the body as Hobbes and Spinoza had assumed them to be. One can even note this in Mandeville, who gave an account of men's motivation in terms of their pursuit of self-interest but who, in spite of being a medical man, couched his whole account in terms of the interplay of ideas. Furthermore, the views of those who, like Butler and Hume, strongly opposed Mandeville's claims also formulated their views in strictly mentalistic terms.[16]

Although the place occupied by self-interest in the moral and social thought of the eighteenth century was an important one, its importance has sometimes been exaggerated.[17] Not only did Butler and Hume attempt to rebut the claim that it was man's sole or even his dominant motive, but one also finds it rejected by Adam Smith. Smith has often been misinterpreted in this respect because of the emphasis he placed on self-interest in his economic theory, but he— like Hume—insisted that motives other than self-interest were important in accounting for the sum total of relations obtaining among men. To be sure, both Smith and Hume held that self-interest had various socially desirable consequences. For example, Smith held that the production and exchange of goods depended upon it, rather than upon any other of men's motives, and he believed that the individual's pursuit of his own economic advantage redounded to the benefit of all. Furthermore, he believed that history had shown that economic growth promotes general social well-being. One can thus understand why—on grounds quite different from whose of Mandeville—Smith regarded self-interest as having highly desirable social consequences. One should also note that Hume had adopted a similar view with respect to political life, holding that self-interest was an indispensable element in it.[18] However, both Hume and Smith insisted that self-interest was not the sole spring of action. For example, in their theories of moral judgment, other motives played a decisive role: in fact, Smith regarded all such judgments as ultimately dependent upon sympathy, and not upon self-interest in any of its forms.

While the attempts of eighteenth-century social theorists to understand the bases of social life in terms of psychological factors represents a form of methodological individualism, their approach differed from the deductive method which had been typical of the political philosophies of Hobbes and Spinoza. This was especially striking in the cases of Hume and Smith, who attempted to shun "metaphysics," adopting a method analogous to the new experimental method in the natural sciences. By abandoning the earlier mode of analysis, which had been distinctly *ahistorical*, they and others who followed the new method set out to compare the actual institutions of different societies in an attempt to discover, through analyzing past successes and failures, what forms of government are best suited to satisfying men's needs. Thus, even though their normative interests were no less strong than those of their predecessors, they differed in attempting to establish their conclusions on the basis of historical analyses, not claiming to derive them directly from what they took to be the essential nature of man.

Whether Hume or Smith, or any of their contemporaries, were explicitly aware of the fact, the "Rules of Reasoning" which Newton had laid down at the opening of book 3 of the final edition of the *Principia* would have furnished justification for their procedure. According to Newton, one must shun general "hypotheses," that is, principles which *could* explain phenomena but which had not themselves been derived by induction from these phenomena; instead, one should base all general propositions on the analysis of individual cases, rendering these propositions general by induction, that is, by showing that they apply to all relevant cases.[19] This was not the method of Hobbes and Spinoza, however apt their hypotheses concerning human nature may have been. Those hypotheses had not been derived by induction from an analysis of individual cases; rather, they had followed from more general metaphysical principles, and were in this respect similar to the hypotheses in physics which Descartes had employed and which Newton was at pains to combat.

Furthermore, the specific policies of government which they were prepared to defend were ostensibly justified in terms of the same general principles. Hume and Smith, on the other hand, viewed themselves as having arrived at a knowledge of the general principles of human nature through direct analyses of men's modes of thought and action, that is, as Hume said in the subtitle of his *Treatise*, through introducing "the experimental method of reasoning into moral subjects." In their social theories they then applied these inductively derived general principles to specific historical examples as a means of explaining what arrangements had in the past been either successful or unsuccessful in the social realm. Because they, like Newton, believed in the constancy of nature (and, in this case, in the constancy of human nature), they held that what had been true of the past could serve as guidance for the present and the future. A passage from section 8 of Hume's *Enquiry Concerning Human Understanding* is particularly revealing in this connection. He said:

> It is universally acknowledged, that there is a great uniformity among the actions of men, in all nations and ages, and that human nature remains still the same in its principles and operations. The same motives always produce the same actions; the same events follow from the same causes. . . . Would you know the sentiments, inclinations, and course of life of the Greeks and Romans? Study well the temper and actions of the French and English: you cannot be much mistaken in transferring to the former *most* of the observations which you have made with regard to the latter. . . . Records of wars, intrigues, factions, and revolutions, are so many collections of experiments, by which the politician or moral philosopher fixes the principles of his science, in the same manner as the physician or natural philosopher becomes acquainted with the nature of plants, minerals, and other external objects, by the experiments he forms concerning them.[20]

This doctrine concerning the constancy of human motives was later challenged by anti-Enlightenment figures, such as Herder and Hegel, who stressed the uniqueness of each people and each age. Yet, even among those who were roughly contemporaneous with Hume and Smith and who shared their interest in explaining social phenomena in psychological terms, there were some who rejected the view that the constancy of the laws of human nature guaranteed that people will always behave in the same ways. Instead, they held that accumulating experience and growing enlightenment had caused the forms of men's thoughts and actions to change in the past and would cause them to continue to change. The foremost early exponent of this doctrine among the associationists was Helvétius; I shall therefore identify this development among the associationists by referring to it under his name.

## The Method of Helvétius

All associationists believe that human thought and action depend upon the association of ideas, and that the laws of association are universal and unchanging. In this they can be said to have held that the laws of association corresponded to Newton's laws, and Hume himself drew this parallel.[21] Newton, however, had a further reason for believing that "nature is very consonant and comformable to herself," for not only did he believe that the fundamental laws of nature were unchanging, but he also held that the ultimate particles of matter were created in precisely the shapes and forms in which they presently exist.[22] No associationist would hold a similar doctrine with respect to human individuals, for it was the fundamental thesis of associationism that the thoughts and actions of each individual depend upon his experiences. Nevertheless, Hartley, Hume, and Smith all believed that the circumstances in which men are placed are, on the whole, so similar that the basic beliefs and modes of action acquired by each individual will come to resemble those of others. It was in this manner that Hume explained the constancy he found in the ways in which men have behaved at different times and in different nations. Thus, to draw an analogy between the individuals who form a society and Newton's view of material atoms, even though each human being changes in the course of his life, all gradually tend to behave in ways that are fundamentally similar. In this sense Hume and Smith, as well as Hartley, can—roughly speaking—be considered "Newtonian."

On the other hand, Priestley, Godwin, and Owen adopted the position of Helvétius, emphasizing the extent to which education is capable of fundamentally altering the characters of men.[23] Such changes in character were not, of course, viewed as random: they occur because a constant set of psychological principles produce varying results. By this time, contrary to the views of Butler, Hume, and Smith, it was widely held that the only universal and constant factors in human affairs were the individual's pursuit of his own interests (usually conceived in terms of pleasure and avoidance of pain), plus the basic principles of the association of ideas. Given these factors, the specific nature of an individual's character was attributable to the way in which he had been affected by the circumstances to which he had been exposed.

Such formative influences, all of which Helvétius had included under the concept of "education," were the sources to which he and others attempted to trace the moral and intellectual differences among men. Helvétius attributed some of them to happenstance, as when two brothers have differing experiences; others he regarded as resulting from deliberately planned regimens, such as those formulated by parents and schoolmasters; still others he attributed to the effects of the laws and the institutions under which individuals live. It was with the last that he was primarily concerned. In the second chapter of *De l'homme* he compared man to a puppet whose actions were controlled by those who govern him. To govern properly, however, one must understand the laws of nature, which are the wires determining how the puppet behaves. Therefore, the art of the legislator, as Helvétius indicates in his poem "Epistre sur le plaisir," lies in so directing men's inclinations toward pleasure that what is in their own interest subserves the public good. When this occurs, each becomes bound to the other, and justice in the social order obtains.[24]

Godwin and Owen shared Helvétius's belief that the association of ideas made men extremely malleable, so that the characteristics of a nation could take on any form, depending upon its laws, just as water conforms to the shape of whatever vase one pours it into.[25] They therefore held that it was possible to alter men's characters in a way that would ensure greater well-being. Thus, like Helvétius (but unlike Hume and Smith), they were concerned to plan and to advocate large-scale changes in social institutions. This was what Owen advocated in his *New View of Society,* where he placed on its title page an epigraph drawn from the first paragraph of that work. It reads:

> Any character, from the best to the worst, from the most
> ignorant to the most enlightened, may be given to any
> community, even to the world at large, by applying certain
> means; which are to a great extent at the command and
> under the control, or easily made so, of those who possess
> the government of nations.

This social interventionism, which was also basic to the thought of Helvétius, was characteristic of the growing faith in the ability of men to control their own destinies. To some extent that faith was also present in later meliorists, such as John Stuart Mill and Huxley, but their efforts were confined to advocating the removal of specific evils and offering opportunities for greater individual growth. God-win and Owen, on the other hand, sought to bring about radical changes in men's characters through their plans to change the basic nature of the institutions under which men had lived in the past and were continuing to live.

What must strike a reader today is the sense of confidence that these associationists displayed with respect to their ability to re-design social institutions, and to do so in a way that would fundamentally alter men's natures. They did not regard their plans as utopian but as capable of being put directly into practice once the basic principles of human nature had come to be understood. What they failed to note was that the reformer himself did not stand outside of his society, but had been formed by his own past experience and could not have escaped its formative power any more than any other man could. Thus, in tending to identify themselves with the ideal legislator who would reconstitute social institutions in forms free of the baleful influence of the past, they fell into what I have elsewhere termed the "self-excepting fallacy": not applying to themselves the same principles they applied to all other men.[26] This fallacy is always common enough in popular thought, and it has sometimes been at least apparently present in sophisticated theories concerning human motivation. For example, on some interpretations of their writings, a charge of this kind has been leveled against both Marx and Freud. However, there was a special reason why the fallacy should have been very effectively concealed from those associationists who shared the dominant standards of the Enlightenment: they judged all other ages and nations with reference to their own standards. Such a lack of appreciation of the values of cultures and forms of organized social life other than their own lay at the basis of their confidence that through a judicious use of education, based on associationist principles, they could remake the world. Not only that faith, but the more modest psychological approaches to social theory, such as that of Hume, came to be challenged by two other types of necessitarian theory, each of which attempted to account for the structures of society in institutional rather than in individualistic terms. It is with them that the next chapter will deal.

# 3 ⇨ Necessity & Purpose
in Institutional Theories

Even though the category of necessity tends to dominate those theories which adopt an institutional approach to social organization, some introduce notions of purposiveness, either openly or covertly, and it is with the relations between purpose and necessity that we must ultimately deal. First, however, we must examine various ways in which those who approach social theory in institutional terms have sought to explain social organization and change. A first, familiar type of necessitarian approach seeks to establish developmental patterns or laws governing the course of human history. A second type attempts to identify the determining factors which are present in any society, and which account for the general character of that society, but does not conceive of these factors as laws of directional change. A third type attempts to explain particular features of any given society in terms of the needs of that society as a whole. I shall deal with some outstanding nineteenth- and twentieth-century examples of each type of theory in turn.

## DEVELOPMENTAL LAWS AND PATTERNS
## OF DIRECTIONAL CHANGE

Although Hegel was not by any means the sole instigator of the revolt against those individualistic theories of society which had dominated the eighteenth century, he stands as the foremost exponent of a new cultural and institutional approach. Not only were his ethical theories and his theory of the state anti-individualistic, but the pattern of historical development which he traced was dominated by the concept of necessity. To be sure, he did not attribute this necessity to a law of development, nor explain it in causal terms. Rather, he viewed it as an unfolding of the spirit of mankind, developing through a series of stages of growth, fulfilling the divine purpose immanent in the world. Thus, Hegel carried on the tradition of theological philosophies of history, but he rejected the traditional view that God's purpose was revealed in single events; rather, it was manifest only in the pattern of development inherent in the world's history as a whole.

It scarcely needs saying that this identification of purpose and necessity, basic in Hegel's idealism, did not appeal to those who, like Comte, attempted to found a science of society that was to be completely free of theological and metaphysical speculation. In this respect Comte returned to a tradition basic to the Enlightenment, even though he, like Hegel, was in most other respects an opponent of Enlightenment modes of thought. For example, both rejected attempts to understand society in terms of the propensities of individuals and also rejected the standards of value by which Enlightenment thinkers had judged the progress of mankind. Similarly, both viewed societies as organic wholes and regarded the degree of unity present in a society as constituting an important aspect of its worth. This unity, however, was not the sole standard used by Comte. Like Hegel, he viewed history as a developmental process in which not all of the values immanent in organic societies were of equal worth: in the course of history there was progress toward higher stages of good. In Comte this doctrine took the form of his law of three stages, according to which change proceeds from a theological through a metaphysical to a positive stage. He traced these stages not only in thought but in successive forms of social organization, holding that all spheres of knowledge, all institutions, and all societies were destined to follow the same stages of growth. Implicit in that conception of human history was the belief that the process was purposeful, that there were ends which human history was ultimately going to achieve. In fact, Comte often spoke of not understanding events unless one were to understand that out of which they had arisen and in terms of that which they were to become.[1] Basic to this quasi-teleological interpretation of the direction of historical change was Comte's conviction that only when societies achieve the goal of the positive stage in all of their institutions, and in their overall organization, would the conflicts within individuals become resolved, with head and heart reconciled and the fullness of human nature achieved.

Such a semi-eschatological notion of social development was closely paralleled in the thought of Marx. This is especially true of the early *Economic Philosophical Manuscripts*, which reflect an ideal of human nature under conditions of freedom, an ideal which remained a motivating force throughout Marx's later analyses of social conditions and social change. Many other parallels can of course be drawn between Comte and Marx; for example, each denied that men's actions are to be explained in terms of psychological propensities that are unaffected by their social relations. On the other hand, there was an important and fundamental difference between their ways of establishing a science of society. That difference lay in the fact that Marx attempted to give causal explanations of the changes in specific institutions, whereas Comte had in fact been content to trace what he believed an overview of human history was able to establish: that there was a single, comprehensive law of social development. This difference reflected Comte's view of science, according to which all causal explanations are vestiges of anthropomorphic conceptions, whereas all adequate explanations are to be formulated in terms of universal laws. Unfortunately, in defining science as "prevision," Comte failed to recognize that the laws characteristic of science—unlike many common-sense explanations—are not simply expressions of a sequence of stages through which one can expect a series of events to pass. Instead, they express functional relationships between various factors present in a wide range of otherwise diverse phenomena, and one can use them to predict what will occur in a particular case only if one applies them to the initial conditions actually present in that case. In contrast to Comte, Marx based his view of the development of human history on an attempt to formulate a law which expressed the functional relationships between various aspects of social organization. Though he, too, viewed the historical process as a single whole, moving in a definite direction, he did not regard this as an ultimate fact concerning human history, but took it to be a consequence of the factors that were responsible for the basic forms of social organization and for bringing about social change.

As we earlier noted, Marx's analysis of these causal factors lay in his doctrine of the productive forces that characterize a society. These forces determine the relations of production obtaining within that society; therefore, changes in the productive forces are what bring about changes in the relations of production. These relations, in their turn, determine the character of the other institutions in a society, which Marx referred to as the superstructure of the society. This superstructure includes, for example, its political and juridical system and its ideology. Thus, according to Marx, the structure of a society, and the changes in that structure, ultimately depend upon the nature and changes in its productive forces, that is to say, on its means of production (its instruments of production and its resources) and upon the labor power present in it.[2] It was to this web of factors, in their interrelationships, that he attributed the element of necessity he held to be present in man's social life.

One obvious presupposition of this view was Marx's thesis that each society constitutes an organic whole, in which no institution and no aspect of culture is unaffected by the basic factors of that society's economic life: when subjected to analysis, each reflects the productive forces present in the society, since the nature of each and the changes which occur in it are ultimately determined by such forces. To be sure, it may seem as if some institutions or some aspects of culture do not reflect the productive forces actually present in the society at a given time, but Marx held that in the long run institutions and cultural features would conform to the nature of the productive forces available to that society.[3]

Here two types of questions arise. First, to what extent is each form of organized social life actually a self-contained whole, all of whose aspects are dependent upon the productive forces available in that society, while remaining materially unaffected by the influence of other forces? Second, how is one to account for such changes as occur within the life of a particular type of social organization, and for the changes that bring about the destruction of one type of social organization and give rise to a radically different principle of organized social life? I shall take up these questions in turn, not with a view to refuting Marx but for the sake of indicating some of the difficulties they suggest.

With respect to the first type of question, there are obvious points at which a Marxist view might be challenged. It might in the first place be claimed that the choices and decisions of individuals can, and often do, alter events. Such an introduction of individual choice and decision is widely and correctly assumed to run counter to the assumption that whatever happens in the social realm happens necessarily and is ultimately independent of the wills of individuals. Marx, of course, was fully aware of objections of this sort, but there were two reasons why he was not inclined to be disturbed by them. In the first place, standing in the Hegelian tradition as he did, it was natural for him to view the individual as a product of society, with the nature and actions of individuals being effective only insofar as they coincided with tendencies which, at the time, were dominant in society. For Hegel, it was the "cunning of Reason" that used individual passions as its instruments, but Marx did not look upon the world as dominated by a divine immanent purpose; instead, he held that whatever might be the causes of an individual's choices, the long-run efficacy of such choices was determined by the institutional factors responsible for the direction of social change. In the second place, Marx was not inclined to regard what we refer to as "choice" as itself being undetermined. On the contrary, he absolutely rejected free will, holding that man was not to be understood in any terms other than those which apply to the rest of nature. For him, this entailed that causal necessity, rather than chance or choice or design, was the only category through which the nature and history of man were to be interpreted.

Although I have more sympathy with Marx's position regarding the role of choice in human affairs than I do with the ways in which the category of purpose has been used by those adopting an individualistic approach to social theory, I find his rejection of the role of choice faulty and ultimately unconvincing.

In the first place, even if one grants, as I would, that every choice of every individual can be said to be causally determined, the question arises as to what determines those choices. This is a question to which I shall direct attention in the fifth chapter. Here I shall simply say that Marx's thesis appeared to him to be plausible only because he was inclined to hold that the factors determining an individual's choices are, in the last analysis, sociological factors, depending upon the nature of society and upon the individual's place in that society. That assumption, however, I find to be palpably false. Put in the simplest terms, two individuals having the same position in a society, perhaps even being members of the same family and engaged in the same way of securing their livelihood, may make different choices in the same situation. This is not to say that their choices are undetermined: it is to say that, to some extent at least, choices are determined by psychological factors such as the nature of an individual's past experience, and perhaps by inherited dispositions, rather than being exclusively determined by sociological factors such as the individual's place in a particular social structure.

In the second place, even though there are limits to the efficacy of a particular individual's choices with respect to influencing the course of events, some choices of at least some individuals may be said to affect the course of social change. This is especially apparent with respect to individuals who, for whatever reasons, occupy a particular status in their societies. For example, the decisions of a prime minister or of a president, or the choices made in a time of crisis by a charismatic leader of a religious sect, may have an immediate effect on political change, or on the forces working for or against social change. To objections of this sort one who is committed to a Marxian analysis often objects that whatever changes individual decisions or group interventions may bring about, the dominant forces in a society will, in the long run, reassert themselves, and the ultimate outcome will not have been changed. To this there is, I believe, an obvious answer. What has sometimes been called the "timetable of history" is of major importance: it is often fateful that a particular event occurred precisely when it did. For example, even if a war between two nations may be said to have been inevitable, the precise time at which one launched its attack may have radically affected the duration or even the ultimate outcome of that war. (And the duration of a war, alone, may affect subsequent history.) Similarly, in economic affairs, the lead time that a specific nation has in the development of a given type of industry does not leave the economic situations of other nations unchanged: how they then react affects their future and also affects economic affairs in the nation innovating the change. One can see the same phenomenon on a smaller scale when one considers how the patenting of a major invention by one individual, or by a corporation, radically alters the possibilities open to others. Once existing conditions are changed, one cannot say that whatever subsequently occurred would "in the long run" have occurred anyway: whatever alters the conditions under which an event occurs much be said to have an influence on what will subsequently occur.

A second major question regarding the adequacy of Marx's analysis is how one is to interpret the relation between those elements which he assigns to the superstructure of a society and the productive forces and the relations of production upon which that superstructure purportedly rests. Are the causal relations such that religious institutions, for example, are ultimately dependent upon the productive forces and relations of production in a society? If so, is the very existence of such institutions dependent upon these factors, or is it only that the varying forms they exhibit in different societies are to be explained in terms of the factors which Marx regarded as basic in social life? An even more obvious and often repeated question is whether Marx held—or should have held—that there is two-way causation between elements in the superstructure and the factors constituting the base on which that superstructure rests. If he were to be consistent, should he have held that causal influences always and only flow from the base to the superstructure, so that even though conflicts within a society are reflected in, say, political conflicts, the latter do not have any effective influence on the direction of social change?

I do not believe that Marx himself formulated a consistent reply to these questions, and I regard Engels' later attempts to reconcile two-way causal influences with long-run necessity as merely muddying the waters.[4] I should be inclined to insist that once one admits— as I think one must—that modes of governance may have an influence on the development of economic life, or that religious beliefs can exert an influence even with respect to what is regarded as food fit to eat or how labor is to be used, one cannot maintain that all causal influences pass from substructure to superstructure, and that none operate in the opposite direction. Once this is admitted, a quasi-Marxian doctrine of substructure and superstructure may perhaps still be defended, but it then becomes a doctrine concerning the relative importance of the substructure and the superstructure, or else it must be restricted in its scope. It would not then constitute a sufficient explanation of the structure of a society, nor of what forces can be effective in bringing about social change.

This brings us to a point at which it appears necessary to criticize Marx's view that each type of organized social life is a self-contained whole, all of whose facets depend upon the productive forces within it. In the first place, it would seem that such a view neglects the effects that geophysical factors (such as changes in climate or the discovery or the exhaustion of natural resources) can have on the life of a society. In the second place, it would also seem to neglect the effects of cultural diffusion, such as are brought about through the introduction of new crafts or of new ideas into the ongoing life of a society. To both of these objections Marxian forms of social analysis have an answer. On the one hand such objections assume that specific peoples or nations constitute the proper units of study, whereas Marx was interested in defining *types* of social organization in general economic terms, such as "feudalism" or "capitalism," neither of which is to be identified with the structure of a single, localized social group. Consequently, the intrusion of outside forces on the life of a particular society was not the sort of change that Marx set himself to explain: he was basically interested only in those changes which represented different stages of economic development. Yet, in using this principle of selection to define the subject matter of his investigations, his explanatory theory threatened to become tautologous: the economic basis of social organization became all-important in explaining change only because the course of change with which he was concerned was the course of changes occurring in economic systems.

Were one to set this objection aside, Marx could offer still another reason for discounting the intrusion of external factors when he was explaining social change. He could hold that the responses of a society to changes in the physical environment depend upon the social organization of that society, and that in many cases previously existing aspects of social organization had led to changes in the geophysical environment itself. Similarly, how a society responds to alien cultures, whether they be introduced through conquest or through the diffusion of new techniques or ideas, will also depend upon the strength of the society that is being subjected to such outside forces, and this will depend on whether its social organization is well-knit or is suffering from internal strains.[5]

Lying behind this answer is the assumption shared by Hegel and Comte as well as by Marx that each society is a single organic whole. Yet, if this be true, one must ask what is responsible for the changes that societies undergo. Hegel's answer simply appealed to the analogy of what occurs in all life: a period of growth is succeeded by the vigor of maturity and then by inevitable decline. Comte's answer, on the other hand, relied on the natural development of new and more adequate forms of thought. The essence of Marx's answer is to be found in a famous passage from the preface of his *Contribution to the Critique of Political Economy*, where he said, "No social order ever perishes before all the productive forces for which there is room in it have developed; and new, higher relations of production never appear before the material conditions of their existence have matured in the womb of the old society itself." Thus, for Marx, there was in each society a tendency to develop all of its inherent potentialities, and only when these had reached the highest point in their development would contradictions set in, and the new forces which were arising within that society could develop and overthrow the old.

This schema for the explanation of change obviously presupposes the existence of some tendency toward the development of all the productive forces present within a society. The basis of that tendency was Marx's belief that people insofar as they are free to do so naturally seek to obtain for themselves greater control over the means necessary for their existence and thus constantly strive to expand and improve the productive forces present in their society.[6]

What therefore ultimately underlies social change, according to Marx, is the nature of man, which is that of a self-fulfilling being.

To be sure, the specific changes undergone by a society are not a direct reflection of individuals' desire to fulfill themselves: rather, that is the hidden spring of their actions, which leads to the growth of new modes of production, to new relations of production, and to the conflicts which are engendered within the superstructure of a society. Yet, without this inherent human drive, there would be no impetus for change within a given social structure and no reason why one form of social structure would be overthrown to be replaced by another. Thus, in the end, Marx's analysis of society rested on an appeal to the category of purpose: the drive of men to improve their lot in the face of antagonistic forces in nature and against the repressive conditions that had developed in the course of all past forms of social life. Thus, according to Marx's view, there is an inherent tendency in history to move from the period when men's needs were frustrated by the recalcitrance of external nature, through a series of stages in which the growth of population and of technology gave rise to a series of internal struggles between classes, until, finally, there was to be achieved the freedom of self-development that all individuals seek. Thus, Marx—no less than Hegel and Comte—regarded the course of history as a single linear developmental process, even though he, unlike them, cannot be charged with not having attempted to explain the causal factors responsible for this course of development. To be sure, as we have seen, his analysis of these causal factors raises a number of crucial problems, and in my opinion some of these problems are so serious that they demand either a radical revision of Marxist theory or its abandonment. Now, however, I wish to focus attention on a major difficulty in *all* theories—whether Marxist, Hegelian, Comtean, or any other—which hold that the proper interpretation of human history demands that one regard it as a single developmental process tending toward a particular goal.

The root error in that view is that all such interpretations view history selectively, resulting in an illusion of linearity, instead of taking into account the relative independence of the histories of different peoples and regions and the tangled skeins of interconnection among them. Perhaps the most common form of this error is attributable to ethnocentrism, where the survey of world history is limited to what the historian sees as the antecedents of his or her own society, omitting from consideration whatever did not directly contribute to it. For example, had Hegel or Comte not placed the values they did on those facets of Western culture in which each was primarily interested, would each have assessed the tendency of world history to have been what he claimed it to be? Or, to take different examples in which ethnocentrism played little or no part, would Toynbee's conception of what constituted the essential aspects of historical change have been what it was had he not regarded the so-called higher religions as the essential aspects of social organization? Similarly, Marx's conviction that the material conditions of existence provide the all-important point of reference for understanding the course of human history prevented him from having an interest in all of the actual interrelations between, say, different nations, and without taking these into account what transpired in each cannot be fully understood. Thus, even if one were to say that Marx was correct in his sociological analysis of the underlying features of all societies, that analysis is not to be identified with *history* and is not a substitute for it. Only historical analyses of actual occurrences can provide an adequate basis for either formulating or testing sociological generalizations, and while Marx's own studies of what was occurring in capitalist countries in his own time *did* provide historical accounts of significant events, they were not sufficient to show that all human history could be interpreted in the same terms, and certainly not that all human history tended toward what he saw as its ultimate goal.[7] Therefore, the supposed necessity present in historical development, taken as a whole, is an artifact of the methods of those attempting to survey all human history from a single point of view and is not a tendency that can be shown to be always and everywhere present.

In this connection it is important to note that when it is held that there is a particular direction in which the historical process viewed as a whole necessarily moves, the stages through which that process passes will take on a purposive aspect: they will be seen in terms of what each contributed to the realization of a definite goal. This connection between the notion of necessity and the attribution of an implicit purposiveness to the stages of a process is by no means accidental: it rests on what I have elsewhere termed the "retrospective fallacy."[8] When one looks back on how a particular process actually developed, one can see the various stages through which it passed, and if one neglects to inquire what would have happened if, at various junctures, events had taken a different turn, the process as a whole will appear to have been a necessary one. Yet, if at some of these junctures events had in fact taken a different turn, each subsequent stage in the process would presumably have been quite different. This is not to say that what happened at each juncture cannot be causally explained; it is only to insist that there is a difference between saying that each event in a series can be explained by the circumstances present when it occurred, and saying that the series taken as a whole had to occur precisely as it did. As we shall later have occasion to note, it is only when one is dealing with a closed system that one can legitimately say that all which occurs within that system was determined. But history nowhere presents us with closed systems: the lives of peoples are affected by other peoples and by what occurs in the natural environment; furthermore, the various aspects of a society affect one another and change in different directions and at different rates. Thus, even though one can adequately explain what occurred in a society at a given time and place and can explain the particular changes which that society has undergone, this does not entail that its development was "determined" in the sense that it could not have proceeded in any way other than that in which it did. And if this be true of any one society, it is true, *a forteriori*, if one is considering human history as a whole. It is only when we look back on a process and grant a privileged position to what has actually happened, assuming that nothing else could have happened, that the process looks as if it were a necessary process and it looks as if history had been inevitably moving toward a particular goal.

This view had characterized most interpretations of man's past in the period of the Enlightenment and had, of course, been present in the thought of Hegel, Comte, and Marx. Its spread was greatly favored by an interest in biological evolution—an interest which antedated Darwin's *Origin of Species*. In this connection one must note the views of Erasmus Darwin and the development of Lamarck's theory, as well as Chambers' widely known *Vestiges of the Natural History of Creation* (1844). However, in addition to this interest in biological evolution there was a tendency to view the evolutionary process as applicable to the history of the world as a whole, encompassing not only geological and organic development but extending into the history of human civilization. The conception of an all-embracing evolutionary development was clearly expressed (perhaps for the first time) in Spencer's essay "Progress: Its Law and Cause," which was published in 1857, two years before Darwin's *Origin of Species*.[9]

Spencer, unlike Darwin, assumed that there was a *law* of evolutionary development—a position for which Darwin had criticized Lamarck. Rather than holding that evolutionary development followed necessarily from a single, basic law of nature, Darwin wanted to establish that biological evolution had in fact occurred and that it was to be explained by variability in the traits of individuals and by the ways in which natural selection operated to preserve or obliterate these traits in successive generations. To be sure, whenever he adopted a retrospective point of view and delineated the whole course of evolutionary development, he did look upon it as a single process, and spoke of the "Tree of Life" which, as it grew, gradually developed higher and nobler forms. Thus, in the closing sentences of the *Origin of Species* he said:

> Thus, from the war of nature, from famine and death, the most exalted object which we are capable of conceiving, namely, the production of the higher animals, directly follows. There is grandeur in this view of life with its several powers, having been breathed by the Creator into a few forms or into one; and that, while this planet has gone circling on according to the fixed law of gravity, from so simple a beginning endless forms most beautiful and most wonderful have been, and are being evolved.

Nevertheless, he did not regard it as a law of nature that there should be definite stages through which the evolutionary series was bound to pass: what had occurred, and was occurring, was brought about through the interaction of a series of independent causes.

When one turns from Darwin's theory of biological evolution to the views of those who attempted to trace the course of social evolution, one notes that they, too, shared the view that there had been gradual progress over time toward the development of higher forms of social life. This was the view of Tylor and of Morgan, as well as of other eminent social evolutionists such as McLennan. However, unlike Spencer, they did not maintain that there was a law of social development, nor did they rely on analogies drawn from the physical or biological sciences to support their views. Instead, Tylor attributed the overall progress of civilization to the development of the arts and of knowledge, while Morgan emphasized the impact of new inventions and of changes in domestic institutions resulting from changes in men's ideas and passions. In fact, one may say that apart from the case of Spencer, there was no direct connection between evolutionism in biology and the theory of social evolution; the resemblance between the two theories was almost exclusively due to a parallelism in method. In both fields the comparative method formed the basis for the development of theories regarding genealogical descent.

By the comparative method is meant the attempt to trace relationships among various phenomena in terms of resemblances between them with respect to one or more of their significant features. As is evident in the case of earlier classificatory systems in botany and zoology, the method need not be interpreted as establishing genealogical connections between the phenomena investigated. It was, however, used in this way by Darwin, who regarded it as wholly implausible to assume that when varieties of plants or animals closely resembled one another, and when their geographical distribution was such that they existed in relatively close proximity to one another, the resemblances between them were not to be explained in any way other than in terms of descent. A similar use of the comparative method provides the basis on which the diffusion of many cultural traits is to be explained. Most social evolutionists, however, were not diffusionists: they attempted to show that all societies passed through certain stages of development and that these stages were paralleled by the stages of development which had been characteristic of the history of mankind as a whole. Unfortunately, their reconstructions were entirely speculative and involved a misuse of the comparative method. Except in the case of material artifacts, there was no basis on which they could reconstruct the history of mankind. No historical records exist through which it could be shown that all existing societies (and all past societies) have passed through the same stages of institutional development: even the most extensive archaelogical remains give only limited clues as to what the institutions of early cultures must have been. What the social evolutionists lacked with respect to such evidence they filled in by means of an illegitimate use of the comparative method.

The procedure they followed consisted in surveying the characteristics of so-called primitive or "savage" societies currently extant; and on no basis other than the fact that these cultures had simpler technologies and no written language, they assumed that the other characteristics displayed by them were to be regarded as similar to those found in earlier stages of the history of mankind. Since the institutions characteristic of these contemporary primitive societies varied greatly among themselves, social evolutionists attempted to hold that some among them represented earlier stages of development, whereas those which more closely resembled features of contemporary Western culture were to be considered as later developments. This procedure, however, was not based on geographical distribution, nor on any serial order which could actually be traced. Furthermore, there were cases in which no contemporary society exhibited the traits that social evolutionists attributed to the earliest forms of culture; instead, these theorists simply extrapolated from the past as they had reconstructed it, assuming what must have been an even earlier stage in human development. The clearest example of this was the hypothesis that there was a stage in the relations between the sexes which could be designated as "group marriage" and which antedated all other forms of social life. Similarly, it was sometimes supposed that there was a period in which all art forms were purely decorative and nonrepresentative, whereas other social evolutionists supposed that all art forms were originally representative, serving magical purposes, and that no sense of pure decoration was to be found. When one surveys these and other variations in the stages of human development which different social evolutionists had attributed to the past, one cannot fail to be skeptical of their claims.

On the other hand, there was a good deal of plausible corroborative evidence drawn from a use of the comparative method that supported the claims of evolutionary theories in biology. In the first place, analyses of embryological development in the higher forms of animal life seemed to suggest that biological forms had passed through analogous stages of development: as the matter was first put by the embryologist von Baer, and later by Haeckel, "ontogeny recapitulates phylogeny." It was not possible, however, to show that the history of individual societies went through each of the stages it was claimed had characterized the progress of mankind as a whole. A second difference—and one which is far more important than any analogies drawn from embryological development—was the geological evidence concerning the sequence of stages through which living forms had passed. Given the geological record, there was strong evidence to show which forms of life had developed earlier and which forms had developed later in the history of the earth. This constituted strong though not conclusive independent evidence that new forms developed from older forms over the course of time, and Darwin's theory offered an explanation of how this could have occurred. The social evolutionists, however, had no equally concrete hypotheses to explain the development of new institutional forms. Nevertheless, the assumption that there had been, and would continue to be Progress was so strong that social evolutionism was not seriously challenged until the end of the nineteenth century.

The first effective challenge came from Franz Boas in his "Limitations of the Comparative Method" (1896),[10] but the chief challenge did not arise until the 1920s with the rise of the functionalist school. That this is so is, to a degree, paradoxical, since an emphasis on function was first formally introduced into sociology by Spencer, the chief representative of the evolutionary school.

Spencer's emphasis on function as applied to both the organization of individual organisms and to societies arose out of his acceptance of a Lamarckian theory of evolution. According to Lamarck (in contrast to Darwin) the structures of organisms developed in accordance with the needs imposed on such organisms by the environments in which they existed. In response to such needs, new structures began to develop and were passed on through the inheritance of these incipient characteristics. When a characteristic was no longer of use in a given environment, it atrophied, and over the course of time it gradually disappeared among the descendents of organisms of that type. Thus, new structural characteristics did not arise because chance variations were preserved insofar as they were useful in the struggle for existence, as Darwin had held. In both theories, of course, structure and function were held to be correlated, but in Lamarckian theory functional needs are primary, and structures develop in accordance with them; in Darwinian theory, on the other hand, structural variations come first and are preserved because they serve adaptive purposes. That Spencer applied a Lamarckian form of explanation to his accounts of social institutions is clear throughout his sociological writings, and this was only to be expected, since the basis of his analysis of societies lay in comparing their characteristics with the characteristics of organisms. In both cases he held that "changes of structure cannot occur without changes of function."[11] His use of this principle is nowhere more clearly evidenced than when he discussed the regulatory system of complex systems. There he said:

> In an animal, along with development of senses to yield information and limbs to be guided in conformity with it, so that by their cooperation prey may be caught and enemies escaped, there must arise one place to which the various kinds of information are brought, and from which are issued the adjusted motor impulses; and in proportion as evolution of the senses and limbs progresses, this centre which utilizes increasingly-varied information and directs better-combined movements, necessarily comes to have more numerous unlike parts and a greater total mass. . . . In a society it similarly happens that the political agency which gains predominance, is gradually augmented and complicated by additional parts for additional functions. The chief of chiefs begins to require helpers in carrying on

control. He gathers round him some who get information, some with whom he consults, some who execute his commands. No longer a governing unit, he becomes the nucleus in a cluster of governing units.[12]

Thus, according to Spencer, functional needs accounted for the evolutionary changes in the structures of both organisms and societies, and he held that these changes had proceeded according to a single developmental law. That law, which he had first sketched in his essay "Progress: Its Law and Cause," was further developed in his *First Principles* and was illustrated throughout his later treatments of the principles of biology, psychology, and sociology. Taken together, these works marked the final and most complete of the nineteenth-century attempts to establish a law of progressive development which accounted for the direction of historical change.

In addition to the previously dominant tendencies in the social sciences, there arose a series of attempts to establish the conformity of social phenomena to a set of underlying laws. Unlike the dominant tendency in the eighteenth century, these were not conceived of as psychological laws. Furthermore, they differed from those of nineteenth-century theories which accounted for change in terms of developmental laws. Instead of interpreting the differences between different societies as representing different stages in a common process of development, they were concerned with forces which operated within every society and could account for the characteristics of those societies. It is with attempts to establish such nondevelopmental laws that we shall now be concerned.

## OTHER SOCIAL LAWS

As we noted with respect to the problem of how Marx's views are to be interpreted, a distinction is to be drawn between laws regarding the direction of social development and laws which simply relate one aspect of the structure of a society, such as its means of production, to other of its structures. I shall refer to laws of the latter type as "functional laws," distinguishing them from "developmental laws."[13] It is with those nineteenth-century social theorists who were interested in applying functional rather than developmental laws to society that we shall now be concerned.

A functional law, unlike a developmental law, does not attempt to say that there is any necessary series of historical stages through which a society, or any of its institutions, will invariably pass; rather, it attempts to relate the presence of some factor or factors in a situation with the presence of some other factor or factors which accompany or follow from them. A failure to distinguish between functional and developmental laws often led to confusion among those who debated the question as to whether there are any explanatory laws that apply to social organization and social change. Too often that question was identified with whether or not there are any universally applicable developmental laws. For my part, I do not believe that there are any irreducible developmental laws.[14] Rather, when one finds what seem to be well-authenticated regularities in the stages of individual or social development, I would hold that their regularity depends upon the operation of some underlying functional laws. In other words, such series of sequential changes as occur in natural phenomena, in human development, or in societies are to be explained through applying some relevant functional law or set of laws to the initial conditions which obtain at each stage in what appears to be a developmental process. Unfortunately, most major social theorists in the nineteenth century did not fully recognize the fruitfulness of appealing directly to functional laws when they sought to explain specific instances of social change. Even Marx did not wholly abandon the view that there apparently was an irreducible necessity in the direction of social change.[15]

There were others in the nineteenth century, however, whose explanations of social phenomena were not focused on tracing overall patterns of historical change. Instead, they were interested in the variations to be found in the characteristics of different societies and in identifying the factors on which such variations depended. Among the more interesting of these thinkers were Condorcet and Quetelet, each of whom attempted to apply statistical methods to the analysis of social phenomena. In addition, there were two influential historical theorists, Buckle and Taine, who sought to generalize concerning the types of factors on which the basic characteristics of nations depended. Of these four, Condorcet was the only one who—like Hegel, Comte, Marx, and Spencer—attempted to sketch a history of the fundamental stages of mankind's social development. There was, however, one respect in which all agreed: each consistently rejected an individualistic approach to social theory. Instead, they took the proper subject matter of historial inquiry to be the characteristics of social collectives. Furthermore, apart from Hegel, all agreed that it was possible to create a genuine science of society based on empirically verifiable laws. There were, of course, substantive differences among them with respect to the actual laws through which they sought to account for social phenomena, and to some extent they also differed with respect to the ways in which they interpreted the status of such laws. For example, Comte denied that lawlike regularities are to be explained through appealing to the concept of causation because he regarded any appeal to "causes" as introducing a metaphysical notion that was incompatible with positivism: such an appeal introduced hidden forces rather than confining itself to that which is observable. Neither Marx nor Spencer agreed with this interpretation of science, nor did Condorcet, Quetelet, Buckle, or Taine; instead, each in his own way sought to explain observed regularities in causal terms. It is important to note, however, that while Marx, Buckle, Taine, and Spencer accepted a complete causal determinism in both nature and society, Condorcet and Quetelet did not. Thus, there were disagreements among them both with respect to their philosophies of science and with respect to the specific causal factors to which they appealed when explaining the nature of different societies and the forces which bring about social change. It is to an examination of these differences that we now turn.

Although Condorcet is now chiefly remembered for his unfinished, posthumously published *Sketch for a Historical Picture of the Progress of the Human Mind*, in his own time he exerted a considerable influence through his advocacy of applying mathematical methods to problems in social, economic, and political theory, as well as through his ideas and his activities with respect to social and political reform. In 1785 he published a major technical work entitled *Essai sur l'application de l'analyse á la probabilité des décisions rendu á la pluralité des voix* in which he set out to show the importance of the calculus of probabilities in its possible applications to practical social and political decisions. Later, in a more popular essay, *Tableau général de la science qui a pour objet l'application du calcul aux sciences politique et morales* (1795), he sketched the uses of mathematical methods in determining what had in fact occurred, in evaluating the reliability of judgments concerning such occurrences, and in drawing conclusions from what had thus been established.[16] In that essay he criticized previous economists for having proceeded deductively instead of through careful analyses of empirical data, and he specifically included among these data the sorts of demographic surveys with which Quetelet was later to be concerned.[17] Nevertheless, Condorcet himself did not carry out any actual inquiries concerning these data, and one can assume that he would not have done so even if his freedom had not been curtailed because of his political views. In large measure, his attention had become focused on the history of the sciences, and his famous *Sketch for a Historical Picture of the Progress of the Human Mind* was a preliminary fragment of what such a work aimed to be. Even though what is now chiefly noticed in that *Sketch* is the confidence with which he extrapolated from his belief in past progress to predict what the future would bring, Condorcet did not hold that the course of human progress conformed to a necessary law. In this respect his views differed from those of Comte. But there was one fundamental point of resemblance between them: both regarded mankind's progress as a truly social achievement rather than attributing it to a growth in the enlightenment of individuals, as Lessing, Kant, and others had done. Both also held that progress depended on the role of science in transforming the characteristics of individual thought and thereby bringing about changed forms of social organization. It was the reorganization of society, rather than the ideal of the cultural emancipation of the individual, that both took to be the goal of mankind.[18] To be sure, Comte carried this emphasis on the social matrix of individual life and thought even further than Condorcet had done, for Condorcet remained too close to the ideals of the Enlightenment to absorb the individual into what Comte called "the Great Being," that is, into Humanity as a single whole. For Comte, the individual human being was in fact a philosopher's abstraction: it was with a society as a whole that social scientists were to be concerned.

Comte attempted to justify this extreme position by claiming that it is far easier to learn the laws governing the nature of and changes in societies than it is to understand the behavior of single individuals.[19] A similar conviction became an important theme among other social theorists at the time. For example, Buckle argued that since we cannot successfully observe the processes occurring in the minds of individuals, if we are to understand their behavior we must first discover the laws which operate in history, and then apply those laws deductively to explain the individual.[20] Quetelet, too, held that contrary to the generally received opinion, it was through a study of the development of peoples that light would be thrown on the intellectual and moral development of the individual.[21] Taine originally shared this conviction as well, concentrating his attention on the characteristics of whole peoples as a means of understanding individuals and their achievements; it was only later, when he wrote *De l'intelligence* (1870), that he shifted his attention from what he regarded as the descriptive psychology of peoples to an attempt to establish principles explaining the operation of the individual mind.

In addition to their common emphasis on an institutional rather than an individualistic approach to the nature of and changes in social life, there was another feature common to the theories of Buckle, Quetelet, and Taine: each believed that social phenomena, like natural phenomena, exhibit regularities which can be formulated in definite laws. To be sure, there was no agreement among them with respect to what these laws were, nor did they agree in their interpretations of the status of such laws. For example, unlike Buckle and Taine, Quetelet interpreted his laws as statistical regularities which vary over time, although they may remain relatively constant within a given society over an extended period. Furthermore, Quetelet held that such variability was to be expected insofar as change occurred in the causal relations upon which these statistical uniformities depended. Among such causal factors he emphasized two: first, the average physical constitutions of men, and, second, the results of the free choices of individuals. Thus, he believed that there were both physical and moral causes which gradually lead to a modification of men's actions.[22] Buckle and Taine, on the other hand, espoused complete determinisms in which the characteristics of a society did not depend upon the characteristics of individuals. They held that societies were directly controlled by physical laws, and that the social world, along with the natural world, formed a single, coherent system. The specific causes to which Buckle attributed the nature of any society were its climate, its food, its soil, and the aspect of nature by which it was faced. He held that these causes operated on the social organization and character of different societies by directly influencing their wealth, their habits of work, the size of their populations, and their religious beliefs—the last being responses to nature's appearance.[23] To be sure, in addition to these physically based causes, Buckle inconsistently held that in favorable environments intellectual factors affect the course of history; in fact, he regarded such factors as the primary agents of change. Compared with them, he regarded the other aspects of a culture, such as its religion, literature, or legislation, as of secondary importance only. As a means of squaring this emphasis on intellectual factors with his determinism, he held that even though intellectual change was primarily due to the thought of outstanding individuals, it was axiomatic that whatever an individual accomplishes is attributable to the effects of antecedent circumstances. Thus, at no point was there to be an interruption in the world's causal determinism: "Every event is linked to its antecedent by an inevitable connexion, [every] such antecedent is connected with a preceding fact; . . . thus the whole world forms a necessary chain."[24]

Taine, too, accepted a total determinism. He regarded the world, including all psychological and social phenomena, as belonging within a single system governed by physically based laws.[25] In applying this universal determinism to social phenomena, Taine—like Buckle—attempted to uncover the basic causes which accounted for the characteristics of a people. Even though he spoke of his method as "psychological," it did not consist in explaining social phenomena through the use of a set of laws concerning the operations of the human mind.[26] Rather, under the influence of Hegel's *Lectures on the Philosophy of History* and Schlegel's *Philosophy of History,* he sought to grasp the characteristics of an age and of a people as this was expressed in the inner spirit (*la faculté maîtresse*) of its institutions, embodied in its eminent men.[27] Unlike Hegel and Schlegel, however, Taine attempted to offer a causal account of the factors which determine such a pervasive spirit. These causal factors were summed up in his well-known formula, "la race, le milieu, le moment." In that formula, which he announced in the introduction to his *Histoire de la littérature anglaise,* the term *race* is not to be interpreted as referring to a set of unchanging, biologically based characteristics which distinguish one human group from another and which remain fixed regardless of historical circumstances. Rather, he believed (along with many of his contemporaries) that the results of past experiences are biologically inherited, and for him *race* included the accumulated effects of the histories of different branches of the human race. As he said, "At each moment of time, the character of a people may be considered as a summary of all antecedent actions and sensations."[28] In his use of the term *milieu,* he had in mind both the physical and the political environments of a people. Like Montesquieu and Buckle, he placed emphasis on the effects of climate, but also included the effects of a nation's geographical position when confronting other nations in its immediate environment. As to his use of the third term, *le moment,* this included all of the accumulated results, in whatever sphere, which the past history of the race and the surroundings had produced in a people up to any given moment of time. Consequently, like Hegel, Taine held that the total spirit of a people, which is present in all of its institutions and without which one cannot understand the great individuals who embody its genius, develops over time. To understand societies we must therefore view them concretely and historically; we cannot do so through any appeal to general principles concerning the individual's mind.

In this respect one is forcibly reminded of Comte, whose views had affected the thought of both Buckle and Taine. For example, in a footnote in the first chapter of his *History of Civilization in England*, Buckle had expressed his admiration for Comte as "[the] living writer who has done more than any other to raise the standard of history." This praise had been directed to the fact that Comte disparaged previous historical work as nothing more than a compilation of incoherent facts that had not been viewed in their inner connections and had not been seen to be governed by laws. Taine, too, was impressed by Comte, for when the second edition of the *Cours de philosophie positive* appeared, he wrote an enthusiastic review of it. Thus, in spite of many substantial differences between them, Comte, Buckle, and Taine—along with Quetelet—may be taken as representing a new tendency in the social sciences.[29] In the first place, each broke with the tradition that social phenomena were to be explained in terms of the psychological principles governing the thought and action of individuals: instead, their attention was focused on uniformities which can be established when one considers collectivities. In the second place, they also shared the conviction that the laws governing these uniformities were not deducible from general facts concerning human nature, but were to be inductively established through appealing directly to historical data concerning the societies themselves. Nevertheless, at least two essential differences separated the methodological principles espoused by Quetelet, Buckle, and Taine from the method which was basic in all of Comte's thought. In the first place, as we have noted, Comte had rejected as "metaphysical" the traditional belief that scientific explanation involves a search for causes underlying the observed phenomena: what science sought were not causes, but laws. *Why* such laws held was not a matter that should, or could, be investigated, according to Comte. As we have seen, however, both Buckle and Taine attempted to identify certain general causal factors on the basis of which the nature of any particular society could be explained, and Quetelet regarded causal factors as providing the explanation of the statistical regularities in social phenomena which his investigations revealed. A second, and even more important difference between Comte on the one hand, and Buckle, Taine, and Quetelet on the other, was that Comte's primary concern was to establish and apply a single overriding law of development, his "law of three stages," which explained the direction in which the history of thought and of social organization inevitably move. As we have noted, the others differed from Comte in not offering any such law of directional change. Instead, Buckle and Taine were attempting to establish what types of causal factors account for the character of a particular civilization, and Quetelet was interested in showing the relative constancy of certain social phenomena within any group. Thus, in contrast with Comte's attempt to establish a directional law in social phenomena, the causal approaches of Buckle and Taine, like the statistical approach of Quetelet, may be said to represent a search for what I have termed functional laws.

The laws which they formulated were in one sense limited: unlike Marx's historical materialism, they were designed to account for the special characteristics of different societies, rather than identifying a set of structural principles which are the same in every society. Since their theories were attempts to account in lawlike terms for the fact that different societies had different characteristics, their theories could not readily be used to show that there was a steady stream flowing through human history as a whole. Therefore, their approach was unable to display previously dominant attempts to establish a single developmental pattern or law of progress, an attempt which had undoubtedly influenced Marx and was capable of absorbing his basic insight into the structure of all societies.

The sorts of laws which Quetelet, Buckle, and Taine had attempted to establish were far too weak to be pitted against the dominant trend, which stressed developmental laws, and that trend was greatly enhanced through the development of evolutionary modes of thought in biology. Even though (as I indicated in the preceding section), Darwin himself rejected the view that there is any law of progressive evolutionary development, others generally interpreted the results of his theory as a corroboration of the existence of such a law.[30] In fact, as we have seen, the manner in which Darwin had sometimes expressed himself when he considered the evolutionary process as a whole, served to fortify the impression that there was such a law. Nonetheless, his actual account of the principles underlying the origin of new species rested on what I have termed the functional mode of explanation, and not on any appeal to a directional law. It was probably Spencer who, more than any other person, popularized the notion that a survey of the results of the sciences established beyond peradventure of a doubt that there was a law of evolutionary change which was manifest in every aspect of nature and, in fact, in nature taken as a whole.

The spread of that view, with what appeared to be its corollary, the acceptance of a complete determinism, was not seriously challenged until scientific developments, primarily in physics, led philosophers of science to question earlier interpretations of the conception of natural laws. When that conception was challenged, confidence in any overriding law of directional change had to be abandoned. Thus, when tendencies which had seemed to be present in the past were interrupted, or were interfered with, by "chance" events, it could not be claimed that, in the end, the law would reassert itself and the course of change would reach an already determined outcome. A view of that sort could be maintained only so long as it was assumed that laws actually control events. Functional laws, on the other hand, are not open to similar objections: they explain events only insofar as they are applied with reference to some specific conditions, and they can be used to predict the outcome of a set of events only insofar as it can be assumed that no other events will intrude to alter those initial conditions. Thus, as we shall see, the necessity which we ascribe to some functional relationships does not entail determinism, and both chance and choice can be acknowledged to affect the course of human affairs. It was their unfortunate neglect of this fact that in part explains the widespread appeal of the view of Buckle and Taine, as well as of Spencer, since at the time it was often assumed that science entailed determinism, and that chance and choice had no place in a scientifically acceptable view of the world.

## THEORIES OF FUNCTIONAL NECESSITY

Before proceeding to a development of the foregoing point, in the next chapter, we must take note of a further type of explanation commonly designated in the social sciences (though not in psychology) as "functional explanation." Theorists of this type were not primarily concerned to establish specific laws capable of accounting for the similarities and differences in the structures of different societies, as were Buckle and Taine, but attempted to account for the various features of any given society in terms of the needs of that society as a whole.

We saw earlier that the notion of "function," used as an explanatory concept, was of fundamental importance to Spencer, and we shall soon see that Durkheim, too, gave it a prominent place in his sociological theory. However, "functionalism" as a distinctive movement in the social sciences was a later development, having its origin in anthropology in the 1920s with the publication of major works by Malinowski and Radcliffe-Brown. Both reacted against social evolutionism and against diffusionist theories regarding the origins and dissemination of culture; both also rejected the widespread tendency of anthropologists to concentrate attention on the similarities and differences between the specific cultural traits present in different societies, either for comparative purposes or with a view to tracing the spread of such traits. Malinowski and Radcliffe-Brown regarded these approaches as springing from a single, fundamental methodological error: the attempt to analyze societies in terms of a congeries of semi-independent traits, rather than viewing societies as single functioning wholes. As Radcliffe-Brown said in criticizing the method of those who followed the comparative method, "by which isolated customs were brought together and conclusions drawn from their similarity," it was necessary to follow "a new method by which all the institutions of one society or social type are studied together so as to exhibit their intimate relations as parts of an organic system."[31] When one stressed the organic unity of a society, as the functionalists did, it was not unnatural to compare societies with living organisms, even if one did not attempt to point out analogies in their structures as Spencer's essay "The Social Organism" had done.

Because of this stress on the organic unity of a society, one might be tempted to link functionalism with the social views of earlier thinkers such as Herder and Hegel, but there was a striking difference between the manner in which Herder and others had used organic analogies, and functionalist modes of thought. In contradistinction to their emphasis on those aspects of the analogy in which cultures, like organic things, apparently had an immanent tendency to grow, develop, and ultimately flourish, functionalist theories were inclined to view organic phenomena in terms of concepts such as adaptation and survival: the various aspects of a society, like the parts of an organism, must have an adaptive function if the society as a whole is to survive. Thus, even though there was an element of purposiveness in both types of theory, functionalism did not interpret purposiveness in terms of an immanent principle of self-development but in relation to survival needs.

These functionalist interpretations fall into two fairly distinct classes, one of which was chiefly represented by Radcliffe-Brown, while the other was brought to the forefront in Malinowski's later works. Originally, each had simply emphasized the unity of a society and the need to understand the interlocking of its various institutions, customs, and beliefs. Soon, however, Radcliffe-Brown stressed the interpretation of all such aspects of a society as mechanisms whereby the society was able to maintain itself. On the other hand, as Malinowski's theory developed, his emphasis shifted from simply stressing the pattern of interrelationships among the various aspects of a culture to attempting to establish certain cross-cultural constants. He attributed these constants to their function in fulfilling universal human needs. Thus, the concept of "function" took on different meanings for Radcliffe-Brown and for Malinowski.[32]

Although there are aspects of Radcliffe-Brown's theory, such as his emphasis on the role of sentiments in social organization, which do not have analogues in biology, he often relied upon an analogy between the two types of functional explanation. Their salient point of similarity was his belief that understanding the elements of a system requires understanding what those elements contribute to the functioning of the system as a whole. As Radcliffe-Brown said in *The Andaman Islanders*, "Every custom and belief of a primitive society plays some determinate part in the social life of the community, just as every organ of a living body plays some part in the general life of the organism." Furthermore, there was an obvious connection between evolutionary interpretations of the functions of the various parts of an organism and Radcliffe-Brown's theory: as he said, "The notion of function in ethnology rests on the conception of culture as an adaptive mechanism by which a certain number of human beings are enabled to live a social life as an ordered community in a given environment."[33]

In evaluating any functionalist theory it is useful to start from a distinction drawn by Ernest Nagel between functional *statements* and functional *explanations*.[34] In biology, for example, a functional statement simply ascribes a particular function to some organ or process; for example, "the function of a fish's gills is respiration." So far as I know, no philosophers of science have objected to statements of this kind, so long as they are not taken as meaning anything more than "Gills function as respiratory organs in fish." It is only if they are interpreted as explanations—that is, as in some way accounting for the fact that fish have gills—that objections have been raised. Similarly, no theoretical objections would be raised to a statement saying that ceremonial customs, as mentioned by Radcliffe-Brown, strengthen the emotional ties of the group. This, however, would simply be a statement of psychological fact; in itself, it would not offer an explanation of the customs themselves. One way of offering a functional explanation of such customs would be to say that a custom of this type was necessary in order to satisfy the needs of individuals, and this (as I have mentioned) is what, in his later writings, Malinowski attempted to do. On the other hand, the type of functional explanation proposed by Radcliffe-Brown consisted in holding that a particular type of custom was needed in order that the society could survive.[35] A functional explanation of this type would not be at all concerned with how a particular custom or institution originated; it would only insist that to account for its continued presence, and for the relations it bears to other aspects of the society, one must show what it contributes to maintaining the society as a stable, continuing whole. It was with this that both Radcliffe-Brown and his predecessor Durkheim were concerned. As Durkheim said, "To show how a fact is useful is not to explain how it originated or why it is as it is. The uses which it serves presuppose the specific properties characterizing it, but do not create them." However, what Durkheim then went on to insist was that, regardless of the origin of some particular societal fact, it remained necessary to explain why it continued to exist, and that in order to do so one had to take into account its beneficial consequences for the society as a whole.[36]

Thus, it is obvious that what Durkheim and, following him, Radcliffe-Brown took to be a functional explanation was a limited form of explanation. Not only was it not concerned with the origin of social usages, but it also made no attempt to explain why such usages (for example, funeral rites) vary in form from one society to another. Instead, it was confined to explaining how such usages function to bind the society together as a stable, continuing whole. Naturally, no explanation is faulty merely because it is thus limited in aim; however, what I first wish to point out is that even granted its limited aim, Radcliffe-Brown's functionalism is subject to serious criticism.

The first such criticism relates to the fact that if we are to take Radcliffe-Brown's theoretical statements at their face value, we should attempt to establish the direct contribution that a specific custom makes to promoting the cohesion and hence the survival of the society in which it is present. This is analogous to indicating the essential role which some specific organ, such as the kidneys, plays in maintaining an organism's life. While this is a perfectly natural way of speaking if one is merely asked "What do kidneys do?" such an answer is only a functional statement, not a functional explanation. To be sure, anyone who wishes to do so may refer to such shorthand answers as "explanations," but *as explanations* they will be misleading: they tend to conceal the fact that organs such as the kidneys contribute to the life of the organism only because of their relations to the functioning of other organs. Similarly, in a society, no social usage can, by itself, account for the continuing life of the society. Both an organism and a society are complex wholes, made up of constitutive parts which are largely interdependent and most of which cannot function at all unless they are directly sustained by the functioning of other parts. Consequently, it is misleading to claim that one can *explain* the specific function of a particular organ, or of a particular social usage, by referring directly to the needs of an organism, or of a society, taken as having a life of its own.

In the case of Durkheim at least, the root error of this conception was a particular interpretation of evolutionary theory in biology. Although he insisted that the beneficial consequences that might follow from the existence of a particular institution could not explain its *origin*, he held that it was because of its consequences that its continuing existence was to be explained. As he said, "Indeed, if the usefulness of a fact is not the cause of its existence, it is generally necessary that it be useful in order that it may maintain itself. For the fact that it is not useful suffices to make it harmful, since in that case it costs effort without bringing in any returns. If, then, the majority of social phenomena had this parasitic character, the budget of the organism would have a deficit and social life would be impossible."[37]

Darwin himself had been largely to blame for the fact that his theory gave rise to this type of interpretation. Throughout all the editions of the *Origin of Species* he held that every variation that was preserved was of positive benefit, that if it were not of use in the organism's struggle for existence, it would not have survived. For example, toward the end of chapter 6 he wrote: "Natural selection will never produce in a being any structure more injurious than beneficial to that being, for natural selection acts merely by and for the good of each. No organ will be formed, as Paley has remarked, for the purpose of causing pain or for doing injury to its possessor. If a fair balance is struck between the good and evil caused by each part, each will be found on the whole advantageous." This appeared to legitimate the view that variations were preserved *because* they were of benefit to the organisms possessing them, and even to this day Darwin's theory is often interpreted as exemplifying this mode of functional explanation.[38] However, when Darwin later wrote *The Descent of Man*, he explicitly recognized that his earlier view had been mistaken, and in chapter 2 of that work he said:

> I did not formerly consider sufficiently the existence of structures, which, as far as we can at present judge, are neither beneficial nor injurious; and this I believe to be one of the greatest oversights as yet detected in my work. I may be permitted to say, as some excuse, that I had two distinct objects in view: firstly, to show that species had not been separately created, and secondly, that natural selection had been the chief agent of change. . . . I was not, however, able

> to annul the influence of my former belief, then almost
> universal, that each species had been purposely created; and
> this led to my tacit assumption that every detail of struc-
> ture, excepting rudiments, was of some special, though
> unrecognized, service.

Thus, the assumption which was at the root of Durkheim's belief
that functional explanations explain why a particular trait persists is
an assumption that finds no support in Darwinian theory. In fact, a
biological trait persists insofar as it is inherited and insofar as (in a
given environment) it is not excessively detrimental to the survival
and reproductive capacity of the individual organisms possessing it.
These conditions—genetic inheritance and reproductive capacity—
have no direct bearing on the transmission of customs and beliefs,
and in this respect evolutionary theory in biology is really irrelevant
to questions of the self-maintenance of societies.

Radcliffe-Brown, like Durkheim, was misled by biological analogies, though in his case it was not primarily evolutionary theory but
holistic thinking in biology that misled him. It is the essence of
biological holism to say that if one is to understand how any organ of
a living body functions, one must relate its functioning to the functioning of the organism as a whole. Aristotle held such a view and
illustrated the point by saying that a person's hand is not in fact a
hand when severed from the body, since it can then no longer function as a hand (*Politics* 1253b19–26). This is of course true, but it is
not true of organisms only: a key can serve as a key only if there are
locks into which it fits, and the parts of any machine can function
only because of their relation to its other parts. This does not mean,
however, that it is the machine as a whole that regulates the operation of its parts; rather, it is the interrelations of the parts that explain
why the machine functions as it does. To be sure, in the case of
organisms, as distinct from fabricated machines, what is particularly
striking is the self-maintenance of the whole and the relation of
various organs to maintaining the life of the whole. Impressed by the
obvious importance of specific organs for the life of an organism, we
are apt to overlook the interdependence of the various organs in con-
tributing to the functioning of the organism as a whole. In short, just
as we are apt in the case of a machine simply to ask "What is this part
good for?" so in the case of a living thing we are apt to pose the
question "What does this organ do?" However, when questions are
phrased in this manner, one tends to overlook the role which an organ
actually plays in maintaining the action of the whole: it is only

through an analytic understanding of the interrelationships existing among the parts that we can in fact understand the whole. In the field of social theory, it would equally be a mistake to interpret particular ceremonials or customs or specific institutions solely with reference to the self-maintenance of the society as a whole: it was this that Radcliffe-Brown was inclined to do, in spite of his early insistence that all phases of a culture tend to be interrelated.

In addition to this criticism, I now wish to point out how limited a form of explanation Radcliffe-Brown's functionalism would provide, even were it accepted. As I have indicated, neither he nor Durkheim claimed that their functional explanations could explain the origin of the cultural traits with which they were concerned. However, no society is a wholly independent entity, to be understood solely in terms of the traits which it displays at any one time. Every society has a history, and if we are to understand its traits and their interrelationships, we must take into account how they developed out of earlier conditions within that society or, if they had their sources elsewhere, how they were changed by the new relationships into which they entered. Thus, functionalist theories may temporarily avoid, but cannot ultimately escape, problems regarding the origin and diffusion of culture traits. Nor can they ultimately avoid the problem of what brings about fundamental structural changes in a society. Thus, even though it was undoubtedly useful for anthropological investigations that functionalism had originally set aside all questions of origins and developmental change, examining instead cultures as presently existing integrated wholes, the functionalist point of view could not banish all of the problems which earlier, historically oriented theories had unsuccessfully attempted to solve.

This general criticism applies no less to Malinowski's work than to Radcliffe-Brown's holistic functionalism. However, in his later writings, as I have pointed out, Malinowski set himself a problem different from that which Radcliffe-Brown had attempted to solve. Instead of accounting for the continuing existence of what might otherwise appear to be strange ceremonies and customs in terms of what each contributed to the coherence of the group, Malinowski attempted to show that there are universal constants in social organization and that such constants rest on a set of basic human needs. Attempts to show that there are important universal social constants was by no means a novel enterprise. For example, in *Patterns of Culture* Clark Wissler had set up a table of those traits which he described as constituting a "universal pattern" found in all cultures. Among the entries he listed were "material traits," "art," "religious practices," "mythology and scientific knowledge," "family systems," and "government." His table was not systematically organized: it was simply a list derived from an empirical survey of the types of traits which anthropologists describe in their accounts of different societies. There are many difficulties in any such list. For example, religious practices cannot be divorced from mythology and scientific knowledge, nor do family systems, property, and government constitute isolates. This difficulty is no mere accident of Wissler's particular list. Any one type of *institution*, such as the family, performs numerous functions in a society: it not only has sexual and child-rearing functions, and not only defines degrees of kinship, but also performs what we, in our society, would refer to as economic and educational functions. Conversely, no specific *function*, such as education, is served by one institution only: in addition to the family, traditions are conveyed through religion and poetry and in conjunction with initiation rites, while techniques are learned from artisans and through communal labor and in some societies through institutions having specific educational aims. Thus, any attempt to characterize a universal pattern of culture by listing a series of distinct institutions is bound to fail. This, in fact, was one of the important implications of the early investigations of both Malinowski and Radcliffe-Brown.

The approach to a universal pattern of culture which Malinowski himself came to adopt had a different foundation. He sought to ground such a pattern in a set of fundamental human needs. He held that all persons, in all cultures, have the same basic needs for food, shelter, security, and the like, and he regarded these as being physiologically grounded. It is of course obvious that if any society failed to provide a sufficient number of its members with the means of satisfying these needs, that society would not survive. However, Malinowski's interest in accounting for the structures of societies in terms of human needs went far beyond this. He also spoke of derived, cultural needs which developed in every society on the basis of the ways in which that society met these more basic physiological needs. He held that such derived needs gave rise to certain types of rules which are to be found in all societies. For example, in every society there will be a rule imposing fidelity on the partners in marriage, even though there will be variation from society to society as to the nature of marriage and as to what constitutes fidelity in marriage. Malinowski sought to explain the universality of such a rule by holding that it rests on a basic need for sexual satisfaction in the marriage relationship. Similarly, he held that in every society reciprocal obligations are demanded of the members of a family or clan and that such obligations are present because of sentiments which develop in the close social relationships involved in the interactions of members of a group. Thus, he claimed that underlying the general rules governing social relationships there are psychological needs; as he said, "Every institution centers around a fundamental need."[39]

There are various ways in which Malinowski's thesis might be attacked. For example, it presupposes that there is in fact a constant and universal set of psychological needs, and that is an assumption which some social psychologists and some anthropologists have explicitly attacked. In addition, some anthropologists would deny the existence of any set of universal rules, such as those demanding fidelity in marriage or enjoining reciprocal obligations between those who recognize themselves as belonging within the same social unit or group. Unfortunately, Malinowski's listing of these rules is too fragmentary, and his account of how they emerge from psychological needs is too tenuous, for one to feel confident that he has either established that there are universal constants in social life, or even that such constants as may be found are in fact based on psychological needs. As we shall see, one might explain at least some of the constants which may be present in social organization in terms of organizational rather than psychological needs.[40] However, setting these issues aside for the time being, there is another line of criticism which is equally appropriate in assessing Malinowski's claims; to it I shall now turn.

Let us suppose that Malinowski had adequately established the universality of certain rules, such as those demanding fidelity in marriage, and let us also suppose that his psychological account of the basis for such universal rules was acceptable; what would then follow? I think that we could say that he had supplied important information concerning human values: that at least some values are common to all cultures. While this would constitute an important contribution to the theory of morality, it would do little to advance anthropological theory, for it remains on too abstract a level.[41] To understand how a particular value functions in a specific culture, we must concern ourselves with the concrete forms in which that value is expressed in that culture.[42] For example, fidelity in marriage is compatible with different sexual practices in monogamous and in polygomous societies, and it can even mean different things within a monogamous system, depending upon whether divorce is a practice to which a stigma does or does not attach. Even more obviously, even if it is true that in all social systems a reciprocity of obligations may be demanded of individuals belonging to the same family or clan, that fact would not carry us any appreciable distance in understanding the specific family obligations which are to be found in different societies. This is a matter of considerable importance, since, as Malinowski showed in his early fieldwork, the obligations which exist in a particular society cannot be understood as isolated elements within that society's culture. To understand these obligations one must, for example, first understand how families are organized with respect to kinship relations and with respect to age and gender; one must also understand how the socioeconomic system functions, and understand the religion, the magical beliefs, and the technology to which these obligations are related. Without such knowledge one cannot understand the specific obligations of reciprocity which bind a clan together. In addition, insofar as such obligations are being modified over time (a problem with which Malinowski did not deal), we must usually look to changes occurring in one or another of these related factors. In short, whatever may be universal in cultures will not, by itself, be sufficient to give us an understanding of the nature of any specific culture, nor of the kinds of differences cultures exhibit.[43]

There is, however, a quite different way in which the twin concepts of purpose and function may enter into the understanding of societies. Unlike Malinowski's approach, it would not rest on a psychological basis, but would more nearly resemble Radcliffe-Brown's approach in one respect: rather than approaching society in terms of the need of individuals, it would stress the needs of society as an organized form of social life. But departing from Radcliffe-Brown, it would analyze such needs in terms of a number of different factors, rather than being primarily concerned with the cohesion and continuity of the social group. Although its emphasis would thus, in the first instance, be concerned with what is essential if human beings are to live together in organized social groups, it would later also be forced to consider the biological and psychological needs of the individuals living in such groups. A consideration of the relationship between individual needs and the needs of society will be one of the topics with which my final chapter will deal: here we shall confine ourselves to problems concerning what constitute the needs of a society as a society.

In addressing this problem we are not concerned with any questions as to the ultimate origins of human social life. A common failing of popular thought, which has also been reflected on occasion in the social theorizing of a few philosophers, has been to postulate that there was a time when individuals lived outside of all societies, and that societies gradually grew as isolated nuclear families banded together to form larger social groups. Such speculations fail to ask where the individuals who first mated to establish these families had themselves originated if not from some preexisting group of individuals. And if we are permitted to take our clue from the observed behavior of colonies of various ape species, it is clear that when groups of some animals exist in colonies, at least rudimentary forms of social structure are to be found. For any such structure to develop, at least two factors must be present, and each is to some degree present even in ape colonies. First, there has to be some form of communication among the members of the group, and second, there must be some differentiation in the roles of various individuals belonging to the group. That this is true of communication should be immediately clear, and though it is less obvious with respect to a differentiation of roles, such differentiation is also present in all cases. For example, there is always some differentiation based on gender, at least in the early care of offspring, and in any colony there also are hierarchical differentiations among various individuals, some (but not all) of which may be based on gender, or on strength, or both. In organized human societies this aspect of groups is manifested in the division of labor and in whatever distributions of power exist. Thus, these two factors—communication and differentiation—may be regarded as the bases of any organized social life. There are, however, other factors which, although they are less foundational, are nonetheless essential to the existence and preservation of *human* societies. Because they do not have equally clear analogues in animal colonies, I am inclined to distinguish them from communication and the existence of differentiation in social groups.

The first of the five factors with which I shall here be concerned is the existence of some system of kinship organization, including within that term such topics as the forms of organization assumed by family life, questions such as matrilineal or patrilineal residence (or neither), divisions (if any) into clans, and rules concerning endogamous and exogamous marriage. These, of course, have no true analogues in any social groups other than human societies; conversely, no human society has ever been described that lacks rules relating to topics such as these. Of course, such rules vary greatly from society to society, though such variations are not so great as to defy classification into meaningful types. Furthermore, it may be the case that there are certain natural compatabilities or incompatabilities between the rules falling under these different types, so that there may, for example, be linkage between rules of residence and rules of descent, in which case one might speak of general "systems" of family and kinship organization. Furthermore, it can be established that some of these rules, such as those governing family organization, are related to other aspects of the social structure, such as the ways in which the materials necessary for subsistence are gathered or produced. The latter constitute a second factor which is essential to the survival of the group as a group.

I am not inclined to include the gathering and production of the means of subsistence as a foundational characteristic of *group* life, since each individual (other than the very young) might in fact forage for himself what may be needful for his own survival; the gathering, producing, and storing of food would not then be a group activity, nor necessary for the survival of the group *as a group*. In human societies these productive activities are linked to rules governing the distribution of the goods produced, and together they characterize the economic system of that society. The influence of such a system on other aspects of social life is not currently apt to be overlooked, thanks in no small measure to the impact of Marx's theories. However, such influences had also been recognized by earlier economists and were frequently noted with respect to primitive societies by travelers and missionaries. The link between a group's economic system and a differentiation of roles within that group is, of course, close; how pervasive such an influence may be with respect to *all* aspects of a society is the question on which Marxists and non-Marxists are apt to disagree. In no case, however, can it be denied that any social group is tied together as a group, and functions as a group, largely in and through its economic system.

The foregoing reference to Marx immediately raises the question as to the extent to which class differentiation, political controls, and systems of belief (which Marx would term "ideologies") are under the influence of whatever economic system prevails in a society. Each of these three systems constitutes a factor which I regard as basic in any form of organized social life. While leaving aside the question of how they may be influenced by the economic system, I shall examine what is to be included in each.

One obvious form of class differentiation—and this is the form which Marx has stressed—is that which results from the division of labor. There are, however, other significant forms of class differentiation, most of which are apt to vary from society to society, though once again there are certain types of differentiation that are so frequently repeated that they are identifiable as important sociological variants. First, there is differentiation in relation to gender. Some such differentiation seems to be present in all societies, even though the tasks performed by males and by females differ from society to society, as do the areas in which each exercises power. In addition, in many societies (though not in all) there is a sharp differentiation according to age groupings. This is evident not only when the elders have great power, but also when adolescents are accorded a special status within the society. The existence in some societies of a sharp transition to a new status by those who have passed through puberty rites, as well as the sharp transition from an unmarried to a married state, also provide examples of class differentiation not primarily based on economic factors. In many societies some persons enjoy a special status defined in terms of their roles in religious practices or because of special capacities or powers that they are assumed to possess. There may be differences based on caste or on other divisions related to descent. In addition to and intermingling with most or all of these is that differentiation into classes according to the place occupied by different groupings of persons within the society's economic life.

Another factor to be found in all societies is the presence of some form of group control. If one thinks in terms of the history of Western societies, one is apt to think immediately (and sometimes exclusively) of various types of government: how the laws of the society are established or change, and how and by whom such laws are enforced. This is not in itself erroneous: even those societies which lack a complex system of laws nonetheless have some locus of authority to adjudicate disputes. What would be erroneous would be to overlook the great role played by custom and by public approval or disapproval in regulating the behavior of individuals living together in a social group. Group life does not have coherence through laws alone; the development of habits and sentiments brings a large measure of order into social life even in the absence of those mechanisms through which authority is exercised in complexly structured societies. In complex societies, however, and perhaps in any society too large to permit a high degree of more or less personal relations among most members of the group, some form of authority is probably essential for the survival of the group as a group. There has been great variety in the forms of authority which have arisen to meet this need, and much of the history of Western political theory has been devoted to normative issues regarding the superiority of some of these forms to others. Such discussions have often (though not always) obscured what should be an obvious point, that which form is best must in part at least be determined in terms of the conditions of life which a particular society may be called upon to face. Even when that fact has been recognized, it has too often been assumed that without the existence of some governing authority no form of social life would in any way be possible. That, however, is to overlook the role played by habit and by sentiments in the processes leading to the enculturation of the individuals born into any particular group.

We come now to a final factor present in every society, one which often serves as stealthily as do habit and sentiment in binding together a set of individuals in a particular social group. This factor is the presence of some widely shared system or systems of belief. Among them would be those beliefs in which a distinction is drawn between a natural and a supranatural environment, as well as the ways in which events belonging to either are to be controlled or explained. Thus, both religion and magical or scientific beliefs and practices are to be included in what I have termed "systems of belief." It is my view that not only are these intimately connected with one another, but that no society wholly lacks some widely accepted set of general beliefs of this sort. In addition, every society shares one or another general view regarding what may be called the human environment, according to which it is inclined to explain its own origin as well as its relation to other societies, either past or present. Such aspects of any system of belief may receive overt expression, while others remain only implicit in the practices of the group. To be sure, in some cases different subgroups within a society will not share the beliefs and practices characteristic of the society as a whole, but such groups tend to become isolated and bound to the others in a social whole only through the network of other reactions, such as the economic system, the mechanisms of social control, and the acceptance of a common system of family and kinship relations.

What has been said with respect to the other essential factors in the social life of a group holds also of systems of belief: no one of these factors remains unaffected by at least some of the others, and there is none which does not affect at least some of the others. Those who believe, as did Hegel and Marx, that all societies are organic wholes would stress these interconnections and would even be inclined to extend them beyond the range of cases where they are empirically verifiable. Such would not be my position. As the next chapters will show, there are in my opinion definite limits to the degree of unity and coherence which can be claimed to characterize any society, for both chance and choice are factors which must also be taken into account.

# PART THREE

# Necessity, Chance & Choice

# 4 ⇨ Determinism & Chance

It is usually assumed that if either chance or choice were to affect the course of human affairs, all hope for arriving at adequate explanations in the social sciences would have to be abandoned. In this chapter and the next that assumption will be shown to be mistaken.

There are many reasons why these concepts were looked upon with disfavor by most social theorists in the nineteenth century; not least among them was the view that for a modern thinker to employ them would be to fall back on prescientific modes of explanation. The reign of law was widely taken to be as absolute in human affairs as in nature, and neither chance nor choice seemed compatible with it. There were, however, two confusions connected with this assumption: the first was most clearly articulated by Comte, that the fundamental nature of science consists in its capacity for prediction; the second was a confusion regarding the meaning of *determinism*.

That science does permit us to predict what will occur under given circumstances, and that this is one of its most significant features, is not to be denied. What must not be overlooked, however, is that such predictions are possible only if we possess sufficient knowledge of the conditions initially obtaining and if we can also assume that the process with which we are dealing will not be interfered with through the intrusion of external factors. In short, laws give us the power of prediction only when taken in conjunction with a knowledge of the relevant initial and boundary conditions. In many cases we are not—and cannot be—in possession of such knowledge; in those cases, therefore, we cannot predict what will occur. Nevertheless, even in such instances it may be possible to offer adequate explanations of what has occurred once it has occurred. For example, it is possible to account for past changes in living forms on the basis of Darwinian theory even though the occurrence of these changes could not have been predicted. Similarly, it is possible to identify the causes of a patient's death through a postmortem examination even though (in the present state of knowledge) there may be no way in which these causal factors could have been discovered while the patient lived: his death, therefore, could not have been predicted. This asymmetry between prediction and explanation undercuts Comte's attempt to identify science with "prevision"; and when that identification is abandoned, it is no longer necessary to deny that either chance or choice can affect the course of human affairs. In fact, as we shall now see, on one meaning of the terms, each is compatible with an acceptance of "determinism."

Perhaps the most inclusive meaning of "determinism" is the view that, whatever happens, there are always conditions which, given them, nothing else could have happened. That meaning, however, does not rule out either chance or choice. For example, if I say that it was a matter of chance that two events happened to occur in the same neighborhood at the same time. I am not saying that, given these conditions, something else might have happened. Rather, I am merely saying that I can find no single set of conditions which accounts for these events' occurring in the same neighborhood at the same time: it was a matter of chance that they did so. Similarly, if I say that an event would not have happened had someone not chosen as he did, I am not denying that it was necessary for this event to have occurred once he had so chosen; rather, I am merely saying that his choice (whatever may have been responsible for it) was one of the conditions which entered into the event's occurring.

In addition to this meaning of "determinism," however, there is another which *does* rule out chance and choice. When a series of transformations takes place within a closed system, and each step in that process is predictable as following from the preceding state of the system in accordance with some applicable law, we are dealing with a process the outcome of which is, in a strict sense, determined. Since, *ex hypothesi*, no factors external to the system intervene in the process and since whatever choice a human being makes with respect to such a system occurs only with respect to its initiation, neither chance nor choice affect the outcome of the process. Thus, carefully controlled experiments provide paradigmatic cases of determinism, whereas events occurring in nature—even though they follow necessarily from the conditions under which they occur—are not in the same sense "determined": their occurrence may not be free of chance influences, nor of interventions due to human choice.

Those who, like Spinoza, hold that the world as a whole forms a single determined system, and thus that every event within it is strictly determined, do so on metaphysical, not on empirical grounds. In fact, Spinoza's attempt to rule out chance and to establish his deterministic monism by means of the example of a tile which falls from a roof and kills a passerby, involves a *petitio principii*. He wished to prove that since neither the tile's falling nor the passerby's presence was an uncaused event, the accident itself was determined. This, however, would have served only to establish what he wished to establish were it true that neither chance nor choice had entered into the series of events which, on the one hand, culminated in the fall of the tile, and which, on the other hand, led to the passerby's presence at that particular point at that moment. Neither of these causal series, however, existed as a closed system: when tracing back either series one finds that the ultimate outcome was dependent on the fact that in a series of events multiple lines of causation intersected. Thus, the problem of whether the outcome was or was not accidental is only compounded and not solved, since it arises once again in exactly the same form at every point in each of the causal series when two previously independent lines of causation are seen to have intersected. It is only when one confines one's attention to the very last stage of what has occurred, when the tile is already falling and the passerby is about to be struck, and it is already too late for anyone or anything to have interfered, that we can say that this outcome, rather than any other, was determined.

While both Spinoza and Laplace held that the world as a whole is to be considered as constituting a single closed system, and while others, such as Buckle and Taine, also took this for granted, there are no empirical grounds to justify such an assumption. Even assuming that there may be some well-attested, universally applicable laws, such as the laws of motion assumed by Spinoza or by Laplace, there are two reasons to doubt that this would justify complete determinism. In the first place, as we have noted, laws can be used in predicting or explaining specific events only insofar as one has knowledge of whatever initial conditions were both present and relevant to the occurrence of the event in question. To claim that we possess any knowledge concerning the totality of the conditions obtaining in the whole universe at any one time, present or past, is to make an absurd claim; therefore, to state that the world as a whole forms a determined system is at best only a speculative ideal, not a matter which can be confirmed. In the second place, even if—as Spinoza and Laplace believed—there are general laws applicable to all forms of *motion*, it is by no means certain that these laws can be applied to all events in nature or in human affairs. For example, it is by no means clear where one should look for the initial conditions to which any universal laws of physics might be applied if one were to explain the choices of individuals, or explain the variations which are to be found in human institutions in different places or at different times. One may wish to insist that there *must be* such conditions, and that there must be such laws, but that is only to say that determinism *must be* true. That there was this insistence on the truth of all-encompassing determinism is readily understandable, since the progress of scientific explanation in terms of laws, especially during and after the seventeenth century, seemed to suggest the possibility of establishing the reign of law throughout nature. Yet, toward the end of the nineteenth century, new interpretations of scientific explanation and of the status of scientific laws introduced a new intellectual climate insofar as the physical sciences were concerned, and this undermined the basic postulates of metaphysical determinism.

The new intellectual climate had multiple roots: among them was the recognition that a law of nature should not be regarded as a force which governs events but, quoting Huxley, should be regarded as "a mere record of experience upon which we base our interpretations of that which does happen, and our anticipation of that which will happen."[1] Such a view had, of course, been anticipated by Hume, but it had not made substantial inroads into the thought of scientists until the middle of the nineteenth century. For example, as late as 1831 one finds Herschel, in his influential *Preliminary Discourse on the Study of Natural Philosophy*, not only speaking of the laws of nature as permanent, but as "consistent and intelligible," and holding that God, in creating the basic materials of the universe, had impressed upon these materials certain fixed qualities and powers "which made all their subsequent combinations and relations inevitable consequences of this first impression."[2] This, it would seem, entailed the acceptance of the world—at least of the physical world—as a single, completely determined system.

Herschel himself, however, was soon led to abandon this view, and he did so under the influence of the new interest in the theory of probabilities as it was being applied in the physical and social sciences. This change is represented in an essay, stimulated by Quetelet, which Herschel published in the *Edinburgh Review* in 1850.[3] In it he explicitly rejects the view that the concept of causation should be used as referring to a force capable of producing an effect; instead, he takes the cause of an effect to be the type of occasion on which a given effect can be shown to occur with a certain frequency. Causes are thus to be interpreted as the *tendencies* of events to occur under a given set of circumstances.[4] While this did not demand that one give up "determinism" in its broadest signification—that, whatever happens, there always are conditions which, given them, nothing else could have happened—it did entail abandoning the stricter form of determinism according to which every event is in principle predictable on the basis of some one law or set of laws, with any apparent irregularities being attributed to human ignorance or error. What had been innovative in Quetelet's work was that instead of denying the existence of such irregularities, he had seen them as a means of discovering nature's basic laws. In order to arrive at these laws he had used tables of frequency derived from observation, and by means of these tables he distinguished between those correlations which represented "accidental causes"; those which, because they varied periodically, represented "variable causes"; and those which were constant, thus representing "constant causes."[5] Herschel accepted this position, and thus abandoned his earlier view that all that happens in the universe is an inevitable consequence of the permanent, consistent, intelligible laws originally impressed on matter by God.

In spite of their rejection of a complete determinism which would rule out all contingency in nature, neither Quetelet nor Herschel was led to suppose that any events are uncaused.[6] Nor was Cournot, another scientist-philosopher who attempted to show the relevance of the theory of probability to both the natural and the social sciences.[7] Unlike Quetelet, however, Cournot directly attacked the metaphysics of determinism, according to which the world as a whole is to be regarded as a single, determined system. In this connection, the view which he developed in his *Essai sur les fondaments de nos connaissances* consisted in arguing—as I have argued against Spinoza—that the meeting of two previously independent lines of causation represents a contingent, or accidental, occurrence. He held that an event should be regarded as determined only when the various series of events which led to it were internally related—that is, when they were interdependent. When, on the other hand, two or more such series proceeded independently, even though they proceeded concurrently, the event resulting from their conjunction was to be regarded as a fortuitous, or chance, event.[8] One might suppose that this thesis would not have provided an adequate answer to the metaphysical determinist, since each of the apparently independent lines of causation would have been known to an omniscient observer, and the event which occurred because of their conjunction would, therefore, in principle have been predictable. To this Laplacean mode of argument, Cournot had an adequate answer. The fact of an omniscient being's foreknowledge would not alter the fact that the two lines of causation *were* independent of one another: their coincidence would remain an example of a chance event.[9] One should in such cases simply say that God (or a mathematical angel) is able to foresee just when and where *chance* events will occur. There should be nothing puzzling in this. When events are determined, one holds them to be determined by the conditions actually obtaining and not by virtue of the fact that God (or a mathematical angel) does have or could have, knowledge that they would occur. The case is precisely the same with respect to the contingent fact that two previously independent lines of causation have met. Whatever occurs in such cases is not to be regarded as having been determined by God's foreknowledge that it would occur. Rather, we must account for it in terms of the circumstances which brought it about, and these circumstances were, *ex hypothesi*, the fact that the lines of causation which met at that particular time and place were previously independent of one another; in short, the event remains, as Cournot claimed, a chance event.

It follows from Cournot's characterization of chance events that one should not identify such events with what is rare or surprising. This can be illustrated through one of his own examples. If one draws a white ball from an urn known to contain mostly black balls, this is a relatively rare and perhaps surprising event; but it is equally a chance event if in such a case one draws a black ball.[10] It was at this point that Cournot's defense of contingency as a fact in nature and in human affairs made contact with his interest in the theory of probabilities. He analyzed many uses to which such calculations could be put, but among them was that of distinguishing between events which were due to chance and those which were not. For example, if, in rolling dice, one die comes up with a six on a whole series of trials, we do not attribute this to chance, but look to some causal factor (such as the conformation of the die) for an explanation. Cournot then extrapolates from such simple cases to the wider uses of probability in the sciences and in everyday life.[11]

In looking to probabilities as an important source of knowledge,

Cournot was in line with strong currents among the scientists of his period. This fact was later stressed by Peirce, who cited Darwin's evolutionary doctrine as a prime example of how chance begets order. In this connection Peirce cited Quetelet, Herschel on Quetelet, and Buckle as representing the new reliance on chance in scientific explanations: to their names he added others, such as those of Clausius and Maxwell, as examples of thinkers who used chance as an explanatory concept in thermodynamics. Although Boltzmann was not cited by Peirce in this connection, he was, of course, the foremost exponent of the statistical method as applied to mechanics. It is of interest, then, that Boltzmann, too, cited Buckle's use of statistics concerning the constancy of voluntary behavior among masses of people as analogous to the molecular motions which engender the large-scale phenomena with which the laws of thermodynamics are concerned.[12] It was Peirce, however, who most completely developed the doctrine of chance as begetting order and extended this contention beyond the sciences to a metaphysics of the world's structure. This was his doctrine of "tychism."

The groundwork for that theory was laid in two articles Peirce published in *The Monist* in 1891 and 1892.[13] In one of them, "The Doctrine of Necessity Examined," he attacked traditional mechanical philosophies, attempting to show that, contrary to what was often believed, the doctrine of absolute determinism was not a necessary postulate of science. In this connection, he argued that scientific method rests on inductive sampling and needs no such postulate. In the same article, he attacked the view that there is adequate empirical evidence for the necessitarian position: he did so by stressing the element of fallibility in scientific measurement, and the steps which scientists take to reduce the range of probable error in their sampling techniques. At one point in his defense of the objective reality of chance, Peirce introduced a dialogue between himself and the necessitarian designed to show that the existence of physical laws does not preclude the existence of chance. Chance, he held, is to be found in diversity, specificity, irregularity, whereas law explains what regularly occurs. The argument runs as follows.

Peirce says: "I must acknowledge there is an approximate regularity, and that every event is influenced by it. But the diversification, specificalness, and irregularity of things I suppose is chance."
The necessitarian answers: "If you reflect more deeply, you will come to see that *chance* is only a name for a cause that is unknown to us."

Peirce presses him, saying: "Do you mean that we have no idea whatever what kind of causes could bring about a throw of sixes?"
To this, the necessitarian replies: "On the contrary, each die moves
under the influence of precise mechanical laws."
But then Peirce makes his point, saying: "But it appears to me that it
is not these *laws* which make the die turn up sixes; for these
laws act just the same when other throws come up. The chance
lies in the diversity of the throws; and this diversity cannot be
due to laws which are immutable."[14]

Peirce then went on to argue that the necessitarian view runs
counter to an acceptance of evolutionary theory, according to which
diversity and specification develop over time. As is well known, his
interest in the scientific and religious implications of evolutionary
theory had been of long standing, and like Spencer and others of the
period, he attempted to build an evolutionary cosmology.[15] His aim
in doing so was to show how it might be possible to account for those
laws which we find to be exemplified in nature, rather than simply
taking them for granted as given. This he did by postulating that
there was a primordial continuum of feeling which gradually differ-
entiated itself and out of which habits developed, these habits being
fixed modes of action that were strengthened through repetition; it
was "from this, with the other principles of evolution, [that] all the
regularities of the universe would be evolved."[16] Thus, instead of
holding—as the necessitarian does—that "chance" is simply a name
for that of which we are ignorant, Peirce regarded it as ultimate, and
regarded order as being derivative from it and to be explained through
it.[17]

This metaphysical cosmology, presented as it was in a highly
abbreviated, opaque, and fragmentary form, seems not to have had
any appreciable influence on contemporary thought except insofar as
it was taken up, in new contexts, by William James. It was James
rather than Peirce who, at the time, did most to undermine the dominance of necessitarianism in popular philosophic thought by extending Peirce's original pragmatism to moral and religious issues. While
the pragmatic theory of knowledge, in all of its forms, did much to
undercut necessitarianism, a far more potent force—so far as technical philosophy was concerned—was the growth of positivistic interpretations of science. It is to them that we now turn.

As we have noted, the view that nature "obeys" fixed laws,
which it is the scientist's aim to uncover, had been deeply ingrained
in scientific thought; it was only gradually displaced by the view that

natural laws are simply generalizations based on observed regularities which appear to hold without exception. This view, implicit
in Hume's analysis of the source of our belief in the causal relation,
became widely accepted only toward the middle of the nineteenth
century. Until then, it was common to speak—as Herschel himself
had originally spoken—of the laws of nature as if they were forces
*governing* the phenomena they explained. Even Comte did not
wholly free himself from this conception, in spite of the fact that he
attempted to rid science of the notion that phenomena were to be
explained in terms of underlying "causes." In fact, it was probably
John Stuart Mill who first clearly formulated a consistent positivistic
conception of the nature of scientific laws. In 1843, in his *System of
Logic*, he wrote, "The Law of Causation, the recognition of which is
the main pillar of inductive science, is but the familiar truth, that
invariability of succession is found by observation to obtain between
every fact in nature and some other fact which has preceded it; independently of all 'considerations' respecting the ultimate mode of
production of phenomena, and of every other question regarding the
nature of 'Things in themselves.'"[18] Similarly, in 1847, Helmholtz
had held that "the principle of causality is in fact nothing more than
the presupposition that in all natural phenomena there is conformity
to law [*Gesetzlichkeit*],"[19] and Kirchhoff, too, rejected the notion
that the task of the scientist was to explain phenomena in terms of
something lying behind them, rather than being content to formulate laws concerning phenomena and to explain these laws not in
terms of underlying causes but through appealing to further laws.[20]

As I have elsewhere shown, scientists such as Helmholtz,
Claude Bernard, and Huxley, who adopted a positivistic view of the
laws of nature and who presumably stripped them of all metaphysical overtones, nonetheless believed—along with Mill—that
the uniformities which found expression in these laws were uniformities existing objectively in nature.[21] By the 1880s, however, this
view was subjected to radical revisions which undercut the assumption that the laws scientists formulate can be assumed to reflect,
directly and unambiguously, the patterning of what occurs in nature.
Two major strains of thought contributed to this altered view. The
first is best epitomized in Mach's interpretation of scientific laws as
originating in our tendency to organize experience in accordance
with the principle of "the economy of thought"; the second was at
first most influentially represented by Poincaré's interpretation of
scientific hypotheses as theoretical *constructions*, a view which had
much in common with some of Boltzmann's theoretical utterances

and received an even more radical interpretation in Duhem.

Mach's concern with philosophical issues antedated his own scientific investigations, having first arisen during his youth when he abandoned the Kantian notion that behind our experience a "thing in itself" is to be postulated.[22] After briefly accepting a Berkeleian position, he challenged the conception of substance not only as it had been applied to material objects but also as it had been applied to the mind or ego. Like Avenarius, he adopted a philosophy of pure experience, attempting to shun all metaphysical notions, whether realist or idealist, claiming that what is given as the material for all knowledge are simple data, or "elements," of which we are directly aware. From the point of view of his interest in physics and in psychophysics, Mach saw this approach as highly advantageous, for it permitted him to investigate the relations among physical events, physiological events, and the data of consciousness, while escaping conventional problems concerning the relations between what occurs in the physical world and what is present in consciousness. According to Mach, the laws of physics, physiology, and psychophysics, and any psychological laws connecting our various ideas with one another, were simply ways in which we relate different sets of elements to one another. Such laws do not in any sense determine the relations among the elements: they merely *summarize* relations which we have regularly observed in the past. Thus, the function of laws is to serve as a means whereby we codify, recall, and anticipate experience, and in this way their function is life-serving.[23] Mach's use of the concept of the life-serving function of thought was connected with the influence that Darwin's theory had exerted on him. It was not, however, the scientific systematization of experience that he regarded as life-serving; as is clear in his *Contribution to the Analysis of Sensations* (1886), he also held that our commonsense categories have an adaptive function, and this function, too, was included in his principle of the "economy of thought." Thus, on his view, neither the way in which science organizes experience nor the way in which we organize experience in everyday life is to be interpreted as reflecting relations which exist in nature independently of us. This marked a departure from the assumptions of such earlier positivistic thinkers as Comte, Mill, Helmholtz, Huxley, and Spencer, and supplemented the influence which was soon to be exerted by Poincaré and later by Duhem.

In the meantime, however, Mach's great intellectual opponent, Boltzmann, attempted to develop a philosophy of science which went beyond positivism, supporting a critical realism (which he called "materialism") based on the procedures and results of the sciences rather than on any form of "metaphysical" argument. In opposition to Mach's phenomenological physics, which reduced all physical concepts to observational terms, and in opposition to Ostwald's energetics, Boltzmann held that given the laws of physics there was every reason to regard atoms as actually existing entities, not hypothetical constructs.[24] In defending this position, he was forced to emphasize that physics could not concern itself simply with observable correlations, but must be allowed to construct a theory that went beyond the directly observable and would be validated only insofar as its constructions permitted one to ascertain relations among observable facts not discoverable in any other way. He recognized that this position forced him to grant the possibility that there could be alternative constructions, and in doing so his statements sometimes seemed to suggest that no particular theoretical construction was likely to present an adequate model of the independently existing world. For example, he said:

> Hertz makes physicists properly aware of something philosophers had no doubt long since stated, namely that no theory can be objective, actually coinciding with nature, but rather that each theory is only a mental picture of phenomena, related to them as sign is to designatum. From this it follows that it cannot be our task to find an absolutely correct theory but rather a picture that is as simple as possible and that represents phenomena as accurately as possible. One might even conceive of two quite different theories both equally simple and equally congruent with phenomena, which therefore in spite of their differences are equally correct. The assertion that a given theory is the only correct one can only express our subjective conviction that there could not be another equally simple and fitting image.[25]

Similarly, he concluded a lecture entitled "On the Indispensability of Atomism in Natural Science" (1897) with the statement:

> Imagine there could be an all-encompassing picture of the world in which every feature has the evidence of Fourier's theory of heat conduction, then it remains so far undecided whether we should reach that picture by the phenomenological method or by constant further development and experimental verification of the pictures of current

atomism. One might then equally well imagine that there could be several world pictures all of which possessed the same ideal property.[26]

Nevertheless, Boltzmann repeatedly argued that while there may eventually prove to be more adequate theoretical constructions than that involved in assuming atomism, the path of science up to the present had increasingly validated that construction, rather than any alternative to it. As he said, "Perhaps the atomistic hypothesis will one day be displaced by some other but it is unlikely."[27] Furthermore, given the successes of the atomistic view in linking a great variety of natural laws in a systematic manner, Boltzmann felt justified in challenging his opponents, saying, "One can ask only what would be more disadvantageous to science: the excessive haste implicit in the cultivation of such pictures or the excessive caution that bids us abstain from them?"[28] On his view the answer was clear: the model of nature proposed by atomism had allowed science to proceed with remarkable success in establishing laws which had thus far proved to be applicable to an ever-expanding range of phenomena. Thus, he insisted that it was in and through science itself, not in terms of subjective criteria nor in terms of philosophic argument, that scientific constructions were to be validated.

There is at least one respect in which the position of Poincaré resembled that which has here been attributed to Boltzmann, and in which it differed radically from the views held by Mach. Poincaré no less than Boltzmann regarded it as the task of science to come to grips with an independently existing world, rather than merely providing a means by which our experience is ordered in an economical way. Like Boltzmann, Poincaré also stressed the fact that science depended upon the use of hypotheses which go beyond observations, yet it was at this point that their views diverged. While Poincaré agreed wih Boltzmann that the success of a hypothesis in assimilating further facts was a test which could serve as a means of validating those particular hypotheses which we designate as *laws*, he drew a parallel between physics and mathematics, insisting that just as it is possible to construct multiple, equally valid geometries, so it is possible to construct alternative physical theories resting on differing definitions and conventions, which he called *principles*. For example, in his treatise *Electricity and Optics* (1901), he said, "If therefore a phenomenon admits of a complete mechanical explanation, it will admit of an infinity of others which will account equally well for all the peculiarities disclosed by experiment."[29] Thus, insofar as the element of convention enters into the formulation of general scientific theories, which Poincaré insisted that it always did, it becomes impossible to choose among the alternatives on the basis of empirical evidence: the more ultimate criterion which he used was that of relative simplicity, and he justified the use of this criterion not in terms of practicality but in terms of aesthetic appeal.[30] While this introduced an element of subjectivity into science, Poincaré insisted that the subjectivity was an impersonal one, for in the end, the decision was one on which many minds agreed.[31]

Poincaré's attempt to shield his theory from subjectivistic interpretations can scarcely be regarded as anything but a failure, and a failure magnified by his insistence that science can never inform us concerning the nature of the entities with which it deals, but only concerning the relations among them.[32] This opened the way for those who, for various reasons, were inclined to limit the significance of science as a means by which we ascertain truths about the world.[33] For example, much to Poincaré's discomfiture, Le Roy combined a conventionalist interpretation of science with a Bergsonian metaphysics, and Pierre Duhem's form of conventionalism made it possible for him to accept as equally valid, though wholly independent of science, an orthodox form of metaphysical theism. Nor was this an idiosyncratic view on the part of Duhem. Toward the end of the century, when interpretations of science became less and less closely associated with epistemological realism, more and more philosophers used the newer interpretations of science as a means of defending their commitments to what they regarded as other, no less reliable forms of truth.

Among those who merit special mention in this connection is Poincaré's brother-in-law, Emile Boutroux. In the preface to the English translation of *The Contingency of the Laws of Nature,* Boutroux described the position he had adopted in the following way:

> Philosophical systems appeared to me as though they might be summed up, speaking generally, in three types, which all had the same draw-back: the idealist, the materialist, and the dualist or parellelist types. These three points of view have this in common: they force us to regard the laws of nature as a chain of necessity, rendering illusory all life and liberty.
>
> Analyzing the notion of natural law, as seen in the sciences themselves, I found that this law is not a first principle but rather a result; that life, feeling, and liberty are

true and profound realities, whereas the relatively invariable and general forms apprehended by science are but the inadequate manifestation of these realities.[34]

This point of view was not, of course, wholly new with Boutroux. Slightly earlier, in 1867, in a survey of nineteenth-century French philosophy, Ravaisson had criticized both eclecticism and positivism, and in his concluding section had proclaimed a spiritualistic idealism reminiscent of Maine de Biran, in which personality and free volition offered the fundamental clues to the nature of ultimate reality. A similar position was developed with somewhat greater rigor by Ravaisson's pupil and friend Lachelier, whose *Foundations of Induction* (1872) was in large part based on a criticism of Mill and ended by saying that "the realm of final causes, by penetrating the realm of efficient causes without destroying it, exchanges everywhere force for inertia, life for death, liberty for fatality."[35] Nevertheless, it was probably Boutroux's essay *The Contingency of the Laws of Nature*, published in 1874, that had the greatest initial impact on the development of that form of French idealism which had as its obverse side a critique and rejection of scientific realism.

At the same time, Revouvier's systematic exposition of a neo-Kantian form of criticism, emphasizing contingency and individual freedom, gave further impetus to the growth of idealism in French philosophy. This movement, which was highly critical of the ultimate adequacy of scientific forms of thought, might have had relatively little impact outside of France at the time had it not been for the influence of Bergson's anti-intellectualism, which began in the early 1890s but grew enormously after 1907, when his *Creative Evolution* appeared.[36] In speaking of this period in French thought, Parodi summarized it as having abandoned the dominant nineteenth-century interpretation of science, seeking instead to exploit other avenues of approach to reality, particularly those in which morality, religion, or intuition played a dominant role.[37]

In one form or another, the idealism present in French philosophy was paralleled in England and in the United States by a great deal of popular philosophic and quasi-scientific thought. It was, however, the development of the positivist tradition—and especially in the form of logical positivism—that did the most to undermine the traditional forms of necessitarian doctrine. It was characteristic of this approach to treat laws as descriptive generalizations, rather than viewing them as expressions of relations which mirrored the underlying forces of nature. While those who stood in this tradition did not generally regard contingency as an ultimate, irreducible aspect of natural events, as had Cournot and Peirce, they relied increasingly on a probabilistic interpretation of scientific laws. Thus, the necessitarian tradition—whether in the form it assumed in seventeenth-century rationalism or in its eighteenth-century formulations—came to an end. Not only was it denied by those who appealed to contingency in nature or to freedom in man, but it was also regarded by positivists as unnecessary metaphysical baggage which scientists and scientifically oriented philosophers would be well advised to discard. At the same time, positivists strongly opposed the legitimacy of appealing to either chance or choice in interpreting the course of human affairs. Their use of statistical probabilities for the purpose of explaining what occurs under given circumstances was not coupled with any assumption that what occurs is not itself determined, nor were they willing to assume—as were the French idealists or pragmatists like Peirce and James—that human action is any less strictly determined than are natural events. What had happened was that a new conception had been introduced into the ways in which most scientists and many philosophers used the concepts of "a law of nature" and "determinism" and "choice": necessity, it was assumed, still reigned. To what extent that view must be accepted insofar as human affairs are concerned is a subject I shall discuss in the final chapter.

# 5 ⇨ Determinism & Choice

Any social theory must at some point face the issue of what weight, if any, is to be assigned to the aims and choices of individuals in bringing about or inhibiting social change. Even those who accept an institutional rather than an individualistic approach cannot deny that individuals act purposively and that they sometimes aim to modify some of the institutions under which they live. Similarly, even those who believe that institutions represent the purposes of individuals must face the question of the extent to which the aims and desires of any set of individuals within a society can effectively alter the social conditions under which they and others live. Thus, when we look at any society as a whole, we can assume that elements of both purpose and necessity are present, and the question arises as to what role each of these play in the actions of individuals and in the social structures within which their actions take place. In the present chapter we shall be concerned with only one side of this issue: that which concerns the action of individuals. Naturally, this raises the traditional issue of determinism versus free will, and few philosophic issues stand in greater need of clarification than questions concerning the sense in which a person's actions may be said to be determined or free.

In discussing this issue it should be noted that what has been regarded as of primary importance has tended to shift over time. For example, in the early period of modern philosophy much of the discussion was interwoven with a variety of theological disputes, but these issues gradually became less central as interest in interpreting man's relation to the world of nature grew. Later, the focus of attention again shifted, and the problems most widely discussed were related to the impact of society on the individual. During the whole of this period, from the seventeenth to the early twentieth century, the meanings of *free* and *determined* as applied to human actions have not remained constant, and one of the characteristics of recent Anglo-American discussions of the problem has been to distinguish among the various possible meanings of these terms and to analyze what their moral implications may be.

Looking back on the history of these shifts, one must note that the problem was at first usually formulated in terms of asking whether or not the individual's will is free. Then, largely under the influence of Hobbes and Locke, this way of putting the question tended to be rejected, and it was claimed that one should not pose the question of whether *"the will"* is free, but under what circumstances a *human being* may be said to be free. While this shift had many advantages, its widespread acceptance gradually tended to obliterate a distinction that had originally been drawn between an *action's* being either free or not free, and speaking of a *choice* as being either free or determined. The difference between these is the difference between asking whether, in a given situation, a person can *do* what he wants to do, in which case we are speaking of freedom of action, and the question of why, in a given situation, a person *chooses* as he does. As both Hobbes and Locke recognized, these are quite different questions and deserve separate consideration. Unfortunately, however, most contemporary Anglo-American philosophers do not seem to regard the question of accounting for our choices as a problem meriting close attention. This is of a piece with their view that the principal task of philosophy is conceptual analysis rather than exploration of empirical questions with a view to tracing their implications. For my part, however, I regard the question of why it is that a person wants to do that which he wants to do as the most fundamental of all the problems related to freedom of action. It is therefore with that question that this chapter will first be concerned.[1] Only later will we be in a position to examine the degree to which individuals may be said to have freedom of action in the situations which they face in the social world.

## THE DETERMINANTS OF CHOICE

Although it is usual to suppose that "determinism" and "libertarianism" offer the two most obvious types of theories with respect to the problem of choice, any reasonably close examination of the alternatives adopted by major philosophers in the past will show that a complete libertarianism regarding choice has rarely been accepted: many positions that pass for libertarianism in fact involve some form of determinism.[2] The major differences are those concerning what have been taken to be the determinants affecting acts of choice.

I find it useful to distinguish four major types of theories concerning the determinants of choice, although each of them may not only be formulated in different ways, but also will have varying implications. These types are (1) theories that regard "subjective propensities" as the determinants of choice, (2) theories that hold that choices are determined by "what is seen as objectively good," (3) theories that hold that "self-fulfillment is the goal of all desire" and that this goal is the one which ultimately determines choice, and (4) theories that hold that choice is determined by "sharply focused attention." As two examples of the first type of theory I shall cite and briefly discuss the views of Hobbes and Hume; of the second, Descartes and Spinoza; of the third, Green and Dewey; and of the fourth, William James, from whose views my own position ultimately derives. As I shall also point out in passing, the views held by Locke and by John Stuart Mill are not those which have been conventionally attributed to them.

### Subjective Propensities and Choice

Hobbes represents a classic form of what has come to be known as the "compatibilist position." According to that doctrine, one's will may be said to be determined, but (under certain circumstances) one's actions may nonetheless be said to be free. As Hobbes said, "*Liberty* and *necessity* are consistent . . . in the Actions which men voluntarily do: which because they proceed from their will, proceed from *liberty*; and yet, because every act of man's will, and every desire, and inclination proceedeth from some cause, and that from another cause, in a continual chain...they proceed from *necessity*."[3] It is clear that in this and in other similar passages, Hobbes was not attempting to avoid the question of choice, which he referred to as "deliberation." Instead, he put forward a theory as to the circumstances under which men deliberate, and he accounted for the outcome of deliberation in strictly deterministic terms. To summarize his view one may say that he held that the behavior of men, like the behavior of all other living creatures, depends on "animal motions," that is, on the internal motion, or "endeavor," of the parts of which living things are composed. Through experience, men gradually learn what is grateful and what is hurtful to them, and thus develop various appetites and aversions, seeking some projects and shunning others. This spontaneous form of response continues until objects are encountered which elicit contrary forces of appetite and aversion, and it is then that men deliberate.[4] If deliberation is absent, there is no choice, and we do not then speak of "willing"; on the other hand, as Hobbes says, "If deliberation has gone before, then the last act of it, if it be appetite, is called *will:* if aversion, unwillingness."[5] In Hobbes's system, the outcome of deliberation simply reflects the relative strength of our appetencies and is therefore determined. All that may be said to be "free" is the fact that we have acted as our appetencies have inclined us to act; we are not free when we are prevented from so acting by physical restraints or by the wills—that is, by the appetencies—of others.

Turning now to the position of Hume regarding liberty and necessity, we may note that it is frequently regarded as being essentially similar to that of Hobbes, and in some respects it was. For both, the crucial question was one regarding freedom of action rather than freedom of choice. On the other hand, Hobbes's rejection of freedom of choice followed directly from his deterministic metaphysics, which reduced all men's activities to the effects of motion, whereas Hume attempted to offer empirical arguments for a necessitarian position. In both the *Treatise* and the *Enquiry,* the argument he used to refute freedom of choice took the following form. He began by calling attention to our reason for holding that natural events are determined, claiming that we do so solely because these events occur in regular sequences. He then argued that since equal regularities are to be found in human behavior, we must admit that they, too, are determined. The regularities which Hume cited in this connection all rested on the fact that individuals act in a consistent manner: on the basis of our knowledge of an individual's past behavior we infer how that person will act in other, similar situations. Since no more than the presence of such regularities can be cited in establishing the necessity which we ascribe to events in nature, we must also admit that human actions are necessitated. Yet this does not preclude us from distinguishing between situations in which a man is able to do that which he wills and those in which he is not. It is the difference between these cases that Hume held to be important for moral judgments and for the ordinary affairs of life. Thus, according to Hume, freedom simply means freedom of action, not a lack of determinism with respect to our choices. As he said in the *Enquiry,* "By liberty, then, we can only mean a *power of acting or not acting according to the determinations of the will.*"[6] But what, then determines the will?

In his analysis of the passions Hume says, "The *Will* exerts itself, when either the good or the absence of the evil may be attained by any action of mind or body," and he identifies the impressions of pleasure and pain as the bases for whatever we find to be good or evil.[7] To be sure, he recognized that on many occasions we experience contrary passions, and he held, as did Hobbes, that it was always the stronger passion that prevailed. For Hume, however, the strength of a passion was not to be confused with what he referred to as its "violence"; in some situations what he termed "the calm passions" are at least equally strong. As he said, "We must distinguish betwixt a calm and a weak passion; betwixt a violent and a strong one."[8] But what, one may ask, are the factors which determine whether, in a given situation, one or another passion—be it calm or violent—will have the greater strength and therefore prevail? Hume usually cites "the *general* character or *present* disposition of the person" as the prime factor at work.[9] In addition, however, he entered into an elaborate analysis of the various conditions under which concurrent passions influence one another, and also of how their strength is affected by repetition, by the imagination, and by the extent to which their objects are either present or remote in space and time. Thus, it was through taking into account *both* "the general character and present disposition of the person," *and* the reasons why passions increase or diminish in strength from situation to situation that Hume attempted to explain the factors determining choice. Thus, Hume's account, though no less deterministic than that of Hobbes, differs from it in the complexity of the factors introduced to explain what determines choice.[10] Furthermore, although his argument against the freedom of the will depended upon an analogy between the regularities in human behavior and the regularity of events in nature, Hume differed from Hobbes in not regarding human actions as following precisely the same principles as those which operate in the physical world. Nevertheless, one may classify Hobbes and Hume together not only because they held a compatibilist doctrine, but also because their views of choice may be characterized as being *subjectively determined*—that is, determined by propensities inherent within the individual, rather than depending upon a cognitive response to what an individual discriminates as a good existing independently of him.

## The Objectively Good and Choice

To clarify this contrast between cases in which choice may be said to be determined by subjective propensities and those cases in which it might be said to be determined by what is seen as objectively good, I should now like to direct attention to the position of Descartes.

In contrast to the compatibilist thesis, Descartes held that men can be said to have freedom of action only insofar as they exercise freedom of choice. In all other cases his explanations of actions were couched in strictly mechanistic terms, assigning no greater freedom to human actions than would be assigned to any machine. Except for the more detailed manner in which he explained the vital functions of living bodies, and except for his abandonment of an irreducible conatus, or endeavor, in explaining animal motion, Descartes's account of the machinelike operations of men's bodies was in principle similar to that of Hobbes. Where he differed, of course, was in the fact that he attributed a mind or soul to man. As a consequence, he was not called upon to explain the processes of thought in physiological terms, nor did he regard choice as being nothing more than a matter of the relative strength of competing appetencies. Instead, he regarded both thought and choice as *actions* of the soul. Descartes divided these actions of the soul into two classes: those of the Understanding and those of the Will. He further divided the activities of willing into two classes: those in which the operations of the will control thought, and those in which they control our bodies.[11] It is with respect to the latter that we most commonly speak of choice, and it is to them that I shall first attend.

Among the more obvious instances in which the soul influences the actions of our bodies are cases such as those in which, when we make up our minds to take a walk, our legs move. Descartes's account of the flow of the animal spirits through the nerves and into the muscles is so familiar that I need not describe it here. What is of more interest with reference to our problem is his explanation of how the soul acts on the body when its volition, instead of terminating in overt action, exercises control over one of its passions, such as fear. Like the other passions, fear is aroused in the soul when some object with which we have had previous experience elicits a flow of animal spirits to those organs which dispose the body to shun that object, or objects of that kind. The reflection of what is occurring in these bodily organs is what we experience as the emotion of fear. Similarly, love is evoked in the soul when an object with which we have had experience elicits a flow of the animal spirits to those organs which dispose the body to seek that object. Yet, just as the soul cannot act directly on the legs when we wish to walk, so it cannot directly control an emotion such as fear through a simple act of will. It can do so only indirectly, by turning its attention away from the past pains associated with the object, noting that on other occasions the object did not cause harm, or by directing its thought to rewards to be gained by not being overcome by fear (*Passions of the Soul*, pt. 1, art. 46).

Descartes recognized, however, that the power of some emotions may be so great as to restrict the capacity of the soul to overcome them merely through redirecting attention to an object associated with a different passion. What occurs in such cases is that the motions of the animal spirits that had caused the original passion are so powerful and persistent that they cannot be overcome for any appreciable length of time by those motions associated with the objects to which the soul redirects its attention. Yet, Descartes holds that even if we cannot actually rid ourselves of the passion, we can prevent ourselves from acting as it would normally lead us to act (ibid.). A case of this sort would be one in which we experience a terror so great that we cannot redirect our thoughts to anything which supplants our fear, yet we can still prevent ourselves from running away from the object we fear. In such a case, the soul has not actually overcome the passion but has simply aided us in holding its consequences in check. This Descartes recognizes as something that all individuals, no matter how weak, are on some occasions able to do: they see that what they truly desire is not in accord with what their passions would lead them to do. And what some persons occasionally do, we should train ourselves always to do: human conduct is to be guided not by passion but by rules of conduct derived from a knowledge of that which is truly good (ibid., arts. 48–49). Thus, it is true judgment, an *action* of the soul, which gives us the ultimate power to act as we should. Here we have a first indication of why I have referred to Descartes's theory as one in which choice is determined by what is seen as being objectively good. In contrast to the theories of Hobbes and of Hume, choice is not determined by the strength of concurrently experienced passions: what determines it is a cognitive acknowledgement of rules of conduct which are taken to be objectively good. This interpretation of Descartes's view of choice can be further strengthened if we now turn our attention from those operations of the will which control our bodies to those which control our thought.

It is at this point—once Descartes is no longer bent on explaining how the will controls the actions of our limbs or how it affects our passions—that we come into contact with his epistemological doctrine concerning the relations of the understanding and the will. In the *Meditations* and elsewhere, he explained the possibility of error as due to the fact that the Will is wider than the Understanding: we sometimes affirm or deny propositions which we have not yet fully understood. This being the case, if we are to guard against error, we must hold the will in check until we have before our minds indubitable propositions, namely those which are intuitively certain or, in the absence of these, those which are seen to follow necessarily from others which are certain. Although Descartes grants the mind the power to refrain from affirming propositions which are not intuitively certain, he believes that when the mind has before it an intuitively certain proposition, assent cannot be withheld. Truth may therefore be said to exercise a compulsion over the will. In this sphere, therefore, choice is not free, and since human conduct is to be guided by true judgment, it would seem that Descartes, like Socrates, was bound to hold that to know the good is to do the good. Thus, in the end, Descartes's doctrine of choice amounts to this: that the will can, under normal circumstances, control our overt behavior; that it can also exercise control over our passions, permitting us to guide our conduct in accordance with true judgments as to the good; and that it has the power to prevent us from falling into error. When, however, we do understand what constitutes human good, we are no longer free to choose evil; but that is a freedom which Descartes, like many others, would gladly give up. At this point the Will is objectively determined, being determined by truths it cannot escape. As Kemp Smith says with respect to Descartes's view of freedom, "True freedom . . . consists in being determined by the true and the good."[12]

Until one examines these moral implications of Descartes's analysis of the mind's control over the body, it would have seemed that no common ground existed between his view of human freedom and that of Spinoza. In all other respects, Spinoza's determinism appears to be essentially similar to Hobbes's. Both rejected the Cartesian dualism of mind and body, and both also rejected Descartes's view that there is a faculty or power termed "the Will" capable of controlling our thoughts and actions. Spinoza parted company from Hobbes, however, in his conception of man's ultimate good and in his conception of that in which human freedom consists. In these respects his views were far closer to those of Descartes than they were to the position of Hobbes.

I shall not here follow the trail of Spinoza's ethical thought to its end, and it is only at the end that he reaches a position similar to the final position of Descartes. The affinity between their ultimate views should be clear from the fact that part 4 of the *Ethics* was entitled "Of Human Bondage," whereas part 5 was entitled "Of the Power of the Understanding, or of Human Freedom." Spinoza held that adequate understanding gives us the only true and lasting good, the ability to overcome the partiality and self-centeredness of our everyday judgments of value, according to which things are good or bad only insofar as they are helpful or harmful to us. When this self-centeredness has been overcome, we shall have freed ourselves from the bondage of our passions and will enjoy the one true lasting good, the intellectual love of God. In short, for Spinoza—as for Descartes—true freedom comes when what we do is not a matter of free choice but is objectively determined by our apprehension of the good. It is therefore fitting that the final section of Spinoza's *Ethics* should be entitled "Of the Power of the Understanding, or of Human Freedom."

This view may be said to have been characteristic of each of the major philosophers of the period, even though the theological metaphysics of Leibniz and of Malebranche introduced complications into the problem, since both were forced to find some way of reconciling the individual's freedom with the fact that whatever an individual does is part of a divinely ordained plan. Consequently, in both Leibniz and Malebranche the earlier theological issues of sin and grace, of freedom of choice and of God's omnipotence and omniscience, were once again thrust into the forefront of attention, but their solutions to these problems in each case rested on the view they shared with Descartes and Spinoza: man is free insofar as his choices and actions are determined by his apprehension of the true and the good.

It might seem that Locke, their contemporary, did not share this view; in fact, he has often been thought to have held a position extremely close to that of Hobbes. This impression derives in part, at least, from the fact that he, like Hobbes, insisted that the question to be raised is not whether the will is free, but whether a man is free to act as he chooses. Furthermore, like Hobbes, he held that choice is determined and is to be accounted for in psychological terms. To be sure, he did not accept Hobbes's hormic psychology, according to which appetency is the dominant force; instead, his psychology was a version of psychological hedonism, according to which we always act to avoid pain, including the mind's present uneasiness. In simple cases, then, Locke—like Hobbes—held that choice is subjectively determined.

On the other hand, this is by no means the end of Locke's analysis of the choices we make. He also insisted that in the ordinary course of our lives we are often beset by "sundry uneasinesses," and in these cases we have the capacity to forego choice until we have considered the future effects of acting in accordance with each of them, thus suspending action while we take account of their effects. As he said, the mind has

> the power to *suspend* the execution and satisfaction of any of its desires. . . . This seems to me the source of all liberty; in this seems to consist that which is (as I think improperly) called *free-will*. For during this suspension of any desire, before the will is determined to action . . . we have opportunity to examine, view, and judge the good or evil of what we are going to do; and when, upon due examination, we have judged, we have done our duty, all that we can, or ought to do, in pursuit of our happiness; and it is not a fault, but a perfection of our nature, to desire, will, and act according to the last result of a fair examination. (*Essay*, bk. 2, ch. 21, sec. 48)

But what, we may ask, gives us the power to suspend action, permitting us to judge which of various alternatives will bring the greatest happiness?

Locke does not explicitly discuss this question, but it is possible to infer what he almost certainly held. When we are beset with sundry uneasinesses, that is, when we encounter conflicts among our inclinations, we have motives pulling in different directions; and since we are seeking our own ultimate happiness, we must suspend action until we see which of the competing uneasinesses it is more important for us to remove to attain that goal. Thus, the very act of choosing may be said to be necessitated by a conflict of forces within us: we do not choose to choose; it is simply something we *must* do. This bears a close resemblance to what Hobbes held regarding "deliberation," but on Locke's view *what* we ultimately choose depends upon an act of judgment, not upon the immediate strength of the competing forces. Thus, Locke allows our cognitive faculty, the understanding, to play a significant role in guiding conduct whenever our immediate impulses have been checked. In such cases, action has been controlled by judgment: what we judge to be better, necessitates our acting as we do. Locke said of this control, that it is "so far from being a restraint or diminution of freedom, that it is the very improvement and benefit of it: it is not an abridgement, it is the end and use of our liberty; and the further we are removed from such a determination, the nearer we are to misery and slavery" (ibid., sec. 49).[13]

In this respect Locke's conclusion resembled the positions maintained by Descartes and Spinoza, in which it was held that an action is free not insofar as it is undetermined, but only insofar as it is determined by the understanding, which apprehends the good. Yet, one cannot attribute to Locke, as one can attribute to Descartes or Spinoza—or to Malebranche and Leibniz—the position that the good which determines those choices we designate as "free" is an objective good, independent of our inclinations. Nor did Locke hold, as did they, that once we have recognized that good, it forces us to choose it. Rather, Locke's position is one more nearly approaching that which we find James describing as the "reasonable type" of decision making.

Before turning to an examination of James's theory, I wish to examine one form of the theory usually referred to as "self-determinism." While "self-determinism" is used in a variety of senses, the form that I wish to examine is the view that self-fulfillment is the goal of all desire; therefore, our choices are determined by a basic need to develop and fulfill the self.

### Self-Fulfillment and Choice

At present, the form of self-determinism related to self-fulfillment is often casually dismissed because it is identified with a form of British and American idealism which flourished at the end of the nineteenth century and the beginning of the twentieth. It is true that the doctrine had Green and Bradley among its most influential exponents, but its appeal had been powerfully influenced by the psychology associated with Darwin and Darwinian theory, which—like the psychology of the idealists—rejected hedonistic accounts of motivation. Yet, even these roots do not fully explain the appeal which the theory has sometimes exerted. For example, odd as it sounds, one can make a strong case for the thesis that John Stuart Mill—whose views are often assumed to have been similar to those of Hume—was to some degree a self-determinist. Let me briefly attempt to vindicate this statement.

When Mill discussed necessitarianism in *Utilitarianism*, he characterized it as holding "that our actions follow from our characters, and that our characters follow from our organization, our education, and our circumstances," and he went on to say that, on this view, a man's character "is formed *for* him, and not *by* him; therefore his wishing that it had been formed differently is of no use; he has no power to alter it. *But this is a grand error.*"[14] In short, Mill held that the necessitarian position was mistaken. Yet, this fact has been widely overlooked, largely, I believe, because his *Utilitarianism* offers no positive alternative to necessitarianism as thus conceived. Unfortunately, most commentators on Mill's ethics have confined their attention to that essay, as if it were the only exposition of his ethical views. However, in his *System of Logic* he explicitly stated his own alternative to necessitarianism. There he said, "The true doctrine of the Causation of human actions maintains . . . that not only our conduct, but our character, is in part amenable to our own will; that we can, by employing the proper means, improve our character."[15] I do not claim that Mill's psychology did actually succeed in allowing him to hold that it is within our power to change our own characters, as he thought it did, but before one dismisses that possibility one has to examine his psychology carefully, and in particular his little-known, anonymous essay on Bentham and his notes to his father's *Analysis of the Phenomena of the Human Mind*.[16] My purpose in calling attention to this aspect of Mill's thought is not to defend him, but to correct misapprehensions as to what his views actually were. In the essay *On Liberty*, as well as in the passages to which I have alluded, it is clear that Mill would have liked to hold a self-determinist position and that he attempted to do so. Thus, his views on what it is that determines choice should not be equated with the views of Hobbes or Hume, and certainly not with the views of other associationists such as Helvétius, Priestley, and his father; much less should we regard them as similar to views which Bentham had held. In short, Mill's actual position regarding choice—though it was by no means identical with the views of such self-realizationists as Green and Dewey—is not the view which has generally been attributed to him. Rather, he was much influenced by the progressivist *motif* prevalent at the time, holding that men had it within their power to make choices that would develop their potentialities, shaping themselves and their society, instead of being shaped by external forces.

I now wish to consider the specific form of self-realizationism which was formulated by Green and received a parallel expression in Dewey, even though Dewey gradually broke with Green's idealism to express his own views in terms of a naturalistic approach to psychology and metaphysics.

What Green took to be the characteristic of an individual, insofar as that individual is viewed as a willing being, is that he experiences wants and impulses to satisfy these wants.[17] In this respect, men resemble other living things. However, regardless of what may be the case with respect to other beings, a human being is a self-conscious subject for whom these wants furnish motives for action; and it is to these motives that one must look for the causes that determine actions. This raises the question of what accounts for the motive inducing a person to act as he or she does. To this Green answered, as other determinists had answered, that this depends upon the character of the person. In saying this, Green differed from those for whom character consisted of a complex set of more or less independent desires and aversions which interacted with one another, and one of which, in a particular situation, proved to be stronger than the others. For Green, the motive of an action was not to be identified with any specific desire or aversion of which the individual was conscious before he willed to act. Instead, Green took the true motive to be the particular self-satisfaction which a person believed he would gain if he attained some particular end or goal. Thus, the motive which an act of will expresses is the desire for self-satisfaction. Green formulated that view in saying that a motive "as an object *of will* is not merely one of the objects of desire or aversion, of which the man was conscious before he willed. It is a particular self-satisfaction to be gained in attaining one of these objects or a combination of them. The 'motive' which the act of will expresses is the desire for this self-satisfaction" (*Prolegomena*, sec. 104).[18] Thus, the individual always acts to develop or realize himself, not to attain any particular, limited end. It is in this way that self-determinism and self-realizationism as the standard of the good became linked in Green's moral system. In a statement summarizing the course of his argument from its epistemological foundations to its conception of the good (ibid., secs. 174–75), Green held that man's self-determinism consists in the fact that, being human and conscious of self,

> he is determined, not simply by natural wants according to natural laws, but by the thought of himself as existing under certain conditions, and as having ends that may be attained and capabilities that may be realized under those conditions. It is thus that he not merely desires but seeks to satisfy himself in gaining the objects of his desire; presents to himself a certain possible state of himself, which in the gratification of the desire he seeks to reach; in short, wills. It is thus, again, that he has the impulse to make himself what he has the possibility of becoming but actually is not, and hence not merely, like the plant or animal, undergoes a process of development, but seeks to, and does, develop himself. (Ibid., sec. 175)[19]

Turning now from the idealism of Green to the thought of Dewey, we find that Dewey's theory closely resembled that of Green. Like Green, he connected self-determinism with the theory that the basic nature of the self is a tendency to self-development, or "self-realization"; it was in this that freedom consisted. Nevertheless, after a time, Dewey felt the need to be more explicit concerning the nature of an agent's self and character than Green had been: he refused to identify a person's character with a self or ego which lay behind experience. Instead, he regarded the self as an integrated system of impulses which had developed and was being modified in the course of experience. In any given case an impulse is accompanied by the idea of its consequences and is seen in relation to the total system of impulses, habits, and ideals that constitute the self. Given this view of an act as being immediately determined by the system of impulses and ends which he identified as the self, Dewey's position was clearly a form of determinism, but one in which, through experience, the self came to determine itself. As he said, "The ethical conception of freedom is the recognition of the meaning for conduct of the identity of self and act, of will and deed. There is no factor in the act foreign or alien to the agent's self; it is himself through and through. . . . The entire voluntary process is one of self-expression, of coming to consciousness of self. This intimate and thorough-going *selfness* of the deed constitutes freedom."20 Thus, in Dewey as in Green—in spite of the differences between their conceptions of the self—the doctrines of self-determinism and self-realizationism went hand in hand: in neither case was deliberative choice between two incompatible alternatives a characteristic moment in morally relevant judgments.21

To summarize what may be said concerning the doctrine of self-determinism, it should now be clear that the self-determinist rejects indeterminism, while at the same time rejecting the traditional necessitarian doctrine. The middle way that he seeks is one which holds that choice is determined, but not as events in the nonhuman world are determined: rather, it is determined by motives. Furthermore, which of conflicting motives becomes operative as the agent's will in a given situation is not a function of their relative strength when considered in isolation; it is a function of the agent's own character. Up to this point, of course, many other determinists might still agree. The self-determinist, however, insists—as did Mill—that the agent's character is not simply a product of his original constitution and past experiences, but that it can gradually be altered by the individual himself. Green and Dewey held this to be possible because underlying all other motives they held that there is one motive which every individual shares: an urge to foster the growth and welfare of the self. Recognizing that actions in accordance with some motives foster growth and welfare, whereas others do not, the individual can choose the former, gradually transforming himself through loss of interest in those which fail to enhance his growth. It is in this way that the doctrine of self-determinism regarding choices is closely linked to the doctrine of self-realizationism as the standard of value.

*Attention and Choice*

Finally I turn to a view of what determines choice which I regard as clearer and psychologically more plausible than the subjective, objective, or self-determinist theories with which I have thus far been concerned. This is the theory that choice is determined through attention, a theory which—up to one final point—was developed by James in the chapter of his *Principles of Psychology* that discusses the will. (Let me say, parenthetically, that in order to understand James's doctrine as he developed it in his *Psychology,* one must, for the moment, forget what he says in his essay "The Dilemma of Determinism.")

To understand James's discussion of choice, one must first recognize the extent to which he stressed the pervasiveness in human behavior of what he and others termed ideo-motor action. That term refers to those occasions on which the presence of an idea unhesitantly and immediately calls forth an action. This he took to be the normal process of volition, which operates in much of our lives. He noted, however, that sometimes conflicting notions are present to the mind, and in such cases action in accordance with one notion is inhibited by the action which the other would ordinarily evoke. It is in such cases that deliberation, rather than immediate ideo-motor discharge, occurs. James notes that while deliberation may be relatively short-lived, at other times it may be protracted over weeks or months, occupying the mind at intervals whenever one of the notions arises and calls forth and is balanced by the other. James found it of great psychological interest to see how such conflicts are ultimately resolved, and he sketched five ways in which deliberation is apt to be terminated so that action can proceed.[22] Of these five, the two with which we shall here be concerned are those in which choice depends upon the fixation of attention, for I agree with James that "we reach the heart of our inquiry into volition when we ask by what process it is that the thought of any given object comes to prevail stably in the mind" (*Principles,* 2:1166). The illustration which he used in each of his several treatments of this problem was that of the drunkard who, after having foresworn drink, thinks of excuses for taking a drink on some particular occasion.[23] James lists a few such excuses, among which are the following: "It is poured out and it is a sin to waste it; others are drinking and it would be churlishness to refuse. . . . It is just to get through this job of work; . . . it is Christmas day; . . . or it is just this once, and once doesn't count." James points out that all these are excuses to keep from thinking of this act as what it is: being addicted to drink. As he says, "*That* is the conception that will not stay before the poor soul's attention. But if he once gets able to pick out that way of conceiving, from all the other possible ways of conceiving the various opportunities which occur, if through thick and thin he holds to it that this is being a drunkard and is nothing else, he is not likely to remain one long" (ibid., pp. 1169–70). Thus, according to James, "the essential achievement of the will . . . when it is voluntary, is to ATTEND to a difficult object and hold it fast before the mind. . . . Effort of attention is thus the essential phenomenon of will" (ibid., pp. 1166–67).

Shortly thereafter—consistently with his whole argument—James said: "The question of fact in the free-will controversy is thus extremely simple. It relates solely to the amount of effort of attention or consent which we can at any time put forth" (ibid., p. 1175). This led him to propose the following alternatives: either the duration and intensity of this effort are "fixed functions of the object," as is the case in "effortless volitions," or else the effort is exactly what it seems to be—"an independent variable" such that "we might exert more or less of it in any given case." As is well known, James opted for the latter alternative; he believed that what he had termed "the dead heave of the will" does count.[24] To be sure, James did not claim that the truth of this alternative could be established within psychology, but he was equally strenuous in denying that psychology (or "science" in general) could rule out the efficacy of effort in determining choice. When discussing this issue in his chapter on attention, as well as in the chapter on will, he insisted that the issue must be decided on other grounds.[25] Some persons, he pointed out, were inclined to decide it on speculative metaphysical grounds, but for him the deciding factor was what he took to be the ethical import of the doctrine that effort *does* count. It is at this point that his treatment of the issue in the *Principles of Psychology* makes contact with the argument of his essay "The Dilemma of Determinism."

Since I do not believe that the alternatives which he outlines are equally balanced, I should like to retreat a step and return to his argument as to the role of attention in choice. What I shall propose is that one can use James's insight concerning the attention (an insight shared, incidentally, by G. F. Stout) and yet hold a deterministic account of choice rather than introducing a special phenomenon identified as an "effort of the will." In short, I wish to propose that choice is determined through attention, but that the concept of effort need not be introduced, as it was by James, when explaining how attention is itself controlled.

When speaking of "choice" in what follows, I am confining my discussion to those cases in which a person recognizes that he is faced by a choice between alternatives, each of which he has some reason for wanting to do. I am not concerned with actions in which an *onlooker* might say that the agent *did* have a choice, but in which the agent—whether culpably or not—failed to recognize that fact. Thus, I am not considering cases in which an agent acts spontaneously, without deliberation, and is not aware, at the time at which he acts, that there is some alternative which it might be to his advantage to pursue. I assume that human infants, until checked by experience, do tend to act in this nondeliberative way. However, experience soon leads them to be somewhat wary of giving spontaneous impulse full play; and what direct experience fails to achieve in this respect will generally be supplemented by the rewards and punishments which their actions elicit from others. Thus, from a very early age, human beings become accustomed to noticing, and even become inclined to search for, alternatives which may be present in the situations they face. In short, it does not take "effort," as a special act of will, to lead human beings to consider at least some of the alternatives in any situation.

Yet, one must ask, when we are aware of alternatives in a situation, what leads us to follow one rather than the other? According to James—and I agree—it is the fact that our attention remains focused on the first rather than on the second. It was at this point, however, that James introduced the notion of *effort* as an "independent variable" which was needed to tip the beam. As his discussion makes clear, the reason he did so was to explain those cases in which "a rarer and more ideal impulse is called upon to neutralize others of a more instinctive or habitual kind" (*Principles*, 2:1154).[26] He held that ideal impulses and remote goals can prevail over the passions, appetites, and ingrained habits only through the exercise of effort on the part of the agent. He illustrated his point diagramatically, saying that the force of an ideal is *per se* less than the force of a propensity, but that an ideal *plus effort* can be greater than the force of the propensity (ibid., p. 1155). The point at which this effort, or act of will, is expended is in holding attention fixated on the ideal goal, in spite of the forces tending to divert it: as he said, "effort of attention is thus the essential phenomenon of will;" it is through effort that we can elect to follow what he termed "the line of greater resistance" (ibid., pp. 1167 and 1154–55).

If, however, we take into account the effects of what is often termed "social conditioning"—that is, the rules, values, and ideals which have gone into shaping our personalities and character—it is by no means evident that it always takes a greater effort to attend to remote goals than to what accords with our desires for objects which satisfy our immediate appetites. The strength of the appeal of an ideal goal and the strength of an appetite will vary from situation to situation, and in such conflicts persons characteristically attempt to judge—as Locke held that they judge—which of the two conflicting tendencies will lead to their greater satisfaction. Or, alternatively put, which of these tendencies will—as Green might have said—best fit with the ideal that the person has of himself or herself. What we do is envision ourselves as acting in accordance with one of these alternatives rather than any other, and envision the consequences which would follow from each. As James said, we mull over the alternatives until one stands out above the others as the one to which we find ourselves committed. James identified this as one type of decision making and distinguished it from those decisions which depend upon an effort of will. In this "reasonable type" of decision making (as he called it) he insisted that no special effort was engaged. Instead, the arguments for and against each of the alternatives are weighed until "they seem gradually and almost insensibly to settle themselves in the mind and to end by leaving a clear balance in favor of one alternative, which alternative we then adopt without effort or constraint . . . the reasons which decide as appearing to flow from the nature of things, and to owe nothing to our will. We have, however, a perfect sense of being free" (ibid., p. 1138). James stressed the fact that "the conclusive reason for the decision in these cases usually is the discovery that we can refer the case to a *class* upon which we are accustomed to act unhesitatingly in a stereotyped way. . . . In general, a great part of every deliberation consists in a turning over of all the possible modes of *conceiving* the doing or not doing of the act" (ibid., pp. 1138–39). When James continues, "The wise man is he who succeeds in finding the name which suits the needs of the particular situation best," we are forcibly reminded that this was precisely his analysis of the situation in which the man who had foresworn drink was able to resist taking a drink; it was possible to resist as soon as the man thought of himself as a drunkard were he to take that drink. Thus, the only difference between the two types of decisions which

James attempted to separate—the reasonable type and that involving effort—was his belief that in the latter case effort was used to control attention, to hold the idea steadfastly in mind. Yet James never elucidated how it is that *effort* can lead us to extrude an idea from consciousness, nor how, through *effort*, we can introduce an idea into consciousness. Of course, it might be said that these are questions which do not permit us to suggest any answer: that the phenomena are *sui generis*, yet recognizable and real. Yet, there is, I believe, an alternative way of explaining such cases if, like Spinoza, one holds that every idea has a conatus: a tendency to persevere in its own being. Thus, each idea will persist until it is displaced by the impetus of another idea. If this is true, then it does not take any effort to allow us to hold an idea fast in our minds.

Yet, even if this be granted, might it not be that effort is needed to expunge an idea to which we are attending, enabling us to introduce another in its place? To be sure, no difficulties arise with respect to cases such as those in which a train of thought has been interrupted by a voice or a noise, and our minds return to what we were thinking before being interrupted. However, a friendly critic suggested to me that there are other, more difficult types of cases. It was his contention that sometimes we deliberately will to expunge an idea from our minds and replace it by some other train of thought. The case he cited was as follows. He had owned a dog of which he was inordinately fond, but which developed a tumor and had to be taken to the veterinarian and put to death. That had occurred over two years earlier, yet every time my friend was about to drive past the veterinarian's, he forced himself to think of other things. Had he not been controlling attention through effort, a special act of will? He would say so, but I think not. I suggest that whenever we have a highly unpleasant or disturbing thought, we cast about for some other thought to displace it—and any unrelated thought will do. I see no reason to regard such an escape from an unpleasant memory as involving an effort of will, any more than withdrawing one's hand from a too-hot object takes an effort of will. (What would indeed take an act of will would be to refuse to withdraw the hand from the hot object, or to force oneself to think of extremely unpleasant things.) And we do this quite regularly. In such cases we *do* say that "we have made an effort," but in all such cases, I submit, we have firmly before our minds some good which will be enhanced by our doing so. It is through fixating that good—whether it be some future consequences to be attained, or some ideal of oneself—that our choice is determined. Thus, it is my claim that while attention determines choice, the focus of attention is itself determined by natural inclination and by the results of past experience, and we need not look—as did James—to an effort to will as an independent variable in our account.

## THE MORAL IMPLICATIONS OF DETERMINISM

While arguments concerning determinism have taken many forms, one common form has involved an assessment of its implications for morality. Such arguments have usually assumed that determinists invariably subscribe to the position that our choices are in all cases determined by those factors that I have termed subjective propensities. It should be clear, however, that if choice were determined by the apprehension of that which is objectively good, all moral objections to determinism would probably be inapplicable. Similarly, the type of self-determinism which I have discussed is inextricably linked with the moral criterion of self-realization, and unless that position can be shown to be psychologically untenable, the usual moral objections to determinism would not apply to that type of self-determinism either. In fact, however, most moral arguments against determinism usually depend upon the assumption that all choices are determined by a person's subjective propensities, and that in any given case these propensities depend upon that particular person's inborn traits and the effects of his past experiences. Given these propensities, the determinist argues, the person could not have acted in any way other than that in which he did act; to this the indeterminist replies that under these circumstances a person should not be blamed—or praised—for acting as he did.

To this, the determinist (in his turn) has usually replied that praise and blame remain appropriate, since they can affect how a person will act under similar circumstances in the future. Thus, for the determinist, praise and blame function as rewards and punishments, and even the indeterminist must admit that rewards and punishments have an effect on a person's behavior. Even though the indeterminist may grant that praise and blame do affect future actions, he may refuse (quite properly, as we shall see) to treat them as being merely special ways of rewarding or punishing past actions. Furthermore, though he can admit that many choices are adequately explained by a person's inborn capacities and his past experiences, and by his hopes of reward and fear of punishments, he would say that this does not prove that *all* choices are determined by these factors: there might also be some which remain undetermined. To this the determinist is apt to reply that it is then incumbent upon the indeterminist to offer reasons for supposing that there are other factors which influence conduct. It is in reply to such a challenge that questions regarding the relation between morality and determinism have most often arisen.

Those who object to determinism on moral grounds may formulate their objections in many ways, but they most often stress the general proposition that morality can be said to presuppose freedom, since if we say that a person *ought* to do something, this implies that we regard it as something which he can do or can forbear from doing. When an indeterminist argues in this way, the determinist has an easy answer: to say that a person ought to do something is merely to say that this is something the person *can* do, that there is nothing which prevents him from doing it. This, however, is merely to say that the person in that situation has, or did have, freedom of action, not that he has or had freedom of choice. Those who insist that individuals do have freedom of choice, and not merely freedom of action, can counter this response by insisting that when we praise or blame a person for that which he has done, our praise or blame refer to him, not merely to what he did. Though we may in fact alter his conduct by our praise or blame, this is not what we intend in our moral judgments: instead, we are assigning merit or demerit to what has already been done, and we need not be primarily concerned with altering his future conduct. For example, our judgments of what is worthy of praise or blame extend to persons long since dead and, as Bishop Butler pointed out, even to the feigned characters of fiction.[27] To be sure, with children we may sometimes use praise and blame to encourage or discourage particular forms of action, attempting to promote what we regard as good habits, but we clearly recognize the difference between using praise or blame in this manner and finding ourselves spontaneously praising or blaming a person for his actions.

Some determinists, such as Hume, do not attempt to interpret praise and blame as if they were forms of reward or punishment, but Hume's psychology of moral judgments has few followers today, regardless of his influence with respect to other matters. Recent formulations of the view that choice is determined by subjective propensities have most often been couched in terms of the concept of conditioning and the affiliated notions of reinforcement and extinction. Originally, of course, the concept of conditioning was developed in connection with explanations of animal behavior and then extended to human behavior. It became further extended when its original physiological orientation was no longer emphasized, and the concept of "social conditioning" was applied to all forms of interpersonal behavior, regardless of whether or not a physiological basis for that behavior could be identified or even readily imagined. Once the concept of conditioning had been thus fully extended, it was widely assumed that moral judgments, too, were wholly the results of the individual's conditioning. Thus, cultural relativism for a time became a widely shared conviction among those affected by developments within the social sciences generally.

To be sure, the influence of Freud's theory of motivation originally served as a counterfoil to this tendency, but gradually most Freudians came to emphasize the impact of cultural factors on personality formation; the norms implicit in Freud's own theory were then challenged in terms of the role played by social factors. As a consequence, cultural relativism became for a time the dominant view among American social scientists and social theorists. In most cases, however, they abandoned it when they recognized it to be incompatible with a condemnation of the Hitler regime. Many of them then sought to establish a moral standard in terms of the existence of some universal needs in individuals or in societies. These attempts, however, did not involve any basic reinterpretation of their previous views concerning human experience: science was still seen as demanding that one explain an individual's actions solely in terms of his inherited capacities and his personal and social experiences.

It was against such an assumption that indeterminists had always directed their arguments. Among recent forms of these arguments, emphasis has often been placed on the fact that science constitutes only one way of looking at the world: that all features of the world need not be interpreted in the same terms as scientists use when describing the particular aspects of things in which they are interested.[28] In line with this criticism, though sometimes for very different reasons, many philosophers have rejected traditional determinism, arguing that while science explains things in terms of their causes, a proper interpretation of human action speaks not of "causes" but of "reasons." This distinction between causes and reasons dovetailed neatly with the position of compatibilists regarding freedom and determinism. When one spoke of why a person acted as he did, one was offering an explanation in terms of the reasons he had for his choices, but this could be wholly compatible with holding that his choices were causally determined by processes of which neither he nor we are aware. Thus, according to the compatabilist, whatever may have caused an action is really irrelevant to whether or not a person should be praised or blamed for what he did. Since compatibilism has been widely accepted in recent philosophic discussions of freedom, the question of whether our choices are determined has shifted, and the questions now most frequently discussed concern the conditions under which one can say that a person has acted freely, or whether his freedom of action has been limited or cancelled by factors such as ignorance, constraints put upon him by others, or inherited or inherited or acquired disabilities. While such discussions have been useful in clarifying ambiguities in the concepts of freedom and responsibility, they have not contributed to the issue as to whether *choices* are in fact determined and, if so, by what. Rather than being solved, that issue has been brushed aside as being an "empirical" rather than a "philosophical" issue. Nonetheless, as I now wish to show, the main philosophical tradition regarding the problem was not mistaken: the issue that is relevant to our theory of morality is not one of when we can be said to have freedom of action, but one of when we can be said to have freedom of choice.

In cases of choice, one is dealing with the fact that a person elected to do X rather than Y. If he did actually *choose* to do X (and was not simply responding to a stimulus or acting out of habit), he will have had some reason for doing so; but if he had chosen Y, he would have had some reason for doing that. We may of course say that he had a reason for choosing X rather than Y, such as the fact that he preferred it or that he felt obliged to choose to do it, or we may cite many other types of reasons why he chose as he did. The question, however, remains; *Why* did he prefer X, or *why* did he feel obliged to do X? In the last analysis, all such questions must be answered in causal terms and cannot be adequately answered simply by citing further reasons.

As I have said, the type of answer traditional determinists have most often given to all such causal questions has been to cite the subjective propensities of the agent, and these have been held to have been caused by his inherited capacities and his past experiences. These having been what they were, an agent could not have chosen to act otherwise than he did. While this has often been claimed to be the verdict of "science"—and is often accepted as such—I wish to show that we need not hold it to be the case; that we can, instead, hold that a scientific account of the causes of human behavior can sometimes take a quite different form, one suggested by James's analysis of willing.

The assumption which I find to be basic to the traditional form of determinism is to hold that in all cases, causal explanations involve finding some event or condition anterior to that which we wish to explain and showing that an event of the type to be explained has always followed when such anterior events or conditions have been present. This sequential, linear view of causation is characteristic of our ordinary commonsense causal explanations and is almost universally shared by philosophers today. Once that view is adopted, the cause of an event which we seek to explain lies in the past, and whatever is to serve as explaining a person's choice is not be to found in the present, nor in the future, but in something anterior to the act of choice.

Elsewhere, I have argued that while this is often a useful enough commonsense view of the causal relation, it breaks down when one seeks to apply it in scientific and historical inquiry, as well as when one attempts to give a reasonably full commonsense answer regarding the "cause" of any event whatsoever.[29] To take a simple example from the behavior of physical bodies, consider the commonsense explanation of what occurs when (to cite an example made familiar by Hume) one billiard ball strikes another, causing it to move. We quite properly say that the motion of the first ball caused the second ball to move, but underlying this explanation is the assumption that each ball is a solid object which resists impact, that motion is transferred by the impact of one solid object on another when that object is not impeded from moving, etc. Yet, even granted these assumptions, which we derive from ordinary observation, such a causal account only explains *that* the ball moves; it does not explain why that motion has the speed it does, nor why the ball moves along the precise path it does. In order to explain the actual motion of the ball, and not merely the fact that it has been set in motion, one must take into account the elasticity of the balls themselves, the spin of the cue ball, and the surface of the table, and in the end, one must restate what had seemed to be an obvious and simple causal relation in relatively sophisticated, fairly technical terms. The need to fill in commonsense explanations through more technical analyses, which are not themselves stated in simple, linear terms, becomes even more obvious when one examines high-speed photographs of the distortions suffered by an object when it is struck by another object and when one then goes on to consider the manner in which physicists account for the fact that an object such as a billiard ball is set in motion when struck. The ultimate inadequacy of a simple, sequential, linear explanation of causation becomes even more evident in the case of physiological explanations, such as what causes a person's fever or what is involved in the case of heart failure. It is still more obvious when one is dealing with societal events, seeking to explain why a political campaign was lost or why one nation has gained economic ascendency over other nations.

Granted that a simple, linear model of causation fails to do justice to the causal relation—however well such a model may jibe with our shorthand commonsense explanations of many physical events —how is this related to the problem of what determines a person's choices? The answer should be obvious: we should not expect to be able to explain such choices solely with reference to that which lies in the person's past, that is, with reference to his inherited makeup and earlier experiences. Nor need we do so, as I shall now attempt to show.

In the first place, insofar as any mental capacities or temperamental dispositions may be inherited, they will not remain wholly unaffected by what happens in the course of a person's life. Furthermore, the results of experience may affect whatever may have been that individual's original nature, and will in turn influence how, as he or she develops, that person will respond to later experiences. Thus, at any time, when we wish to explain a person's responses to a given situation, we must do so in terms of his *present* nature, and not with respect to one or another factor in his past. In short, one must say that it is not to a person's original heredity nor to any specific past experiences that one must appeal in explaining his behavior; rather, it is with reference to his present nature as it has been formed by his inheritance and his past experiences that appeal must be made. It does not matter whether one thinks of the present effects of past experiences as being present to consciousness, or as buried in the unconscious, or as embedded in traces in the nervous system; what is essential when one seeks to explain a person's choices is to take into account what constitutes his nature at the time that he makes whatever choice he does make.

In the second place, one must, in explaining any choice, also take into account the nature of the specific situation which the person confronts and be aware of how the person himself sees that situation; how we or another outsider might describe it is irrelevant: it is his choice that we wish to explain. In many cases, of course, how an individual views a particular situation will depend upon his past experiences with similar situations; for example, he will have learned to prefer one type of food to another and may therefore choose it, and he will have learned to fear some object and will thereafter be inclined to shun others resembling it. One should not seek to minimize the very great degree to which an individual's past experience determines his present choices. Nevertheless, traditional determinists have so overestimated the effects of past experience that they are willing to deny that the specific nature of the situation an agent confronts may itself serve to determine how he will act. It is this form of determinism, which regards the past as being in all cases dominant over the present, that I wish to refute. I contend that one can consistently hold to a determinist position and yet not place exclusive emphasis on that which has occurred to a person prior to his act of choice.

To be sure, traditional determinists can admit that a person's choices are affected by the nature of the situation he or she faces, but they can still maintain that the way in which the alternatives in that situation are viewed will depend upon the person's past experience. For example, a person will not choose to do that which resembles what has in the past brought him suffering, unless he foresees that making that choice will, in the end redound to his benefit. Thus, according to the traditional determinist, it would be on the basis of past experience that present choices are always made. While such an analysis is in many cases undoubtedly correct, it is not in all cases plausible. Among the most obvious exceptions would be those in which a present context radically changes an agent's previous way of looking at one of the alternatives. This occurs, for example, when some type of action which he has previously performed in a habitual, thoughtless manner is suddenly seen as harmful to a person he respects or loves. Similarly, an action which seemed innocent enough so long as it was he who did it may appear in a different light when a similar action is performed by another and causes either him or some friend to suffer embarrassment or discomfort. In all such cases, the way a particular type of action is viewed has been changed because it is seen in a different context from that with which the person had previously been familiar. If this did not occur, we could not explain how new ways of acting and new moral judgments are sometimes inculcated by unfamiliar situations, or by the examples of others.

There is nothing mysterious about these claims. The first follows directly from the fact that when we wish to explain why a person acts as he does, we need to take account of his present nature, not of whatever past events may have contributed to his having the beliefs, dispositions, or temperament that he presently has. It is in terms of his present nature that he responds to whatever situation he faces. Since his present nature may be different from what it was in the past, we should not expect that he will always view any particular situation in the same light as he had previously viewed other similar situations. In the second place, the context in which something is seen may lead a person to recognize previously unnoticed aspects of an otherwise familiar situation, or it may accentuate aspects of one of the alternatives which had not formerly stood out prominently for him. Both of these reasons for insisting on the possibility of novel types of responses in otherwise familiar situations are needed to explain learning in animals as well as in human behavior.[30]

Of course, what is essential if a person is to respond in a non-stereotyped way to any situation is that he should closely attend to that particular situation. It is at this point that James's emphasis on attention in willing is of the utmost importance. While humans, as well as animals, naturally attend to their environments, humans are in most cases apt to respond to the familiar aspects of their environments. They must therefore learn, in one way or another, that it is sometimes undesirable to act entirely spontaneously, without considering alternative possibilities for action. This demands that people be in some way conditioned to look before they leap. In fact, such conditioning begins at an early age through painful experiences, and through the admonishments and rewards and punishments administered by their parents; it is then reinforced through interactions with their playmates, and by the praise and blame they receive, even from strangers. In a sense, one can truly say that, initially, individuals are *conditioned* to take notice of the fact that in many situations choices are to be made. The range of their awareness of such choices grows as their experience grows; thus, paradoxical as it may seem, one can say that it is through conditioning that individuals gain whatever autonomy they come to enjoy.

Yet, were it the case that our actual choices were wholly determined by our inherited capacities and the consequences of whatever specific experiences we have had, one could not claim that we are acting autonomously, even though we may feel that we are. That sense of autonomy would be justified only if it had been possible for us, at the time, to have elected to follow either of the courses which appeared to be open to us—that is, if our actual choices were not beyond our control, having been determined by what had already occurred. If, on the other hand, a choice is determined by our view as to which of the possible alternatives is of greater intrinsic importance, or of greater importance to us, then it is truly we who are choosing: it is not the past, but that which is here and now presented to us which determines how we shall act. Of course, were it not for our past experience, we would not be aware of the choices that exist in any situation, nor would we be in a position to understand the nature and probable consequences of the alternatives confronting us. Yet, as I have indicated, what we see when we truly attend to a situation (rather than simply reacting in a habitual or stereotyped way) is not exclusively determined by past experience. Instead, what we then see will be situationally determined, and the fact that it is *we* who must act is seen as part of that situation itself.

Because of our individual experiences in the particular environments in which we have grown up, each of us carries certain self-images of what we are and of what we would like to be; when we are faced with choices, our self-images often play a crucial role in that which we choose to do. Thus, in the situation James discussed, it is when the reformed alcoholic sees himself as a drunkard were he to succumb to the temptation of taking a drink that he does not do so; but so long as he does not project that image of himself into the situation he faces, it will seem of no importance whether or not he takes just one drink: there will then be nothing to deter him from doing that which his former habit tempts him to do. In such cases, as James insists, he will think up excuses to justify himself, trying to put his mind at rest. Yet, if he really attends to the situation, and he takes his own past and future into account, he will refrain. Thus, we often say, "*I* cannot do that," and we feel obliged to abstain.[31]

That our self-images can, in principle, be explained by whatever dispositional properties we inherited and by the ways these have been transformed in and through our experiences cannot be denied. It must further be admitted—as I have admitted—that were it not for our past experience we would not be in a position to see what alternatives there may be in whatever situations we face. All that I insist upon is that we cannot—even in principle—explain all of our choices in terms of identifying any set of conditions or events which existed in the past. Some situations in which we are aware of alternatives between which we must choose are—for us—novel situations, and so long as we actually attend to them, they—being novel—do not permit us to respond in a habitual or stereotyped way. There is nothing mysterious about claiming that in novel situations a person is determined by the nature of his present situation and by the way in which he sees his role in that situation, rather than being determined by what lies in his past.

Indeed, the past can be a determinant of our action only insofar as it is present within us. It will, of course, be present in our present memories of what had occurred or what had failed to occur; it will also be present insofar as the situation evokes certain aspects of our self-image which—though they depend upon the past—are always present within us; and it will be present because the reservoir of our acquired knowledge is always more or less accessible to us. It is only so long as we think of causation in terms of simple, linear, common-sense models of how one physical object appears to affect another that we will be inclined to retreat to the past in order to explain present actions. Once we abandon thinking in terms of that model, we will recognize that the past can only be effective if there is some form in which it operates in the present.[32]

In short, though I am a determinist, I am unlike the traditional determinist in not accepting what Mill criticized when, in a some-what different context, he criticized "necessitarianism": I do not believe that what we choose is wholly determined by what lies in the past. If my view is correct, then our choices, even though they are determined, must in many cases be said to be codetermined by the actual nature of the situation we face, rather than being the inevitable outcome of that which lies in the past and is therefore beyond our present control.

It is my contention that determinism, as thus conceived, has important implications for moral theory. Traditional determinists have always been attacked for failing to give adequate accounts of moral praise and blame, and for failing to offer morally adequate justifications of rewards and punishments. I believe that, in general, such criticisms are warranted.

Take the case of praise and blame. Opponents of traditional de-terminism have held that if a person's actions are determined, no person can have helped doing what he did; under these circum-stances neither praise nor blame are due him: it has simply been his lot to do what he did. Determinists have countered this argument by saying that these actions—however they may have been caused—*were* his actions, and he must be held accountable for them. Further-more, on this view it makes sense to praise or to blame him, since in that way we are providing incentives for him to act in one way rather than another in the future. Unfortunately, however, such a justifica-tion of praise and blame can be accepted only if we forget that if determinism is true, then it is not only true with respect to the action of others, but also with respect to our own actions.[33] Thus, when we praise or blame a person, even though our praise or blame falls on that person for what he or she has done, the fact that we find such an action to be praiseworthy or blameworthy will itself have been deter-mined; and it will have been determined not by the nature of that which is praised or blamed, but by whatever aspects of our own past experience prove at the time to be dominant over us. This involves a complete relativization of moral praise and blame. Consequently, when traditional determinism goes beyond explaining the actions of others to explain how we ourselves react, we must drastically revise our usual interpretations of what is involved in moral praise and blame.

The inadequacy of traditional determinism when confronted by the nature of moral judgments can be even more clearly seen when we consider the question of how we are to justify the rewards and punishments administered in a judicial system such as ours. The traditional determinist has usually justified legal punishments by appealing to some form of utilitarian theory, claiming that such punishments serve to deter others from commiting similar crimes, or are needed to protect society from the likelihood of future wrong-doing by the criminal himself, or—ideally—will serve to reform the criminal, making him a useful member of the community. In addition, determinists can hold a "social theory" of punishment, pointing out that laws are necessary for there to be any stable form of social life, and that laws necessarily entail socially defined sanctions. All such theories of punishment rest on a utilitarian or consequentialist justification of punishment; what the traditional determinist rejects is any form of retributivist theory, considering it immoral to inflict suffering on an individual unless that suffering is justified by whatever further good it promotes. Assuming the truth of a utilitarian theory of punishment, it is entirely reasonable to punish a lawbreaker even though his actions were wholly determined by what had befallen him and could not at any point have been different from what they were.

Plausible as it may seem, such a justification of legal punishments falters when one applies the theory of determinism to the behavior of judges as well as to the actions of those who are judged. If a judge's decision is determined by his own past, this will include not only the results of his training in the law and by what has influenced his social orientation, but may be deeply affected by attitudes he has formed toward persons other than those presently on trial, by whether he has been privately or publicly criticized for some earlier decisions, and even by the most random incidents that set the tone of his disposition at the time of the trial. There is no end to the variety of factors which might play a role in his reaching whatever decision he does reach, and we should regard this as unjust to the person on trial. On our view, a judge's decision should be formed on the basis of the specific circumstances under which an action was done, and what the law that he interprets and applies holds to be appropriate under these circumstances.

It is at this point that one can most clearly see the difference between the form of determinism which I accept and the position of traditional determinists. Instead of holding that our actions (or our judgments) are determined by events that lie in our past, I have argued that the determinants of choice lie in the present and, in particular, in how we react to what is present before us. What I hold—and have elsewhere argued[34]—is that the basic notion running through all of our moral judgments is what appears to us to be fitting in the situation by which we are confronted. And, as I have indicated, it is psychologically false to hold that what we perceive in a situation is, in all cases, to be accounted for by our past experience in other situations, even though they may be similar in many respects to that which we now confront. The specific context in which a given situation is seen is often a novel context, and what may appear objectively to be the same action will, in a different context, take on a new meaning, calling forth a judgment different from those which have been made before.

As I indicated in discussing James's analysis of willing, no special effort is needed to force us to act in one way rather than another, once we view the alternatives before us and see the consequences to which they are likely to lead. Thus, when we freely choose one action rather than another, our decisions are of the sort which James called the "reasonable" type; they are of the sort upon which Locke ultimately relied when he held that though men are determined in their actions, they may also be said to be free. Granted that we are not dealing with persons of impaired intelligence, or with those compulsive psychopaths who lack the necessary self-control, or with children whose experience is too limited for them to recognize that there are alternatives in a given situation, that which impedes and imperils our freedom is a careless lack of attention to the alternatives present in a given situation. To be sure, there will be differences among the moral judgments made by different persons, but how to resolve such differences (insofar as they can be resolved) is not our present problem. My aim has been confined to showing that insofar as a person has deliberately chosen one course of conduct rather than another, it is entirely justified to hold him responsible for his choice, even though that choice is determined. Were it determined by what lay in the past, rather than in the choice itself, I should consider it unreasonable to blame him for what he has done. On the other hand, insofar as that which determines what he chooses is his acceptance of one alternative in a situation, preferring it to all others of which he is aware, we can consider his action to be a responsible one, and we hold him accountable for it.

## THE EFFECTIVENESS OF CHOICE

The fact that we have the ability to choose, and that our choices are not in all cases forced upon us by our past, should not suggest that these choices are in all cases effective. Many factors limit our capacity to change the course of events by our choices. Obvious cases of this sort are those in which we choose to do X, unaware that doing it is beyond our power, either because we lack the requisite strength or because external forces, such as the will of another or some unforeseen change in circumstances, preclude us from doing it. Such cases as this can apply in almost any type of situation in which an individual has chosen to do some particular thing: what he has chosen to do is something that he, as an individual, happens to be unable to do. Yet, there are many other situations in which our individual choices are effective, and we can do exactly what we have chosen to do. Ordinarily, nothing inhibits me from taking a walk when I decide I would prefer to walk rather than remain at home to wait for a telephone call which may or may not come. In such cases the decision is mine, and it is unlikely that anything will prevent me from doing what I have decided to do.

To be sure, not all things that we may choose to do are things which we are able to do, and this is not only because we lack the physical strength or the knowledge necessary, nor is it in all cases because external forces act upon us to prevent us from carrying out our plan. In some cases our expectations themselves may be wholly unrealistic, and in those cases what checks the effectivess of our choices is not attributable to personal incapacities or external hinderances, but to a failure to recognize that, given the world as it is, we cannot through a single act of choice alter its constitution. Thus, it does not lie within our power to avoid ageing, nor to remain wholly unchanged by experiences we have had; nor does it lie within any individual's power to prevent all human suffering, nor to bring about a complete change in the social systems of even one nation, much less to wipe away all causes of distrust which have grown up among the different peoples of the world.

I assume that all this is obvious and will not be challenged, though many refinements of what has been said could be introduced. If, however, the issues it raises are to be clarified, we must recall the distinction to be drawn between freedom of action and freedom of choice. The question of freedom of choice (as I have indicated) is one as to why I choose what I choose; the question of freedom of action concerns whether, having chosen, I can do what I have chosen to do.

In the preceding section I contended that it is not our past which, in all cases, wholly determines our choices: that when we have learned to see alternatives in the situations we confront, our choice is determined by what seems to us to be the most appropriate way to respond to that situation. What appears to be appropriate will depend upon our preferences, our self-image, and our assumptions as to the consequences of each of the alternatives. To be sure, we may wish that we had not been placed in a situation which forces such a choice upon us, and under such circumstances we do not feel free. Yet, so long as we recognize that we *must* choose, we do not regard that which we chose as having been chosen for us or as having been determined against our will. To this extent we feel that the choice we are making is free and that it is we who are responsible for what we have chosen.

To choose is not to perform a purely mental act, however; it is to set ourselves to do something.[35] In short, as Dewey insisted, choice flows into action and is merely the initiating moment in that which we do.[36] Nevertheless, the aspect of an action which we designate as "choosing" does not constitute the action itself: we may choose to do X, setting ourselves to do it, but we may be unable to do it because we lack certain abilities or are hindered by circumstances, or because any number of things may interfere with our doing it. Thus, even though choosing may constitute the initiating phase of an action, it is to be distinguished from the action, and even though we exercise freedom of choice, this does not entail that we have in all cases the freedom of action we may wish that we had. Even so, it makes sense to speak of the effectiveness of choice. In the first place, when choosing to do X rather than Y, even if we are unable to carry out our choice and attain that which we had anticipated when we chose X, we have for the time being foreclosed the option of doing Y. That may be fortunate or unfortunate, but in either case our choice of X did make a difference. To be sure, we may at a later time have a chance to pursue Y, if we then desire to do so, but by then the situation under which we act will almost always be attended by new circumstances, including the fact that we and others may be mindful that doing Y was not our original choice. In many cases, of course, such choices may not be very consequential, but in others they may make a great deal of difference to our welfare and to the welfare of others.

There is a second way in which choices frequently prove to be consequential, and that is with respect to what we may learn through them, once their consequences have been brought home to us. For example, if my physician advises me to change my eating, drinking, or smoking habits, and I first start following his advice, but then, at some point, am tempted to disobey his warning and revert to my former habits, I may quickly learn that I should not have done so. This should constitute a learning experience, leading me to a better knowledge of my weakness of will, and it may help me to resist similar temptations in the future. To this extent choice can break what Mill called "necessitarianism," making it possible for us to change our own characters. Of course, I may not have had the lesson of succumbing to temptation driven home strongly enough, and I may revert to my former habits, and that, too, involves my having been responsible for the character that emerges, perhaps becoming even more addicted to my former habits and forfeiting—or making more difficult—the possibility of later change.

Totally apart from how our choices affect our own welfare or that of others, some of our choices may be effective as examples to others. When, for example, we see a person who chooses to hold fast to his ideals at great cost to his personal well-being, that example may not only stir our admiration but may also force a moral lesson upon us, altering our own future conduct. Similarly, when we see a person overcome by greed, we may be revolted and may become more aware of the selfishness which characterizes much of our own conduct. Since what is morally incumbent upon us becomes far clearer in most cases through examples than through moral precepts, one person's choices may have effects which not only directly affect the welfare of others but also substantially alter their moral views.

The effectiveness of example is nowhere clearer than in the extent to which an individual may develop a leadership role in founding and sustaining a charitable organization or in leading a revolt against some form of injustice. Although one person's dedication to a cause is not the only factor which leads others to devote their energies to that cause, it is in many ways one way of mobilizing the help of others to enlist in the same cause. Herein lies much of the truth of purposive interpretations of many voluntary social organizations and of the changes individuals can bring about in their societies.

Yet, in spite of these and many other ways in which the choices of individuals must be regarded as efficacious, there are limits to their efficacy. It is with some of these limits that we shall next be concerned in noting the complex interplay of necessity, choice, and chance in human societies.

# 6 ⇨ Necessity, Chance & Choice in Human Affairs

I

In the preceding chapters I have discussed issues related to necessity, to chance, and to choice as these have arisen in the history of modern social theories. Having shown how these concepts were often interpreted, I criticized some of the uses to which they have been put. I now wish to argue that, properly interpreted, they are compatible and that, together, they are important for understanding the organization of societies and the changes that societies have undergone.

First, let us consider the concept of "necessity," which provides the background against which chance and choice must be viewed. There seems to be no other term which is in all cases substitutable for *necessity* and for its various derivatives. To be sure, *inevitable* and *unavoidable* can be used as synonyms for "that which is necessary," but these terms implicitly contain a reference to possible human action, and no such reference is present in all uses to which the concept of necessity is put. Another term which, along with its derivatives, is often substitutable for *necessary* is *determined*, and this locution resembles our use of *necessity* in being applicable to both human actions and situations which do not involve reference to what human beings can or cannot do. *Necessity*, however, is a term that is also used with respect to nontemporal relations, as is the case when one speaks of logical or rational necessity, and in such cases the concept of being determined or of being inevitable or unavoidable do not have applicability, except in the extended sense in which one may say that certain conclusions are inevitable or unavoidable if one reasons aright. Thus, necessity may be taken as a basic notion in our interpretation of the relations between things or between states of affairs whether they involve human actions or proceed independently of what any human being may do.

However, as we have noted in discussing determinism, a distinction is to be drawn between holding that, whatever happens, there are always conditions which, given them, nothing else could have happened, and another view, namely that which may be called "metaphysical determinism." The latter holds that anything which does in fact happen, or has happened, or will happen, happens necessarily. Metaphysical determinism, as one finds it in Spinoza or Laplace, or in some of the contentions of Buckle or Taine, presupposes that the entire world, in all of its aspects, forms a single closed and coherent system, such that every specific event not only has its determining conditions, but that every event is ultimately related to all other events, and nothing could happen otherwise than it did. This metaphysical determinism obviously rules out both chance and choice as factors that need to be taken into account in order to explain what in some cases occurs.

If one accepts metaphysical determinism, the notion that chance is an objective fact in nature or in human affairs will disappear: events which appear to be the result of "chance" are events whose causes are not known. This Spinozistic interpretation of chance is, however, mistaken. We often know the causes of events which we take to be chance events, and we can trace these causes back to their causes, and can sometimes continue to do so almost indefinitely. Nevertheless, we regard such events as chance events if they represent a conjunction of different lines of causation which are independent of one another and whose coincidence at any particular point in time could not have been predicted on the basis of what occurred in either of these lines alone, no matter how fully we understood them. This view, which we saw to be the view of Cournot, is important in understanding the history of any society: it is almost never possible to understand what has occurred in any society independently of all references to what has occurred in other societies with which it has had points of contact; yet each of these societies will have its own history which is to some degree independent of what has occurred in the other.

Similarly, the concept of causal necessity does not exclude a belief that human choices affect history. In the first place, even though each choice has some determining conditions, one cannot have known all of these conditions in advance, nor can one know, under varying circumstances, how they will interact to produce the results they do. Furthermore, the choices of any individual may alter the situations in which others are placed, and will thus affect the choices they make; therefore, the consequences which any choice may have cannot be said to follow directly from whatever conditions originally determined it. Under these circumstances one cannot say that the outcome of those events in which the choices of individuals play a role is "determined" or "inevitable"; consequently, a complete or metaphysical determinism will have no plausibility if one attempts to apply it in explaining human affairs.

On the other hand, it would be a serious mistake to hold that the concept of necessity is without meaning and applicability when dealing with human affairs. There is a sense in which we can speak of something as being "necessary" and mean that it is a condition *sine qua non* for the presence of some characteristic or for the occurrence of some type of event. As I have elsewhere argued, when necessity is taken in this sense, that which is necessary is not to be identified with the cause of an event, even though a necessary condition may be among the conditions which, together, constitute the event's actual cause.[1] When all these conditions are present, the event necessarily follows, or may be said to be determined by them; yet no one of these conditions may be a necessary condition for the occurrence of events of that type. In fact, there may not be any single factor common to a number of similar events, that is, to events which we are apt to classify in terms of their resemblances. While each such event will have its own determining conditions, there need be no condition which is characteristic of every event that we subsume under a particular type.[2] Nevertheless, one can discover certain features of social organization which are universal and are presumably necessary for the continued existence of each and every society. Such features would be necessary factors of organized social life, and I have already indicated, in the last section of Chapter 3, five different factors of which this might be claimed. It was my contention that each of them had to be present in one form or another if any human society were to exist. In addition, when discussing Malinowski's later functionalism in Chapter 3, I had also held that for the continuing existence of any society, that society must be able to satisfy at least some of the basic needs of the individuals living in it. Thus, it is my claim that two sorts of necessary conditions must be present in any human society: it must be so organized that the needs of a large number of its members are met, and its basic institutions must be so organized as to be compatible with one another. In the following section I shall begin by spelling out what this second, institutional necessity involves.³

II

Every social institution involves a patterning of relationships among individuals: if their behavior were not to a large extent regulated by commonly recognized rules, so that each person had a notion of what was to be expected with respect to the actions of others, there would be no institutions and no organized social life. Since one cannot speak of institutions without speaking of rules according to which individuals behave, it would seem that we should regard societies simply as a congeries of individuals who behave in a certain way. This, however, would be a mistake. For example, the rules defining the nature of a game are not identical with the behavior of those who play that game: they play *according to the rules,* and the rules are not simply summary statements of how they actually behave. This is clear every time a foul is called in a game, and every time an individual breaks a law, committing a crime.⁴ It is therefore a mistake to think of a society in terms of the actual behavior of individuals, even though it is clear that were it not for the existence and activities of individuals, the society would not exist.

That the individuals themselves are not to be considered the elements constituting a particular society becomes evident when we consider what is involved in describing a society: we proceed by describing its various institutions and their relations to one another, rather than by referring to the individuals who participate in its life. (In fact, not only do societies and their institutions survive the death of any particular group of individuals, but we could not possibly either enumerate or identify the individual members of those societies which we can describe.) Conversely, when we describe any individual, we do not simply describe his physical appearance, his capacities, his character and temperament, but we also refer to his status within his society. Thus, in the case of our own society we not only characterize a person's physical appearance and mention that he is, for example, intelligent and high-strung, but we will identify him as a clergyman, a banker, or a teacher, as a citizen or resident alien or illegal immigrant, as married or unmarried, and as belonging to some particular subgroup within the society because of his ethnic origin, because of his religious affiliation, or because of the socioeconomic class to which his speech, clothing, and habits suggest that he belongs. In fact, an individual's institutional status is in many respects as important as his inherited traits and temperament in determining his behavior. Consequently it would be mistaken to assume that institutions are to be regarded as nothing but the ways in which anthropologists and others summarize certain aspects of the ways in which a particular set of individuals behave; rather, a society should be regarded as being composed of both individuals and the institutional structures under which they live.

In attempting to explain the nature of a society's institutions, we must view them in two different ways, but these ways are fully compatible. From one point of view they can be considered with reference to the needs of individuals, while from the other they are to be viewed as essential to the formation and continued existence of organized social life. Institutions capable of performing this dual function differ widely from society to society, with respect both to their specific nature and their patterning. For example, kinship and familial relationships assume a great variety of forms and need not in all cases be of equal importance with respect to their relationships to such other institutional structures as the religious, educational, or economic life of the society. What is necessary is only that, whatever forms they assume and whatever their patterning, they must satisfy some needs of many individuals and must be such that they are mutually consistent if the society is in the long run to survive. It is with the problem of the compatibility or incompatibility of institutions, and the relation of this problem to societal change, that I shall now be concerned.

It has long been recognized that in any given state of technology, there is a relationship between the type of family organization that is present and the ways in which food is obtained. Furthermore, as Tylor seems to have shown, within different types of kinship relationships and family organization there may be correlations with respect to certain practices, such as rules of residence and rules of descent. Whether there are invariant relationships of this kind and, if there are, how extensive they may be is an empirical question that cannot be settled out of hand. However, one may be in a somewhat better position to see what *cannot* be the case than to come up with positive generalizations as to what is in all cases true: it sometimes seems intuitively certain that some types of institutions are incompatible, and cannot coexist. For example, while small communities may govern themselves through the direct democracy of town meetings, or while conflicts within a tribal group may be resolved by the dictates of the tribal chief, no such instrumentalities can formulate laws governing a large and complex industrial society. Similarly, an economy dependent on barter or on other face-to-face economic relationships will not provide the capital needed to establish industries dependent on a large number of workers and complex machinery to produce goods. It is also clear that the division of labor within a society may make it impossible for certain groups of individuals to participate in all of the same activities as are available to other groups. This is often a function of the density of a population and its mode of gaining a livelihood. For example, those who live in rural agricultural communities will not be in a position to engage in all of the same types of activity that are open to those who live in major urban centers, while those living in large urban centers will not be able to develop the same forms of social interrelationships that naturally occur in small, semi-isolated communities.

If one turns one's attention from the institutional structures of different societies and considers various facets of human culture, such as language or technology, one also finds interrelationships that place limits on what can coexist in any given society at any one time.[5] For example, the absence of a written language limits the range of knowledge that the members of a society can possess, and the state of technology in every society obviously plays a part in that society's economic life. Thus, with respect to specific types of institutions and also with respect to some aspects of culture, there may be incompatibilities which limit the forms in which these factors coexist. It is convenient to refer to such limiting possibilities as "objective possibilities" and to distinguish them from what I shall term "subjective possibilities," which concern the compatibility or incompatibility of certain of the activities of individuals.

Earlier I granted what was stressed by Malinowski in his later works: that societies must be so organized as to be capable of fulfilling the basic needs of individuals. However, as he insisted, different societies fulfill this condition in different ways: human beings are malleable with respect to the ways in which their needs can be fulfilled, even though they are not so malleable as to have no basic needs which are constants. What is important to note is that when a society is so organized as to fulfill some need in one way rather than another, there will be pressure on individuals to develop some traits rather than others, and these individuals may then suppress tendencies which they might have exhibited had their society not channelled their actions as it did. To be sure, tendencies which are suppressed in connection with certain forms of action may manifest themselves in other ways in other situations. For example, if signs of tenderness and affection between certain classes of individuals are not countenanced in a particular society, such displays may be permitted or even encouraged in situations involving other classes of individuals.[6] This is true with respect to the attitudes and behavior of individuals toward those whom they take to belong to another social class. For example, in our own society it has been the case—and to some extent still is the case—that the attitudes and behavior of whites toward blacks, and of blacks toward whites, differ from attitudes shown by whites toward whites or blacks toward blacks. It is therefore a great oversimplification to speak of national characteristics, or of patterns of culture as Ruth Benedict has done, assuming that certain values or sets of values characterize the basic character of those living in a particular society. Rather, what is directly affected by the social structure of a society are the occasions on which, and the ways in which, the various needs of individuals are fulfilled.

Nevertheless, any given individual may find himself caught in basic conflicts between traits which have been fostered by one of his institutional roles and those traits which he is called upon to display because of the demands placed upon him by other institutions. Thus, even though two forms of institutional organization may, in principle, be entirely compatible, some individuals will find themselves in a stressful position because they are called upon to exhibit opposed modes of behavior. To be sure, one often readily adjusts to exhibiting some form of behavior when placed in one type of situation and exhibiting quite different behavior in other situations; yet, if either of these forms is sufficiently entrenched in an individual's character, that individual will become uneasy in whatever situations presuppose that such traits be suppressed. Therefore, when a society is so organized that conflicts of this sort persist, its stability will be threatened: it will tend to frustrate individuals who are trapped in affective or behavioral dilemmas, and they will either evade some of their institutional responsibilities or reinterpret them. The presence of such conflicts will therefore tend to introduce institutional change.

While this may be one important factor making for institutional change, other significant factors must also be taken into account. Thus, not all change is due to changes in people's attitudes, as some idealistic theories of the state have tended to suggest. For example, radical changes may be introduced because of changes in the physical environment, or may follow from contact with other societies. When such changes are not due to anything which has occurred within the society itself, we may legitimately speak of them as chance occurrences. Of course, many changes in the physical environment may be brought about by the activities of members of the society, and contacts with other societies may have been initiated by the society which has been changed by such contacts. In these cases we would not say that the changes were brought about by chance, since the society itself was indirectly responsible for them. But whether change is brought about by chance or is indirectly brought about by the society itself, whatever changes actually occur will depend in part upon the already existing state of the society undergoing that change. This is simply an instance of what should be recognized as being in all cases true: the cause of a specific result never consists of some one factor only, but always involves the conditions present in the situation into which that factor has been introduced.[7] Thus, in considering whatever changes follow from changes in the physical environment, or those which follow from contacts with other societies, we must do so with reference to the previously existing state of the society which has thereby been changed.

All of this, I should suppose, is so obvious that it will now readily be granted. What is not equally obvious is whether or not there are any principles of development that are present in a society independently of what occurs outside it. Social evolutionism, of course, held that there was a necessary pattern of development within societies, and most social evolutionists even attempted to show that there was a pattern to which each type of institution conformed. For them, that pattern was evidenced in all societies, regardless of whatever other characteristics these societies may have possessed. While Spengler and Toynbee were not social evolutionists, they too regarded certain principles of development as inherent in each of the world's great civilizations. Even historians who are justly suspicious of the structures erected by Spengler, Toynbee, and other philosophers of history have sometimes written as if institutions naturally develop in one direction rather than another, so long as nothing interferes. On that assumption, it is not always necessary to find the specific causes that account for the overall changes societies undergo. Such a view, however, involves a spurious, circular form of explanation, since it starts with what results from a process and seeks to explain the various steps in that process as if both the steps and the result had been predetermined. This teleological mode of explanation is as spurious as explaining the institutions present in a society as due to some persisting national characteristics, whereas these institutions themselves are responsible for the characteristics through which they are purportedly being explained. As I indicated in Chapter 3, it was just such a misconception that underlay Aristotelian explanations in biology and the organic analogies used by Radcliffe-Brown. In general, those who fall into this sort of misconception tend to overstress the element of necessity in historical processes, ruling out the pervasive influences of chance and of choice.

It is not difficult to see why such a misconception arises, and why it is especially difficult to avoid when looking back upon a temporal process in terms of that to which it has led. Once the outcome of a process is given, one can follow each step that led to that outcome; as a consequence the process as a whole appears as if it could not have had any other result. This I regard as the retrospective fallacy, for it overlooks the fact that had conditions at any point been different from what they actually were, the outcome might have been extremely different, yet in that case too, the end result would have seemed to be no less inevitable than what actually occurred.[8]

## III

There is good reason why one should stress the role of chance when considering the nature of any society and the changes it undergoes. In any society each institution will to some extent have its own history. Its changes will not at all points run parallel to the changes that other institutions undergo, even though change in one institution may contribute to change in another. For example, as closely connected as the technologies and the economic systems of every society are apt to be, one cannot explain specific technological changes in terms of economic factors alone, nor explain economic institutions solely in terms of technology. In each of these fields there are bound to be autonomous developments; furthermore, in each field, other institutional or cultural changes will have an effect on what occurs. The junctures at which, and the ways in which, one field influences another are not foreordained: in many cases one must acknowledge such influences as chance occurrences.

To be sure, some would say that it is misleading to introduce the notion of chance in situations such as this, since even if these influences had not occurred when they did, the ultimate result would sooner or later have been the same. This, however, would be a mistake. Even if economic and technological factors always affect one another in some way, the other aspects of a society will not have remained in the same state as they were, nor will a technology and economic conditions always remain the same. Consequently, there will be differences between what comes about if two lines of causation meet at one time rather than another: in short, *when* an event occurs makes a difference with respect to *what* occurs. It is this which justifies regarding chance as playing an inexpungeable role in human history.

The same conclusion follows, and can be even more readily seen, when we turn our attention from what occurs within any particular society and consider what has occurred in the course of human history as a whole. Unfortunately, we have an inveterate tendency to think of the past in terms of whatever has led to the present state of the society to which we belong: we are therefore apt to view other societies only in terms of their relations to our own institutional and cultural history. Yet, when we seek to understand how these societies themselves developed, we find that their histories were in many ways independent of our own. Thus, insofar as we can free ourselves from a provincial, ethnocentric point of view, we realize that the human past does not form a single, continuing stream leading up to what *we* have become; rather, we come to see it as a highly complex reticulated network in which the history of each society will to some degree be independent of the others. Of course, there will be many points at which these otherwise independent strands intersect, with no single strand following a wholly independent course throughout its history, and when we take these cross-influences into account we must grant importance to the factor of chance in dealing with world history.[9]

Even those who view societies in holistic terms, assuming that all institutions within a given society form a completely integrated system, are unable to rule out the influence that catastrophic natural events or the spread of virulent diseases may have on particular societies, nor can they dismiss the historical importance of the invasion of a society by an alien band, even though the ways in which a particular society reacts to such events will in large measure depend upon the nature of the society itself. From the point of view of the institutional history of a society, each of these must be considered a chance event, which need not have happened when it did and which, when viewed in terms of what led to its occurrence, was actually unrelated to any of the consequences it may have had on the society it changed. To repeat, in understanding the history of any society we must take into account chance events—events which, up to that point, were unrelated to the prior nature of that which they changed and which would not have been predictable no matter how much we knew about the prior history of the society that was changed by them.

I V

What has been said about chance is also applicable to questions concerning the role of individuals in bringing about societal change. Of course, this contention would be challenged by those who regard all individuals as having been wholly determined to act as they do because of the nature of a society's institutions and because of their roles in their society's social structure. I shall comment on that contention shortly; first, however, I must attempt to show that an individual's choices, whatever may be their sources, do in fact influence historical change.

Choice, as I have argued, in large measure depends upon how a person sees the situation in which he is placed, by what he sees as his alternatives, and how he reacts to the contrast between them. His recognition of alternatives in a given situation depends upon his past experience, which is in large measure different from the experience of those in other societies, and likely to be in many respects different from the experience of others in his own society. This being so, we may expect that even if two individuals were to be placed in identical situations, they would often make quite different choices. Since the influence an individual has upon his society tends to vary according to his status and role, the functioning of a society will be affected by the character of whichever individuals occupy dominant positions within that society. In some societies the status and role of a person are due to his lineage; in others, a similar status is ascribed to persons because of some powers they are assumed to possess; in some cases, too, there may be a selective electoral process which determines who shall occupy a particular position. In each case, however, it will to some extent have been a matter of chance, rather than a matter solely of character, that a person has come to occupy a particular status and play a particular role in the society to which he belongs. In this way, too, chance must be admitted to be an ineluctable element in any society's history.

While one must take chance into account in understanding who has come to occupy various positions in a society, chance alone does not determine what a person will be able to achieve: there will be boundaries within which he must operate, regardless of his role. Those boundaries are set by the organization of his particular society and by the actions which its members will tolerate, or—if they are discontented—by the forces they can muster to resist what he undertakes to do. Here, once again, we come upon the distinction between freedom of choice and freedom of action: a leader or a ruling elite may choose to follow one course of action but may be unable to carry out that choice. The possibility of doing so is sometimes limited by the attitudes of others in the society, and it will also be limited by the ways in which various institutions can function—that is, by what I have termed "objective possibilities." While it is always in part a matter of chance that one rather than another institutional form has developed in a particular society, the compatibility or incompatibility of that form with other institutions cannot be attributed to chance. The institutions present in a society have an effect on each other, and changes within one will to some degree affect how some other institutions change. Consequently we must view the history of any society in terms of both necessity and chance, neither concept being dispensable for historians who wish to explain how societies change.

V

Thus far, what has been said concerning the role of individuals in historical change has been confined to stressing the fact that an individual's influence will vary according to the place he occupies in the structure of his society. What has been neglected has been any attempt to assess the influence that the personal capacities of individuals may have in forming and changing the life of a society. From the point of view of individualistic theories this would be regarded as a fatal mistake, since such theories regard the aims and capacities of individuals as the basis upon which our understanding of social structures must rest. When such a contention is narrowly interpreted—so that it merely means that all societies presuppose that human beings possess certain traits—I regard it as obviously true, but when taken as providing the basis for understanding the nature and changes in specific societies, I regard it as entirely false.

What I of course grant is that human social life presupposes that men have certain traits in common: for example, that they are not asocial beings, that they can and do communicate with one another, and that there are many other traits which they possess in common. Precisely how far this commonality in human nature extends is not easily ascertained, but that is not a question with which I need here be concerned. What is important to recall is that in any society different individuals are called upon to perform different tasks, and traits that are important for performing one sort of task may not be important, or will be less important or even a hindrance, to those individuals who have different tasks to perform. Of course, no matter how rigid a social structure may be, every individual will have more than one role to play in the society; nevertheless, a person's particular place in, say, the economic system will impose demands upon him which those occupying different places will not face, even though when they are considered as citizens, their roles may be the same. Consequently, if one attempts to assess the ways in which possession of certain traits affects the nature of and the changes in a society, one must do so in terms of the importance of such traits with respect to the functions that different individuals perform: one cannot offer sweeping generalizations as to the characteristics which all individuals must possess in order for there to be efficiency or harmony or adaptability in a community.

In the earlier part of this century social theorists as different as Bosanquet and Hobhouse tended to share the view that the common purposes of individuals and their fellow-feelings and rationality were sufficient to explain the gradual development and coherence of organized social life. Later, however, the importance of differences in the character of different cultures came to be stressed, and while some anthropologists, such as Franz Boas, held that in spite of these differences, human nature was relatively constant, others held that human nature was molded by culture, with individuals reared in different societies coming to be totally different, depending upon what values dominated particular societies.

In such discussions, the term *values* was generally taken as referring to a monolithic system of feelings and beliefs that underlay the way of life of a given society. That use, however, involved a great oversimplification of the nature of societies. In the first place, and most importantly, the structure of any society is complex and can be understood only in terms of the specific nature of its various institutions. In the second place, it cannot rightly be supposed that there is some one system of feelings and beliefs that is universally shared within a society and that distinguishes it from all others. To be sure, some beliefs will be more widespread and more deeply held by the various members of one society than by the members of other societies, but this is also true *within* societies: some beliefs are more widespread and deeply held by some classes of individuals than by others. Furthermore, within any class of individuals (no matter how that class is defined) various individuals will differ with respect to whatever beliefs they share. In short, no society should be treated as if it constituted a homogeneous entity, dominated by any single system of distinctive values.

This should be obvious from the role which experience plays in our individual lives. To be sure, what we experience and what we absorb in the course of that experience does not depend upon experience alone: it also depends upon what we have inherited and upon our earlier experiences. Consequently, one must expect that different individuals will react differently to what they experience, but this variability should not be overstressed. Not only do all persons have some traits in common, but one must look below the surface of behavior to be certain that what appears to be great variability does not conceal an underlying common trait, since exactly the same basic trait may find expression in different (and seemingly incompatible) ways of behaving. For example, what elevates a person's self-esteem in one society or under one set of circumstances may lead to feelings of inferiority in other societies or under differing circumstances. Even the ways in which some physiological needs obtain satisfaction varies from society to society, and varies even among individuals belonging to the same society. It is for this reason that it is difficult to say precisely what motives, if any, are fundamental in human nature and are shared by all.

The attempt to identify such motives has sometimes taken the form of finding some one underlying psychological force capable of manifesting itself in a variety of ways, and this is what theories of psychological hedonism or of self-realizationism have attempted to do.[10] Another equally common approach to the problem has been to start from a small list of physiologically based needs and then show how, under differing circumstances, these organic needs give rise to complex forms of behavior in which the original motivation is no longer directly recognizable.[11] A third type of motivational theory has resemblances to each of the others. Like the first, it aims to establish a single principle underlying all human motivation, but like the second it is also physiologically oriented, seeking to connect the basis of human behavior to characteristic aspects of animal behavior.[12] Without entering into controversial detail, I shall indicate why each of these types of theory is flawed.

As theories of motivation, both hedonism and self-realizationism are to be criticized on the ground that "pleasure" and "self-realization" are concepts lacking in explanatory power. This has frequently been pointed out with respect to self-realization. If whatever is done springs from an underlying drive toward self-realization, then self-realization must explain self-abasement as well as actions that arise from ambition or greed or a desire to help others. To class all such actions together, claiming that each expresses the same underlying tendency toward self-realization, is not to explain them. An explanation of any specific action presupposes an understanding of the individual's character and of the particular situation in which, at a given time, he was placed: nothing is added to such an explanation if one then says that each of his actions contributed to his self-realization. Therefore, no matter how enticing the concept of self-realization may be when interpreted as the ideal end of all human action, it fails as a psychological theory that throws light on why, under particular circumstances, given individuals act as they do.

Unlike the theory of self-realization, the theory that we always act to gain pleasure and avoid unpleasantness or pain does serve to explain many of our actions. On the other hand, it fails as a comprehensive theory of motivation, since many actions spring from other sources. This has often been pointed out with respect to those cases in which pleasure arises due to the satisfaction of a preexisting desire: for example, when we are hungry we do not eat for the pleasure of eating but we eat because we are hungry. Under these circumstances, pleasure is to be considered a by-product of our action rather than the goal. The same situation obtains with respect to any desire and extends beyond those desires which are clearly biologically based; the pleasure that comes from winning a game, or from helping a friend, is a by-product of success rather than being the reason the action was undertaken. As Sidgwick pointed out in discussing what he termed the "hedonistic paradox," in many cases we derive pleasure from an action only insofar as it was not for the sake of pleasure that the action was undertaken.[13] In the face of such facts it may seem strange that a desire for pleasure and the avoidance of pain have so often been supposed to be the goal of all human actions. In part at least, this question is answered when one realizes that "pleasure," like "color," is a general term applied in a wide range of greatly varying instances, whose common characteristic cannot be indicated in any way except by saying that they have the property of being pleasurable, or of being colored. In the terminology made familiar by W. E. Johnson's *Logic*, "pleasure," like "color," is a *determinable*, not a *determinate*.[14] However, the fact that all of these experiences are pleasurable need not explain why we seek them, any more than the fact that most solid objects are colored explains why we see them.

One reason hedonism may have been regarded as a tenable psychological theory is that most of our experiences (and perhaps all) have some degree of hedonic tone, either positive or negative; further, there can be no doubt that we prefer pleasant to unpleasant experiences. Therefore, *if* one were to insist that there must be some factor which is in all cases capable of accounting for human action, it would

not be implausible to locate it in the degree of pleasantness or unpleasantness attaching to the alternatives in the situations we face.
This, I believe, is what led Locke to his form of psychological hedonism (see Chapter 5, above) and led Mill to recast Bentham's psychological hedonism in the way that he did.[15] Yet, why should we
assume that there is some one factor which is adequate to explain
why we seek those objects or experiences that we do? Given their
variety, why not explain each in terms of whatever conditions obtain
with respect to the natures of different individuals and the nature of
the situations in which they are placed?

In response to such a suggestion it might be held that even were
we to give up the view that there is some single explanatory factor for
all our actions, there are at least a few distinct drives which human
beings must possess if they are to survive. When we recognize our
kinship with other forms of animal life, the importance of satisfying
these needs will loom large in our explanations of human behavior.
To be sure, human beings appear to have many needs other than
survival, and such needs become evident when we consider our lives
as members of a society; however, as Darwin pointed out, some of the
same needs seem to be present among animals and give rise to various forms of social animal behavior.[16] Although this parallelism is
suggestive, it should not be taken as establishing that the needs of
human beings are precisely the same as those of the higher animals.
It would be entirely consonant with Darwin's discussion and with
what is now taken to be established by evolutionary theory in biology
for there to be needs which are present in man but not in other animal
species, or present in some animal species but not in man. Furthermore, in Darwin's own discussion of some of these parallels, it is
clear that although there are resemblances between various aspects
of human behavior and the behavior of some animal species, these
resemblances are not so close as to preclude many important differences, both with respect to their strengths and their specific man-
ifestations. Therefore, however suggestive it may be to look for the
roots of human behavior in animal behavior, it is a mistake to assume
that an adequate account of human motivation will become available
through investigating the behavior of any other species. Yet, as was
evident in McDougall's *Social Psychology*, this is precisely what
some instinctivist theories formerly attempted to do.

To be sure, it is tempting to try to relate human motivation to
some theory of basic physiological needs, since unless these needs
are satisfied individuals cannot survive. Yet, this does not force one
to assume that other human needs must have developed out of these

more basic needs: there is no reason to suppose that the whole range of human motivation is to be understood as deriving from some set of physiological needs. Of course, even when this is recognized, it remains possible to try to explain human motivation in physiological terms. Instead of attempting to identify some particular set of basic needs or drives, one could attempt to formulate a general theory of the factors underlying all needs or drives, as earlier behaviorists and B. F. Skinner have done. Such a theory would in principle be similar to the associationism of Helvétius, who linked associationism with a psychological hedonism in order to explain why, under varying circumstances, human beings behave as they do. Today this type of theory, unlike its eighteenth-century analogues, is most often formulated in a strictly physiological manner, relying upon the concept of conditioning, or (in a few cases) on principles of homeostasis or tension reduction. The difficulty with formulations in terms of homeostasis or tension reduction is similar to that which we found in the case of self-realizationism, for when these concepts are extended beyond their application to specific organic processes and are used to explain all forms of human action, they lose explanatory power, since they fail to show how disparate forms of action all exemplify one and the same motivational force. This, however, would not be true of the uses to which the concept of conditioning has been put. Its difficulty lies elsewhere: it presupposes the existence of other motivational forces which are not themselves conditioned; so that in and of itself conditioning is insufficient to account for the behavior which it purports to explain.

That this is true becomes readily apparent when we recall the original Pavlovian experiments out of which more recent conditioning theories arose. After repeated trials in which the presentation of food was accompanied by the sound of a bell, Pavlov was able to condition dogs to salivate at the sound of the bell in the absence of food. Yet, this conditioning could not have taken place had it not been for some unconditioned connection between food and salivation; absent that connection, the conditioned response could not have been induced.[17] Even in Skinnerian experiments, in which apparently random links connect the stimulus and the response, and then become reinforced and persist, there must be a natural bond, such as the satisfaction of a particular need, which is not itself the result of prior conditioning; if there were not such a need, what would be "reinforced"? It then becomes a question as to what these natural, unconditioned needs may be. Skinner was entirely correct in refusing to identify them with any set of overt bodily needs, as instinctivist theories had tended to do, but the experimental situations on which his theory was based were far too restrictive to prove that the range of such needs was as limited as his behaviorism demanded they be. To extrapolate from what is true of, say, caged pigeons to how pigeons and other birds behave in their natural environments, in which they are constantly exposed to innumerable stimuli and in which they have freedom of movement, is to make a hazardous leap. To proceed further and apply the results obtained when dealing with caged pigeons in an attempt to explain adult human behavior is, I should think, to defy all theoretical self-restraint. Yet this is what Skinnerian theory, and even Skinner himself, has been inclined to do.

Let us admit, with Skinner, that we should not try to pry into the "black box" of the organism in order to develop a theory of human motivation. In that case, however, we must start from the behavior that actually characterizes human action and seek to determine under what circumstances it occurs. In doing so, we need not assume that all human motivation springs from some one source, nor even that it is all derived from just a few basic needs, as the instinctivists claimed. In fact, even those aspects of human behavior which arise out of the most basic biological needs, such as hunger or sex, cannot be understood simply in terms of the satisfaction of those needs: the ways in which they are satisfied are intelligible only if we also take into account other needs which have no obvious biological source. For example, as Hutcheson long ago pointed out, the satisfaction of hunger is not in any way sufficient to explain the pleasure we get in dining with friends; similarly, few of our actions can be understood without taking into account what has often been termed a need for self-esteem, with which our desire for the approbation of our fellows is intimately connected. Thus, human nature must be acknowledged to be extremely complex, and human needs are not to be restricted to those few needs for which we can find direct physiological correlates.

Whatever may be the case in psychology, this contention is not likely to be disputed by those social psychologists and anthropologists who use the concept of "social conditioning" to explain human behavior. Although this concept had little to do with the Pavlovian theory of conditioning, it found ready acceptance and became widespread in popular thought because it suggested that there was at last a hard scientific way of explaining the almost indefinite variability that characterizes the behavior of different individuals and serves to explain the norms for behavior in different cultural milieus. As a consequence, a certain form of cultural relativism developed: not only was it held that each society must be understood in terms of its own systems of belief, but it was also claimed that the values embedded in these systems were not commensurable. These, however, are quite different theses, and the second need not follow from the first. Given different situations and different beliefs about the world, it is to be expected that differing systems of value will develop. Yet, these differing systems might be expressions of the same underlying needs, so that a relativistic conclusion would not necessarily follow from the very striking differences that are in fact to be found when one compares one culture with another.

To be sure, some have held that it is not because of differences in beliefs that one finds differing sets of values in different societies, but that differences in belief are themselves reflections of differences in valuations. For example, Nietzsche was not alone in claiming that valuation is primary, and that judgments of fact in all cases conform to more basic motivational forces. In fact, this thesis has become one of the hallmarks of much recent philosophical-psychological speculation, even though the experimental evidence used to support it provides a very shaky foundation for such a radical revision of traditional theories regarding the relations of fact and value.[18] What separates most recent discussions of the primacy of value from the earlier formulations of, say Schopenhauer, Kierkegaard, Mach, and Nietzsche is the emphasis placed on how the individual's values are formed by the system of cultural values in which his life has, from the first, been embedded. Yet, in the end, no social theory will be adequate if it approaches the individual solely in terms of the culture to which he or she belongs: it must also take account of whatever characteristics are fundamental in human nature.

On the other hand, any universal human needs, being very general, can be satisfied in many different ways: consequently, they will not suffice to explain why some specific set of values has come to permeate a particular society. This can be explained only in terms of the history of that society, and its history will have been channeled by necessity and by chance, as well as by the choices of individuals who, at specific times, learned what they did learn and made the choices they actually made. Thus, in the end, one cannot escape combining necessity with chance and choice in explaining what have been termed the values of any society.

## VI

To give point to what has been argued in this chapter, let us start from the fact—or what I take to be the fact—that it is impossible for us to undo the past. This is not simply a metaphysical thesis (though it is that too), but has direct application to the life of any individual, and also to what in any situation it is possible for the state to do.

When, for example, we examine how we ourselves have acted in a given situation, or when we consider the actions of others, we see that what has been done will have changed the situation which we or they originally faced. Given that change, any subsequent action will represent a response to a new situation which will not in all respects be the same. At a minimum, it will have been changed because we or others will be able to recall what had been done before, and we may feel shame or pride, and others may rejoice at or may regret what had originally been done. Even more obviously, the situation which is then to be faced will either offer new opportunities or will close off opportunities which had formerly been present, or both. This transformation will occur whether we may be said to have been able to choose what we wished to do, or whether our action had been forced upon us by circumstances: in either case, the situation which originally obtained will no longer be wholly the same. To be sure, if we regret what we had done, we may attempt to rectify it, but that will simply lead to another new situation, rather than allowing us to return to what the past had actually been. Similarly, if we happen to take pride in having done what we did, we ourselves will have been changed by recalling with pride that which we had done. In these cases, too, the attitudes of others toward us will in all probability have been changed.

Although such transformations are important in the ordinary affairs of our individual lives, usually they make little difference to the world at large. This, however, is not the case when an individual happens to occupy some key position in a society, for then some of his actions will have wider repercussions than will those of most individuals. It is at this point that individual actions sometimes deeply affect the fate of societies: once an opportunity is lost, it will never be wholly regained. For example, in the relations among nations, former injuries will not be readily forgotten or forgiven, no matter how a nation may attempt to make restitution for its deeds. Even the help which one nation can provide another may have unintended consequences which lead to ill will. All such reactions can be more or less adequately explained once they have occurred, but they cannot always be clearly foreseen: to some extent nations, like individuals, must act without knowing precisely what consequences their actions will bring.

It is at this point that one can see that there is a third type of necessity with which we have not yet dealt. I have indicated that any society must be so organized as to fulfill basic human needs; I have also noted that every society must possess certain types of institutional structures in order to survive. Neither of these types of necessity involved the temporal dimension of social life, whereas the third type, which I have now recognized, does so; it supplements the other two in providing an essential factor in explaining historical change.

Historical change is never merely repetitive. For example, adjustments that take place in order that a society may better satisfy one or another human need will create a situation which could threaten the stability of the society if those adjustments are not offset by changes in some other institutions that had been affected by them. Yet, once such adjustments have occurred, a new situation will have emerged, and any future actions will have to take account of that situation if they are to succeed. Thus, insofar as individuals are in a position to bring about some change in social organization, the choices they make will have many unforeseen consequences. Since such consequences are never completely reversible, any decisions to bring about change may be fateful. Yet—as William James insisted—it may be equally fateful not to act at all. This is the dilemma persons occupying positions of great authority must face: the choices they make will have an important bearing on the future of their society as well as on the future of any other societies with which their own history is linked.

Yet, as we noted, when we consider how a particular person has come to occupy a position of power in his society, we see that it was in large measure a matter of chance. This is true whether he came by that position through his lineage, or whether it was ascribed to him because of the capacities or powers he was believed to possess. In either case, how he acts once he has achieved his position, and what decisions he makes, will be influenced by his temperament and experience, neither of which will have been solely responsible for his having come to occupy the position he holds. When one person rather than another is elected to office, or one son rather than another succeeds to a throne, he is in a position to exert a profound influence on the history of his nation and on its place in the world; yet in either case it will have been partly through chance that it was he, rather than another, who occupied that position at that particular time.

This is not to say that any single person, however great his authority, is in a position to change a society in whatever ways he may choose. Not only must others be willing and able to act as he would wish them to act, but the objective possibilities inherent in the societal situation must permit him to do what he wishes to do. This is not always the case: not every change—even if all thought it desirable—could be grafted onto whatever social structures are already in place. In short, both the needs of individuals and the conditions actually obtaining within a society will set limits on the ways in which even the most powerful members of a society can be effective in bringing about change.

Nevertheless, revolutionary figures rallying groups of like-minded individuals around a common purpose have often started movements which have radically altered what had previously been taken to be unalterable states of affairs. Even in the absence of such leadership, groups of ordinary individuals with a common concern have sometimes successfully founded voluntary associations which have gradually become rooted in the social structure, and have become so well established in one place that they have been widely replicated and later taken for granted as permanent factors in the social life of succeeding generations. Such possibilities have lent plausibility to attempts to explicate the existence of social structures in terms of the confluence of what individuals will. What these explanations overlook, however, is that such associations can survive only insofar as they fill an empty niche in the previously existing societal structure. Furthermore, the success of revolutionary figures in organizing movements for radical social change presupposes serious strains within the institutional system they are seeking to alter; in the absence of such strains, they would not attract followers to their cause. Thus, purposive change always takes place within the context of a system of institutions which are not themselves the direct outgrowth of choice and will.

It is probably not necessary that those seeking to institute social change should at the outset have a clear vision of what their goals are to be: they may simply be aware of an unmet need, or of a situation so oppressive that it must be changed. In the course of their action, however, they must proceed pragmatically, taking into account the nature of already existing institutions, and adapt their tactics to that which they are in a position to change. This will involve both an understanding of the unfulfilled needs and the temper of the people as well as an understanding of the ways in which their society's institutions are structured. Contrary to what has often been claimed, past history is not the best source of such knowledge. What is needed is an analysis of the actually present situation. Only if one were to accept an individualistic theory of social institutions, and then also accept—as did Hume—that human nature remains constant, could one look to the past in order to understand how the present can be changed.[19] If one rejects either of these postulates, it is not to past history but to an analysis of the contemporary scene that one must look for guidance as to the ways in which one can presently bring about change.

Given such knowledge, even granting that the slate of the past can never be wiped clean, choice can be effective in bringing about some forms of societal change. The importance of that knowledge is readily seen once one recognizes that choice involves a decision between open alternatives. To be sure, how well one succeeds in what one then attempts to do is not merely a function of having made an intelligent choice; in the field of societal change it also depends upon whatever traits of character one must possess in order to attract followers and on one's perseverance in implementing what one has set oneself to do. Unfortunately, there is no point at which chance may not intervene, transforming the situation that was originally faced, closing off possibilities that once were open. While the intrusion of such unforeseen events will often wipe out all hope of realizing a well-conceived plan, it need not always do so: one may find alternative paths toward the same end. History, however, does not suggest that this is always the case; catastrophes have not always been avoided. That is one lesson history seems to have taught, though it is not through past history that we can learn how to solve present dilemmas.

# Notes

## 1. The Analysis of Social Theories

1. Maurice Mandelbaum, "Societal Laws," in *Philosophy, History, and the Sciences* (Baltimore: Johns Hopkins University Press, 1984), pp. 184–94.

2. Because the presuppositions of individualism were first formulated on the model of analytic mechanics and the initial institutional alternative was based on a wholesale revolt against that model, there has arisen the unfortunate assumption that if one rejects "methodological individualism," one is committed to accepting "holism" as its only alternative.

3. Especially in Maurice Mandelbaum, "Societal Facts," republished in *Philosophy, History, and the Sciences,* pp. 171–83.

4. Hume, *Inquiry Concerning Human Understanding,* sec. 8, pt. 1 (Selby-Bigge ed., p. 83).

5. From Rousseau's "Letter to M. d'Alembert on the Theater," translated by Allen Bloom in *Politics and the Arts* (Glencoe: Free Press, 1960), p. 17.

6. Unfortunately, the wholesale attacks on holism and historicism which one finds in Popper's *Poverty of Historicism* and in Berlin's *Historical Inevitability* do not make it sufficiently clear how widely disparate the views of Hegel, Comte, and Marx actually are.

7. See "Darwin's Religious Views" in my *Philosophy, History, and the Sciences,* pp. 307–21. For other points regarding Darwin's views, see the entries under "Darwin, —on man" in my book *History, Man, and Reason* (Baltimore: Johns Hopkins University Press, 1971).

8. An extreme example of this argument is to be found in Floyd Allport's *Institutional Behavior* (Chapel Hill: University of North Carolina Press, 1933), pp. 3–4 and 13.

9. See Melville Herskovits, *Man and His Works* (New York: Knopf, 1948), ch. 2.

10. Ibid., p. 21.

11. Ibid., p. 28.

12. Ibid.

13. To be sure, a language can be studied by linguists as if it were a self-subsisting entity, but that—as Herskovits would contend—is simply a heuristic device.

14. In a brief note entitled "The Concept of Culture and of Social System" (*American Sociological Review* 23 [1958]; 582–83), A. L. Kroeber and Talcott Parsons criticized using these terms as interchangeable and attempted to characterize the difference between their referents. The distinction they drew is in several respects similar to that which I shall draw, but is not identical with it.

15. These paraphrases and quotations come from Herskovits, *Man and His Works*, pp. 289–90.

16. Ibid., p. 21.

17. Ibid., p. 55. At another point (p. 25) Herskovits states his view as one which does not assign objective reality to culture, but views it as having "psychological reality," for it "can have no manifestation except in human thought and action," and it exists as an entity "only in the mind of the student."

18. I have elsewhere remarked on the origins of this concept and its connection with the founding of the Center for Advanced Study in the Behavioral Sciences (see *Philosophy, History, and the Sciences*, p. 209, n. 4). For the fullest account of the introduction of the term and for its adoption in recent literature, see the article "Behavioral Science" by Bernard Berelson in the *International Encyclopedia of the Social Sciences*.

19. For a brief exposition of this as the goal of his theoretical system, see Parsons' *The Social System* (Glencoe: Free Press, 1951), esp. ch. 1.

20. There are, of course, striking differences in what is "seen" or "heard" (i.e., *noticed*) by individuals whose experiences have been formed in different cultural and social environments, but there is no clear evidence that their visual and auditory processes are for that reason inherently different. The same may be said about other sensory processes, as well as about learning processes, the effects of habituation, etc.

21. A parallel situation may be said to exist in the natural sciences, with physics, geology, and biology all being concerned with different aspects of the physical world. To be sure, there is a tendency to think that the natural sciences are not really autonomous sciences but part of a single hierarchical system for which physics and chemistry provide the basis. Though some arguments in favor of such a view are relatively strong, the same cannot be said with respect to establishing a hierarchical order among the social sciences. Earlier attempts to regard psychology as the basis upon which politics and economics and the other "moral sciences" rested were based on the unhistorical, analytic method, which, as I have tried to show, was untenable. Marxism may be interpreted as providing a more recent alternative by which the discreteness of the various social sciences has been challenged, but

whether Marxist theory has been able to assimilate all fairly well established generalizations of the social sciences into a single system is surely open to doubt.

22. This difference between the historical treatment of the cultural and the institutional components of societies parallels the distinction between "general" and "special" histories which I drew in my *Anatomy of Historical Knowledge* (Baltimore: Johns Hopkins University Press, 1977), pp. 11–13.

## 2. Individualistic Theories of Purpose & Necessity

1. In his early *Outlines of a Critical Theory of Ethics*, Dewey held that "institutions are organized modes of action, on the basis of the wants and interests which unite men. They differ as the family from the town, the church from the state, according to the scope and character of the wants from which they spring. . . . The moral endeavor of man thus takes the form not of isolated fancies about right and wrong, not of attempts to frame a morality for himself, nor of efforts to bring into being some praiseworthy ideal never realized; but the form of sustaining and furthering the moral world of which he is a member. Since the world is one of action, and not of contemplation like the world of knowledge, it can be sustained and furthered only as he makes its ends his own, and identifies himself and his satisfaction with the activities in which other wills find their fulfillment" (*Early Works of John Dewey, 1882–1898*, ed. Jo Ann Boydston, 4 vols. [Carbondale: Southern Illinois University Press, 1967–72], 3:347).

2. For the view of Bosanquet, see especially *The Philosophical Theory of the State* (London: Macmillan, 1899), chs. 7 and 11; for those of Hocking, see *Man and the State* (New Haven: Yale University Press, 1926), especially chs. 11 and 24.

In his earlier work, Robert M. MacIver also accounted for social institutions in terms of the purposes of individuals. In this connection, see *Community: A Sociological Study* (London: Macmillan, 1917), bk. 1, ch. 1, and bk. 2, ch. 2. He, too, viewed conflicts as superficial in contrast to the underlying commonality of interests within the social order. As he said, "The deepest antagonisms between interests are not so deep as the foundations of community. Every opposition on analysis turns out to be partial, not absolute. What is true of the whole universe, that differences prove to be but differences within unity, is true of our social world" (p. 114).

3. Grotius explicitly grounded the law of nature in the "dictates of right reason," not in God's will. As he said, "The law of nature is a dictate of right reason, which points out that an act, according as it is or is not in conformity with rational nature, has in it a quality of moral baseness or moral necessity; and that, *in consequence* [emphasis added], such an act is either forbidden or enjoined by the author of nature, God" (*De jure belli ac pacis*, bk. 1, ch. 1, sec. 9, no. 1 [Kelsey trans., The Classics of International Law, no. 3]).

4. Ibid., Prolegomena, sec. 39.

5. Pufendorf, *De jure naturae et gentium*, bk. 1, ch. 2, sec. 2 (Oldwater trans., The Classics of International Law, no. 17).

6. Spinoza, *Tractatus politicus*, ch. 1, sec. 4 (Wernham trans.).

7. Nevertheless, as Mugnier-Pollet has pointed out, it is striking that given the importance of commerce for Holland, Spinoza had nothing to say concerning the role of economic institutions in the life of the state. See Lucien Mugnier-Pollet, *La philosophie politique de Spinoza* (Paris: Vrin, 1976), pp. 62, 70, 79–80.

8. Spinoza held that only three forms of state were possible: monarchy, aristocracy, and democracy; see *Tractatus politicus,* ch. 1, sec. 3, as well as the author's Prefatory letter. Chapters 6–11 discuss the three forms, though the treatment of democracy is fragmentary owing to the unfinished character of the work.

9. Both Leibniz and Wolff also depended upon the method of rational deduction, but they differed from Hobbes and Spinoza in at least two important respects. First, and of major significance, their theories were grounded in a doctrine of natural rights rather than in a naturalistic, egoistic psychology. Second, the questions they addressed were more wide-ranging and more concrete because they were writing on jurisprudence rather than focusing on philosophical questions concerning the foundations of the state's authority. Thus, both Leibniz and Wolff, following Althusius, dealt with society as containing a whole hierarchy of forms of organization, rather than being confined to the sovereign state. On this aspect of Leibniz's thought, see Otto Gierke, *Natural Law and the Theory of Society,* trans. Barker (Cambridge: Cambridge University Press, 1934), 1:164 and 175, as well as 2:368, n. 6. Also, cf. Leibniz's fragment "On Natural Law" in Loemker, *Philosophical Papers and Letters* (Chicago: University of Chicago Press, 1956), 2:702–6.

10. Cf. *Second Treatise,* chs. 5, 6, and secs. 77–86 of ch. 7. Locke's treatment of the family was cursory and uninfluential. In these respects it differed from his discussion of property, which laid a basis for the labor theory of economic value. His interest in more specific economic questions is evident in his lengthy discussions of interest and money, which were connected with his membership on the Board of Trade from its very inception. These discussions are to be found in the nine-volume edition of his *Works* (1924), 4:3–205.

11. On the other hand, as we shall later see, Locke's influence on the social thought of those who followed the method of Helvétius was profound. That influence, however, was due not to his political writings but to the empiricist side of his theory of knowledge, and to the consequences of that theory for his doctrine of education.

12. The original reads: "Les Loix, dans la signification la plus étendue, sont les rapports nécessaires qui dérivent de la nature des choses, dans ce sens tous les Etres ont leurs Loix."

13. Montesquieu, *Considérations* 18, in *Oeuvres complètes,* ed. Roger Callois (Paris: Gallimard, 1949–58), 2:69–209. In the next generation, John Millar formulated a similar position in a different context. His views on necessity were summarized by one of his critics, Francis Jeffrey, who said, "It was the leading principle . . . of all his speculations on law, morality, government, language, the arts, sciences and manners—that there is nothing produced by arbitrary or accidental causes; . . . everything, on the contrary, he held arose spontaneously from the situation of the society, and was suggested or imposed irresistably by the opportunities or necessities of their condi-

tion." (Quoted in W. C. Lehmann, *John Millar of Glasgow* [Cambridge: Cambridge University Press, 1960], p. 122.)

14. In support of the claim that these interconnected factors were to some degree independent of one another I might cite book 19, chapters 21–27, of the *Spirit of the Laws*, in which he argues that in order to be effective the laws of a nation should be in conformity with its customs, but he is then at pains to point out that customs may also be affected by the laws. Thus, though connected, the various factors in a people's life are to some degree independent of one another: they are not mere reflections of a single, underlying "spirit of the people."

15. Cf. book 19, chapter 4, where, for example, he holds that nature and the climate almost completely dominate the life of savages, whereas codes of manners were dominant among the Chinese, and maxims of government and traditional customs were of prime importance in Rome.

16. One useful analysis of the psychological theories of the period is to be found in A. O. Lovejoy's *Reflections on Human Nature* (Baltimore: Johns Hopkins Press, 1961). His own account of the role of pleasure and pain in motivation (like the views of many eighteenth-century thinkers) is discussed primarily in relation to how these feelings attach to other ideas, rather than in terms of how they attach to bodily processes.

17. A corrective is to be found in Albert O. Hirschman's *The Passions and the Interests* (Princeton: Princeton University Press, 1977), in which it is shown that in the economic thought of the period, the passions and self-interest were viewed as antagonistic forces. Self-interest was seen as resting on a calculation of means-ends relationships, and one which more often than not served to check the passions.

18. Cf. Hume's essay, "The Independency of Parliament," in *Essays: Moral, Political, and Literary* (London: Henry Froude, 1904), 1:40–47.

19. For a discussion of Newton's use of the term *hypotheses* and of his four "Rules of Reasoning," see my *Philosophy, Science, and Sense Perception: Historical and Critical Studies* (Baltimore: Johns Hopkins Press, 1964), pp. 66–88.

20. Hume, *Enquiry Concerning Human Understanding*, sec. 8, pt. I (Selby-Bigge ed., pp. 83–84). Cf. Hume's *Treatise*, bk. 2, pt. 3, sec. 1 (Selby-Bigge ed., pp. 402–3).

21. Hume, *Treatise of Human Nature*, bk. 1, pt. 1, sec. 4 (Selby-Bigge ed., pp. 12–13). Hume, however, did not carry this comparison as far as did Hartley and Priestley, who regarded it as relatively exact. For example, in the concluding chapter of volume 1 of his *Observations on Man*, in which Hartley is discussing freedom and determinism, he says, "By the mechanism of human actions I mean, that each action results from the previous circumstances of body and mind, in the same manner, and with the same certainty, as other effects do from their mechanical causes" (5th ed. [London: R. Cuttwell, 1810], pp. 514–15). He even held that the vigor of an action corresponds to the intensity of its motive, so that "if a master be actuated simply by anger, he will beat his servant more violently and continue the correction longer, in proportion to the degree of his anger," and that "opposite motives, as causes of love and hatred, are known to balance one another, exactly like weights in

opposite scales. According to all appearance, nothing can act more invariably, or mechanically" (ibid. pp. 30–31).

Priestley, too, used analogies between mechanical and mental causation, especially in sections 1 and 4 of his *Doctrine of Philosophical Necessity* (London, 1777).

The difference between Hume's position and the closeness of the parallel that Hartley and Priestley drew between the laws of association and the law of gravitation was connected with the fact that, unlike Hume, they attempted to correlate the association of ideas with underlying physical processes ("vibrations") in the brain.

22. Both the quoted phrase and the discussion of this point are to be found in query 31 of the *Opticks*. The passage on the immutability of the atoms is worth quoting: "All things being considered, it seems probable to me, that God in the Beginning formed Matter in solid, massy, hard, impenetrable movable particles, of such Sizes and Figures, and with such Properties, and in such Proportions to Space, as most conduced to the End for which he formed them; and that these primitive Particles being Solids, are incomparably harder than any porous bodies compounded of them; even so hard, as never to wear or break in pieces; no ordinary Power being able to divide what God himself made one in the first Creation."

23. For a more extended treatment of this aspect of the history of associationism, see my discussion in *History, Man, and Reason*, pp. 151–62.

24. These verses are probably most accessible in Lovejoy, *Reflections on Human Nature*, pp. 45–46.

25. Cf. Helvétius, *De l'esprit*, discourse 3, ch. 30 (*Oeuvres*, 5:69–70).

26. Maurice Mandelbaum, "Some Instances of the Self-Excepting Fallacy," in *Philosophy, History, and the Sciences*, pp. 60–63.

## 3. Necessity & Purpose in Institutional Theories

1. For discussion and documentation of this point, see two paragraphs in my book, *History, Man, and Reason*, pp. 68–69.

In that passage I also indicate that it is a mistake to hold (as is often held) that Comte's doctrine of three stages is based on, and reflects, the natural stages of development of the individual's mind. Rather, as I said, "he claimed that the dynamic tendency of history derives from general conditions which are necessary if men are to fulfill each of their three basic faculties: thought, action, and feeling."

2. For a careful analysis of these factors with which, on the whole, I agree, see G. A. Cohen, *Karl Marx's Theory of History: A Defense* (Princeton: Princeton University Press, 1978), ch. 2.

3. In its emphasis on the organic unity of each type of society, Marx's social theory resembled those of Hegel and of Comte, even though the factors which each took to be basic in this unity were different. Also, although Marx was more concerned with analyzing specific historical institutions in detail than were they, he too tended to dismiss as irrelevant to the ultimate course of history whatever events fell outside the framework of his explanatory schema.

4. For Engels' view of the problem, see his well-known letters to Joseph Bloch, Franz Mehring, and H. Starkenburg, parts of which are included in Robert C. Tucker's *Marx-Engels Reader*, 2d ed. (New York: Norton, 1978), and are also included (along with parts of two letters to Conrad Schmidt) in Lewis S. Feuer, *Marx and Engels: Basic Writings on Politics and Philosophy* (Garden City: Anchor Books, 1959), pp. 395–412.

5. A similar view was espoused by Toynbee, who held that a civilization is never overthrown by outside forces, but may always be said to have committed suicide. For a succinct general statement of this view, see his *Study of History*, abridgement by D. C. Somervell (New York and London: Oxford University Press, 1947), 1:274; also cf. 1:246.

6. This is what G. A. Cohen refers to as Marx's "Development Thesis," and he quite properly gives it an essential place in Marxist theory; see *Karl Marx's Theory of History*, pp. 134–36.

7. For a further discussion of this point, from another point of view and with other illustrations of the fallacies inherent in it, see my *History, Man, and Reason*, ch. 7.

8. Ibid., pp. 134–36.

9. In fact, the view had already been adumbrated in part 4 of Spencer's *Social Statics*, which was published in 1850. For Spencer's own account of the development of his evolutionary views, see his *Autobiography*, 2 vols. (New York: Appleton, 1904), 2:6–16.

10. Reprinted in Franz Boas, *Race, Language, and Culture* (New York: Macmillan, 1940).

11. This statement is the opening sentence of chapter 5, section 228, of volume 1 of Spencer's *Principles of Sociology* (New York: Appleton, 1899–1900).

12. Spencer, *Principles of Sociology*, 1, sec. 252:528–29. For a general statement of his view of the priority of function over structure in biology, see *Principles of Biology* American ed. (London: Williams and Norgate, 1863–65), vol. 1, ch. 3, esp. secs. 55 and 61.

13. For a more extended discussion of this distinction, see my *History, Man, and Reason*, pp. 114–27.

14. For my critique of the methodological assumptions of the contrary view, see ibid., pp. 113–27. With respect to Hegel's view that there is a necessary pattern of historical development, see ibid., pp. 127–33.

15. The notion of historical inevitability in Marx and especially in Engels took this form, but this aspect of their theory has too often been overstressed. While their philosophy of history did appear to entail the acceptance of an ultimate law of directional change, controlling the sequence of stages through which all societies pass, one might also view the changes they predicted as consequences of their acceptance of two nondirectional, functional laws: first, that the superstructure of a society is functionally dependent upon its economic substructure; second, that there always is pressure to create new instruments of production in order to satisfy human needs.

In *History, Man, and Reason*, I offered this type of interpretation of Marx. On reading Cohen's *Karl Marx's Theory of History*, and also noting the preface to the German edition of the *Communist Manifesto* published in 1872 and the preface to the Russian edition of 1882, I have become even more convinced that such an interpretation is warranted: that the doctrine of historical inevitability which looms so large in many passages could well be excised from Marx's theory, leaving it stronger, though perhaps less moving as propaganda.

16. This essay was republished in *Oeuvres de Condorcet*, ed. Dominque F. J. Arigo (Paris: Firmin, Didot Frères, 1847–49), 1:539–73.

17. For Condorcet's criticisms of deductive reasoning, ibid., pp. 541–42 and 567, and for his interest in demographic data, ibid., pp. 544 and 546–47.

18. Although Comte severely criticized Condorcet with respect to his periodization of history and his failure to break with Enlightenment standards of value in judging other periods of the past, he did recognize Condorcet as having been his own progenitor in approaching the history of mankind as he did. See Comte, *System of Positive Polity*, 4 vols. (New York: Franklin, 1967, reproduced from London edition of 1875), 4:570. Also, 3:xviii–xix, and 4:27.

19. Regarding these and allied statements, cf. my *History, Man, and Reason*, pp. 171–74.

20. Henry T. Buckle, *History of Civilization in England*, 3 vols., "New Edition" (London: Longmans, Green, 1871), 1:22–23.

21. Adolphe Quetelet, *Du systéme social et les lois qui régissent* (Paris: Guillaumin, 1848), pp. 238 and 239.

22. Quetelet believed that freedom of choice was compatible with the existence of such regularities in social phenomena as the changes of crime rates in different seasons and the distribution of crime by sex and age, since the free choices of individuals will cancel each other out in the population at large, resulting in the existence of statistical uniformities. As he said, "Toutes les observations tendent également à confirmer la verité de cette proposition, que j'ai énoncée depuis longtemps, que ce qui *se rattache à l'espèce humaine considérée en masse, est de l'ordre des faits physiques;* plus le nombre des individus est grand, plus la volonté individuelle s'efface et laisse prédominer la série des faits génerauz qui dépendent des causes, d'après lesquelles existe et conserve las société" (Quetelet, *Sur l'homme*, 2 vols. [Paris: Bachelier, 1835], 2:247). Also see *Du systéme social*, pp. ix–x.

For Quetelet's acceptance of the view that one could expect a gradual change in the correlations he established, as a result of changes in the causal factors responsible for them, see *Sur l'homme*, 1:15.

23. Buckle, *History of Civilization in England*, 1:39.

24. Ibid., 1:9.

25. On the unity of the natural world, see the concluding paragraph of Taine's *Les philosophes classiques du XIXᵉ siècle en France*. In the preface to the same work, Taine acknowledged Hegel's influence on him with respect to this view of the world. He failed to note, however, that his own conception of what determines that unity was totally at odds with Hegel's views.

For another, later expression of his determinism, see the concluding section of *De l'intelligence* (*On Intelligence*, trans. T. D. Haye [New York: Holt and Williams, 1872], pp. 498–99).

26. As I have noted, when Taine later wrote *De l'intelligence*, he did

attempt to establish specifically psychological laws. In that work, however, he related them to physiology rather than social phenomena. He explicitly acknowledged the difference between these two points of view in the preface to *De l'intelligence* when he said: "The historian notes and traces the total transformations presented by a particular human molecule; and to explain these transformations, writes the psychology of the molecule or group. . . . Every perspicacious and philosophical historian labors at that of a man, an epoch, a people, or a race: the researches of linguists, mythologists, and ethnographers have no other aim; the task is invariably the description of a human mind, or of the characteristics common to a group of human minds; and what historians do with respect to the past, the great novelists and dramatists do with the present. For fifteen years I have contributed to these special and concrete psychologies; I now attempt general and abstract psychology" (*On Intelligence*, pp. ix–x).

27. With respect to the influence of Hegel and Schlegel on Taine, see Victor Giraud, *Essai sur Taine*, 7th ed. (Paris: Hachette, 1932), pp. 40–41.

28. Hippolyte Taine, *History of English Literature*, trans. Henry van Laun, The World's Great Classics (New York, 1899), p. 14.

29. With respect to my linking Quetelet with the thought of Buckle and Taine, not only did Buckle cite Quetelet's early work with approval, but in a later revised edition of that work Quetelet took note of Buckle's praise and quoted him at considerable length: see Quetelet, *Physique sociale* (Brussels: C. Muquardt, 1869), pp. 139–41.

30. For a more extended discussion of this point, see my *History, Man, and Reason*, pp. 80–83.

31. Alfred R. Radcliffe-Brown, *The Andaman Islanders* (Cambridge: Cambridge University Press, 1922), p. 324.

32. For a more detailed study of this contrast and the stages of its development, see my essay "Functionalism in Social Anthropology," in *Philosophy, History, and the Sciences*, pp. 213–40.

33. Radcliffe-Brown, *The Andaman Islanders*, p. 229. Cf. *A Natural Science of Society* (Glencoe: Free Press, 1948), p. 154.

34. Ernest Nagel, *Teleology Revisited* (New York: Columbia University Press, 1979), p. 294.

35. Naturally, it would be possible to combine both types of functional explanation, but if each is faulty, as I hope to show, there is no point in attempting to use them in tandem.

36. Emile Durkheim, *Rules of Sociological Method* (Glencoe: Free Press, 1938), pp. 90 and 95–97.

37. Ibid., p. 97.

38. This, for example, is G. A. Cohen's interpretation of it in chapters 9–10 of *Karl Marx's Theory of History*. For my criticism of him on this point, see "G. A. Cohen's Defense of Functional Explanation," in *Philosophy, History, and the Sciences*, pp. 247–50.

In an article entitled "Adaptation," Richard C. Lewontin also stressed the fact that Darwin's theory, properly interpreted, in no way justifies regarding it as an example of the functionalist mode of explanation. His article originally appeared in the *Encyclopedia Einaudi* (Milan, 1980); it has been reprinted in Elliott Sober, ed., *Conceptual Issues in Evolutionary Biology* (Cambridge: MIT Press, 1984). For the relevant discussion, see especially pp. 235–44 in Sober. For the similarity between this misleading interpretation of the concept of "adaptation" in biology and the theory of functionalism in the social sciences, see Lewontin's remark on p. 235f. of the same article.

39. Malinowski, "Culture," in *Encyclopaedia of the Social Sciences*, ed. by E.R.A. Seligman and Alvin Johnson (New York: Macmillan, 1931), 4:626a.

40. The constants which I take to be fundamental for the existence and continuity of a society will be seen to be different from those stated by Wissler in his "universal pattern" in that they are not to be identified with specific types of institutions, but with very general basic needs underlying the possibility that human beings can live in organized social groups. Although I take these needs to be essential for the cohesion and continuity of any society, my approach differs from that of Radcliffe-Brown in that it emphasizes the various aspects of social organization which contribute to that end: I would not interpret the specific nature of particular practices in terms of it. As I shall later indicate, the practices which characterize different societies have diverse and often accidental origins, and each is itself likely to perform a variety of different functions. What I take to be common to all societies are simply certain very general organizational features which every society must possess. I do not regard it as helpful to interpret the specific practices which are to be found in different societies as if each had the purpose of promoting cohesion and continuity in the group.

41. Malinowski indirectly admits this at the end of his *Scientific Theory of Culture* (Chapel Hill: University of North Carolina Press, 1979), pp. 175–76. There he acknowledges that his functional theory simply provides a chart to help guide the fieldworker in isolating and relating what he is to look for: it does not offer an explanation of the concrete nature or the interrelations of the specific features which the anthropologist actually describes.

42. This point has been made by Max Scheler in several of his writings, and it conforms to the distinction between *values* and *specific goods* which Nicolai Hartmann drew in his ethical theory.

43. In *Experiments in Living* (London: Macmillan, 1952), Alexander Macbeath used a series of anthropological studies of diverse cultures to arrive at an analogous conclusion regarding morality, but his point of view was different from that of Malinowski, since he was primarily concerned to develop a theory of morality, not to make an original contribution to anthropological theory. It differed also in that he relied on a self-realizationist interpretation of human nature rather than invoking a number of distinct needs each of which derived from physiological constants.

## 4. Determinism & Chance

1. T. H. Huxley "Science and Pseudo-Scientific Realism," reprinted in Huxley, *Science and the Christian Tradition* (New York: Appleton, 1894), p. 74.

2. John Herschel, *Preliminary Discourse* (London: Longman, Green, Brown, Longmans, 1851), paragraphs 33 and 27. In the same vein Herschel

said: "Among all the possible combinations of the fifty or sixty elements which chemistry shows to exist on the earth, it is likely, nay almost certain, that *some* have never been formed; that some elements, in some proportions, and under some circumstances, have never yet been placed in relation with one another. Yet no chemist can doubt that it is *already fixed* what they will do when the case occurs" (par. 26).

3. Later, Quetelet republished Herschel's essay, in translation, as the introduction to his *Physique sociale* (Brussels: Marquardt, 1869), which was a revised edition of *Sur l'homme* (Paris: Bachelier, 1835). Quetelet's own preface to the *Physique sociale* briefly sketched the growth of interest in probability theory following Pascal's early concern with it.

4. Herschel's introduction to Quetelet's *Physique sociale*, pp. 6–7, 50.

5. Ibid., pp. 50–54.

6. Herschel, however, attributed this conviction to the psychological effects of past experience and, unlike Mill, denied that it could be justified by any form of inductive argument. It was this that opened the way for his discussion of the concept of probability (ibid., pp. 1–4).

7. In what follows, no attempt will be made to offer an interpretation of the basic aims of Cournot, nor of the structure of his philosophic position. For an exposition of these matters, the reader should consult the essay on Cournot by D. Parodi in *Du positivisme à l'idealisme: Philosophies d' hier* (Paris: Vrin, 1930). I am here solely concerned with his position regarding the status of contingency.

8. Antoine Cournot, *Essai sur les fondaments de nos connaissances* (Paris: Hachette, 1851), sec. 31. In section 32 Cournot gave illustrations of the differences between these two types of series.

Cournot's usage conforms to what Mill held to be the meaning of chance, though Mill himself rejected that notion as representing an objective category of existence. Mill's characterization follows: "But we may say that two or more phenomena are conjoined by chance, that they coexist or succeed one another only by chance; meaning that they are in no way related through causation; that they are neither cause nor effect, nor effects of the same cause, nor effects of causes between which there subsists any law of coexistence, nor even effects of the same collocation of primeval causes" (John Stuart Mill, *System of Logic*, bk. 3, ch. 17, par. 2, in *Collected Works*, ed. John M. Robson et al. [Toronto: University of Toronto Press, 1963–], 7;526f.).

9. Cournot, *Essai*, sec. 16.

10. Ibid., sec. 32.

11. Peirce, whose thought regarding chance sometimes parallels that of Cournot, makes a similar point, saying: "That a pitched coin should sometimes turn up heads and sometimes tails calls for no particular explanation; but if it shows heads every time, we wish to know how this result has been brought about. Law is *par excellence* the thing that wants a reason" (Charles S. Peirce, *Collected Papers*, ed. Charles Hartshorne and Paul Weiss [Cambridge: Harvard University Press, 1931–58], p. 12).

12. The analogy is to be found in Boltzmann's 1886 lecture, "The Second Law of Thermodynamics," in Ludwig Boltzmann, *Theoretical Physics and Philosophical Problems*, ed. Brian McGuinness (Dordrecht and Boston: Rei-

del, 1974), p. 20. In the foreword to this volume, the physicist S. R. de Groot, speaking of two major contributions made by Boltzmann, says: "The first is his interpretation of the notion of 'entropy' as a mathematically well-defined measure for what one might call the 'disorder' or 'probability' of a collection of atoms. His ideas on this topic gradually evolved from tentative ones of a purely mechanical character to the final concept of a statistical property" (p. ix).

13. Peirce, *Collected Papers*, vol. 6, chs. 1–2. In all, there were five articles related to tychism in the series, the others being included in volume 6 as 12 chapters 5, 9, and 11. For our purposes, however, only the first two are crucial.

14. Ibid., sections 55–56.

15. See specially Peirce's "Architecture of Theories," the first of his *Monist* papers, printed as chapter 1 in *Collected Papers*, vol. 6.

16. Peirce, *Collected Papers*, 6.33. (Cf. 6.101[g].) Here, too, there is a parallel between the thought of Cournot and that of Peirce. It was Cournot's belief that whereas many phenomena originally arose through chance, once they had originated their form of action was to be explained in terms of the interaction of their parts. See chapter 5 of his *Essai*, which, in the English translation, bears the title "On the Way in Which Probability Enters into the Critique of Our Ideas of the Harmony of Results and of the Finality of Causes."

17. These were not Peirce's only criticisms of necessitarianism. Among the others was the inability of a mechanical philosophy to make room within its system for mind, and its rejection of the freedom of the will. For some expressions of his views on these points, see *Collected Papers*, 6:36, 59, and 61.

18. Mill, *System of Logic*, bk. 3, ch. 5, 2 (*Collected Works*, 7:326–27). Similarly, in book 3, chapter 4, section 1, he said, "The expression Laws of Nature, *means* nothing but the uniformities which exist among natural phenomena" (ibid., p. 318).

19. Hermann Ludwig von Helmholtz, *Ueber die Erhaltung der Kraft* ed. Wilhelm Ostwald (Leipzig: Engelmann, 1889), p. 53.

20. For Kirchhoff's views, see Boltzmann, *Theoretical Physics and Philosophical Problems*, pp. 16 and 104, and Boltzmann, "Gustav Robert Kirchhoff," in *Populäre Schriften* (Leipzig: Barth, 1905), pp. 70–71.

21. Mandelbaum, *History, Man, and Reason*, pp. 13–16.

22. The following is a very truncated account of how Mach's position developed; for a more thorough discussion, see my *History, Man, and Reason*, pp. 304–10.

23. There are frequent discussions of the nature of laws in Mach's *Science of Mechanics* (1883), but for the fullest discussion of how the methods of science contribute to the economy of thought, see "The Economical Nature of Physical Inquiry" (1882), in his *Popular Scientific Lectures* (Chicago: Open Court, 1894).

24. In *Vorträge und Erinnerungen* (Stuttgart: Hirzel, 1949), Max Planck recalled the controversy over a realistic interpretation of atoms and noted the overwhelming influence of Ostwald, Helm, and Mach against which

Boltzmann's views had to contend. (Cited by E. Broda in his "Philosophical Biography of L. Boltzmann," in *The Boltzmann Equation, Acta Physics Austriaca,* Supp. 10 [1973], p. 19.)

25. Boltzmann, "On the Development of the Methods of Theoretical Physics in Recent Times" (1899), in *Theoretical Physics and Philosophical Problems,* pp. 90–91.

26. Boltzmann, "On the Indispensability of Atomism in Natural Science," ibid., p. 50.

27. Boltzmann, "The Second Law of Thermodynamics," (ibid., p. 17.

28. Boltzmann, "On the Indispensibility of Atomism," ibid., p. 49.

29. Quoted by G. B. Halsted, Poincaré's translator, in his preface to Poincaré's *Science and Hypothesis* (New York: Science Press, 1905).

30. Jules Henri Poincaré, *Science and Method,* trans. Francis Maitland (London and New York: Nelson, 1914), ch. 1, "The Choice of Facts."

31. It was on this basis that Poincaré rejected the extreme subjectivity, or "nominalism," which he attributed to the conventionalism of Le Roy. See Poincaré, *The Value of Science,* trans. G. B. Halsted (New York: Science Press, 1907), ch. 10, "Is Science Artificial?" and ch. 11, sec. 6, "Objectivity of Science."

32. In his introduction to *Science and Hypothesis* Poincaré says: "Some people have been struck by this character of free convention recognizable in certain fundamental principles of the sciences . . . and have asked themselves if the savant is not the dupe of his own definitions and if the world he thinks he discovers is not simply created by his own caprice. Under those conditions science would be certain, but deprived of significance.

"If this were so science would be powerless. Now every day we see it work under our very eyes. That could not be if it taught us nothing of reality. Still, the things themselves are not what it can reach, as the naive dogmatists think, but only the relations between things. Outside of these relations there is no knowable reality."

33. Cf. Schopenhauer's criticism of science as etiology, as giving us only the relations among things and never the inner nature of things themselves (*The World as Will and Representation,* trans. E.F.J. Payne [New York: Dover, 1958], esp. vol 1, bk. 2, sec. 17, pp. 95–99).

34. Emile Boutroux, *The Contingency of the Laws of Nature,* trans. Fred Rothwell (Chicago and London: Open Court, 1916).

35. *The Philosophy of Jules Lachelier,* translated and introduced by Edward G. Ballard (The Hague: Nijhoff, 1960), p. 56.

36. The influence of Renouvier on James, and the deep admiration James expressed for Bergson, did much to make this tendency in French thought better known in the United States.

37. Dominique Parodi, *La philosophie contemporaine en France* (Paris: Alcan, 1919), pp. 186–87. One may also note the manner in which J. A. Gunn summed up one basic aspect of the same period in his *Modern French Philosophy* (London: Unwin, 1922): he said, "Belief in creativeness and spontaneity replace the older belief in determinism" (p. 133). These two characterizations are not, of course, in any way contradictory, and both are true.

## 5. Determinism & Choice

1. I am pleased to note that in 1985, Rogers Albritton's presidential address to the Pacific Division of the American Philosophical Association (*Proceedings and Addresses* 59, no. 2: 239–51) was entitled "Freedom of Will and Freedom of Action," and that in it he showed that many recent analytic philosophers, with whose work he is in many ways sympathetic, have mistakenly confused these distinct problems. He held, however, that through separating the problems he was able to defend the doctrine that man's will is free. As I shall suggest, this does not follow.

I have previously published two articles which utilize this distinction, and which discuss the determinants of choice. They are "The Determinants of Choice," in *Philosophy Research Archives* 11 (1986): 355–78, and "Determinism and Moral Responsibility," in *Ethics* (1960): 204–19. The present discussion is in line with both, but it treats the historical and psychological aspects of the issue in less detail.

2. The usual dictionary definition of *libertarian* refers to those who uphold the doctrine of free will. But what does this mean? Given the ambiguities besetting variant uses of concepts such as "to cause" or "to determine," it is extraordinarily difficult to characterize what a purely libertarian position would be. I should say that, in the first place, the position presupposes that human choices depend upon some activity of the mind that cannot be attributed to any present bodily states nor be accounted for in terms of any antecedent bodily conditions. It also presupposes that—as Descartes and others have held—it is meaningful to speak of "the will" as an activity of the mind distinct from "the understanding." Finally, it holds that *what* "the will" wills is not in all cases due to past experiences, nor to constraints placed upon it either by the individual's understanding or by the nature of his total character. This final proviso rules out a number of positions that have often been taken to be examples of libertarianism rather than being special forms of determinism. For example, it rules out the Socratic position that to know the good is to choose the good, and the self-determinist position that choice is determined by one's whole self. On the other hand, on most interpretations of Aristotle, Clarke, and Reid, they can presumably be classified as libertarians, and the libertarian position has been defended in a number of ways by some contemporary philosophers, such as J. R. Lucas, C. A. Campbell, Roderick Chisholm, and Karl Popper.

3. Hobbes, *Leviathan*, pt. 2, ch. 21 (*English Works*, Molesworth ed., 3:197–98). Cf. the following passage from *Concerning Body*, ch. 25, sec. 13: "Such a liberty as is free from necessity is not to be found in the will of either men or beasts. But if by liberty we understand the faculty or power, not of willing, but of doing what we will, then certainly liberty is to be allowed to both."

4. In *Liberty, Necessity, and Chance*, contraverting the position of Bishop Bramhall, Hobbes points out that in this respect "horses, dogs, and other beasts" may be said to deliberate in the same sense as do men, for they too "do demur oftentimes upon the way they are to take: the horse retiring from some strange figure he sees, and coming on again to avoid the spur. And

what else doth man that deliberateth, but one while proceed toward action, another while retire from it, as the hope of greater good draws him, or the fear of greater evil drives him?" (Animadversions no. 8 [*English Works*, Molesworth ed.] 5:80).

5. *Concerning Body*, ch. 25, sec. 13. Cf. *Tripos I: Human Nature*, ch. 12, sec. 2, and *Tripos III: Liberty and Necessity (English Works*, Molesworth ed., 4:68 and 275). Also, *Leviathan*, pt. 1, sec. 6 (ibid., 3:48–49).

6. Hume, *Enquiry Concerning Human Understanding*, sec. 8, pt. 1 (Selby-Bigge ed., p. 95).

7. Hume, *Treatise of Human Nature*, bk. 2, pt. 3, 9 (Selby-Bigge ed., pp. 439 [quotation] and 438 [on pleasure and pain in relation to good and evil]). Hume's *Dissertation on the Passions (Philosophical Works*, Green and Grose ed. [London, 1882], vol. 4) opens by laying down the same basic principles.

8. Hume, *Treatise*, bk. 2, pt. 3, sec. 4 (Selby-Bigge ed., p. 419).

9. For this terminology, see ibid., sec. 3 (Selby-Bigge ed., p. 148). In other places Hume uses such equivalent terms as "the temper and disposition of a person."

10. Helvétius, Hartley, and Priestly—the other major associationists of the period—also offered deterministic accounts of choice in terms of association of ideas, but their accounts, like the account of Hobbes, were greatly simplified as compared with that of Hume.

11. Descartes phrases this distinction as one between those volitions which "terminate in the soul itself" and those which "terminate in our bodies" (*Passions of the Soul*, pt. 1, art. 18).

12. Norman Kemp Smith, *New Studies in the Philosophy of Descartes* (London: Macmillan, 1952), p. 262. Also, cf. section 6 of Descartes's Reply to the Sixth Set of Objections (*Philosophical Works*, Haldane and Ross ed. [Cambridge: Cambridge University Press, 1934], 2:248).

Furthermore, Kemp Smith points out that Descartes repeatedly insisted that the relation between the Will and the Understanding is different insofar as God and man are concerned: God's will is not bound by his understanding, whereas man's is (*New Studies*, pp. 268–69 and 169). In the same connection, Kemp Smith quotes at length from Descartes's Reply to the Sixth Set of Objections, cited above.

13. If it be assumed that Hobbes, too, attributed this control over action to man's cognitive faculty, it would be difficult to explain such passages as those cited in note 4, above, in which he compares human deliberation with the responses of "horses, dogs, and other beasts."

14. Mill, *Utilitarianism*, in *Collected Works*, ed. John M. Robson et al. (Toronto: University of Toronto Press, 1963–), 8:840; italics in the last sentence added.

15. Mill, *System of Logic*, in *Collected Works*, 9:463.

16. For a discussion of Mill's psychology, see my essay, "On Interpreting Mill's *Utilitarianism*," in *Philosophy, History, and the Sciences*, pp. 259–71.

17. Thomas H. Green, *Prolegomena to Ethics*, ed. by A. C. Bradley (Oxford, 1883), sec. 85, p. 97. In this characterization of man's basic motivation it is obvious that Green's theory, like Darwin's, starts from antihedonistic premises.

18. For a further elucidation of Green's position, see his essay "On the Different Senses of 'Freedom' as Applied to Will and to the Moral Progress of Man," in *Works of T. H. Green*, ed. R. L. Nettleship, 3 vols (London, 1885–88), 2:308–33.

19. This is identical with what Mill sought to establish.

20. *Early Works of John Dewey*, ed. Jo Ann Boydston, 4 vols. (Carbondale: Southern Illinois University Press, 1967–72), 4:341–42. In the following section, entitled "Determinist and Indeterminist Theories" (pp. 344–49), Dewey holds that once the dualism between self and motive is overcome, the whole controversy between the Free-Willist and the "Predeterminist" vanishes. Their futile arguments, he holds, rested on the fact that both accepted the same faulty psychological anaylsis, according to which the question was one between "mechanical causation on one side, and arbitrary interference on the other, forgetting that *both* alternatives arise from the unexamined assumption of the dualism of self and ideal and ideal and motive." (p. 349).

21. In this respect, as we shall see, James's theory of the will differed radically from Dewey's views. In fact, Dewey, in the essay "The Ego as Cause," was highly critical of James. (Cf. *Early Works*, 4:93, on "attention," as well as the footnotes appended to pp. 93 and 95.)

22. All citations to James are to the now standard edition, *Works of William James*, ed. Frederick Burkhardt et al. (Cambridge: Harvard University Press, 1976–). James's discussion of the five types is to be found in *Principles of Psychology*, 2:1138–42, and in *Psychology: Briefer Course*, pp. 370–73.

23. Cf. *Principles*, 2:1169–70; *Talks to Teachers on Psychology*, p. 110; and *Psychology: Briefer Course*, pp. 388–89.

24. In fact, in one passage James claimed that the basic characteristic of a moral action "consists in the effort of attention by which we hold fast to an idea which but for that effort of attention would be driven out of the mind by the other psychological tendencies that are there" (*Talks to Teachers*, pp. 109–10). For his use of the phrase "the dead heave of the will," see *Principles*, 2:1141.

James's view presupposed his further belief that "thinking exists as a special kind of immaterial process alongside the material processes of the world," a belief to which he firmly adhered (*Principles*, 2:1174–75; cf. 1:141–45 and 2:1185–86).

25. Cf. the section entitled "Is Voluntary Attention a Resultant or a Force?" in the chapter "Attention," *Principles*, 1:423–30 (esp. pp. 424 and 428–30), and the section entitled "The Question of 'Free-Will,'" in the chapter "Will," *Principles*, 2:1173–82. Also, *Talks to Teachers*, pp. 111–12.

26. See *Principles*, 2:1143 for a fuller statement of the same point.

27. Butler's argument that it is natural for men to view actions as being worthy of praise or blame or, as he put it, of "being of good or ill dessert" is worthy of quotation. In his second Dissertation, "Of the Nature of Virtue," he said: "That we have this moral approving and disapproving faculty, is certain from our experiencing it in ourselves, and recognizing it in each other. It appears from our exercising it unavoidably, in the approbation and disapprobation even of feigned characters . . . from our natural sense of gratitude,

which implies a distinction between merely being the instrument of good, and intending it: from the like distinction, every one makes, between injury and mere harm, which Hobbes says, is peculiar to mankind; and between injury and just punishment" (in L. A. Selby-Bigge, *British Moralists* [Oxford: Clarendon Press, 1897], 1:245–46).

28. Although this type of criticism had originally been most often used by those interested in the philosophy of religion, it more recently became fairly widely accepted among philosophers who adopt an ordinary-language approach to analytic philosophy.

29. For example, in my *Anatomy of Historical Knowledge* (Baltimore: Johns Hopkins University Press, 1977), chs. 3 and 4, and apps. A and B.

30. For example, once rats have learned to run a particular type of maze, they can no longer be used as a source of information concerning the ways in which rats learn to run similar mazes: they are now, in a sense, different subjects, having been changed by their earlier experiences. Moreover, there are cases in which rats respond differently to what is objectively the same stimulus when it is placed in a different context. For example, in one experiment when rats were conditioned to respond positively to a horizontal row of dots, rather than to a vertical one, they then responded positively to horizontal lines, rather than to the same horizontal rows of dots to which they had formerly been conditioned. (Similarly, when trained to respond to a vertical row of dots, rather than to a horizontal row, they responded positively to vertical *lines*, rather than to the vertical rows of dots to which they had been conditioned.) See the findings of I. Krechevsky in his experiments on one group of rats (Group I) in "An Experimental Investigation of the Principle of Proximity in the Visual Perception of the Rat," *Journal of Experimental Psychology* 22 (1938): 497–523. While this paper shows that under other conditions (used for Group II), the visual perception of rats depends upon factors other than proximity, the point I here wish to make is clearly exemplified in Krechevsky's summary of Group I behavior (pp. 516–17) and in his concluding statement, item 2 on p. 521. In this part of Krechevsky's experiment, it was "horizontality" (or "verticality"), and not a specific horizontal (or vertical) pattern with which the rats were already familiar, that served as the effective stimulus in the situation. In such cases, the rat is responding to a general characteristic which can be exemplified in more than one specific situation, and learning is "transferred" rather than being tied to specific past experiences. This obviously obtains—and to a higher degree—in humans as compared with animal learning. Cf., for example, Max Wertheimer's analyses in *Productive Thinking* (New York: Harper's, 1945), and George Katona, *Organizing and Memorizing* (New York: Columbia University Press, 1939).

31. In my former analysis of the sense of moral obligation in *The Phenomenology of Moral Experience* (Glencoe: Free Press, 1955; rpt. Baltimore: Johns Hopkins University Press, 1969) I used the concept of "fittingness"—an important concept in earlier British moral theory—in my analysis of our moral experience. At the time, however, I somewhat overstressed analogies to aesthetic fittingness and to other forms of perceptual experience as investigated by Gestalt psychologists; I failed to stress the role of our self-images in guiding our conduct. That is an omission I now regret.

32. It is possible to offer differing conceptualizations of the mode in which the past is present and affects our choices. For example, one might speak of the unconscious or of neurophysiological traces left by past experience. In any case my contention would still hold: that if the past has an effect on the present, this effect can be exercised only indirectly, through the way in which it has modified our minds, our bodies, or our characters. It will not directly determine what we now do.

33. To forget this is to commit what I have elsewhere called the "self-excepting fallacy" (cf. *Philosophy, History, and the Sciences*, pp. 60–63).

34. In *The Phenomenology of Moral Experience;* also, cf. note 31, above.

35. As James pointed out in "The Will to Believe," if we have a choice forced upon us and we wish to avoid choosing either alternative, we can refrain from taking any action, but that, too, would constitute a choice. In this case we would be setting ourselves against taking any action.

36. For example, Dewey said: "The deed cannot be distinguished as act in contrast with mere getting ready to act. The whole process of working out ends, of selecting means, of estimating moral values, of recognizing duty, is . . . one of activity at every point; it is dynamic and propulsive throughout. The deed is simply this activity focused, brought to a head" (*Early Works,* 4:337).

## 6. Necessity, Chance & Choice in Human Affairs

1. In particular, see my *Anatomy of Historical Knowledge*, pp. 97–108 and app. B; or, more briefly, my "Historical Explanation: The Problem of Covering Laws," *History and Theory* 1 (1961): 229–42.

2. Cf. my discussion of Hempel's view in the article on historical explanation cited in the preceding note.

3. I first discussed this topic in the third section of my paper entitled "Psychology and Societal Facts" (*Philosophy, History, and the Sciences*, pp. 206–9). There, I developed my thesis in the context of discussing the autonomy of sociological categories with respect to psychological concepts; in the present context I shall take the autonomy of sociological categories for granted, confining myself to the question of the compatibility or incompatibility of different social institutions.

4. Cf. the second section of the paper cited above (ibid., pp. 200–206). There I argued that institutions exist as "representations" defining codified forms of behavior that individuals are expected to acknowledge and respect. "Representations," however, are not to be identified with the individuals who hold them in mind, any more than the proposition "Seven plus five equals twelve" is to be identified with the boy whose teacher has taught him to add and subtract.

5. That not all institutional forms and all facets of human culture are mutually compatible is a point explicitly recognized by Simon Kuznets in the opening paragraph of his Nobel Prize lecture, "Modern Economic Growth: Findings and Reflections" (*Les Prix Nobel en 1971* [The Nobel Foundation, 1972]). In illustrating this point he said: "Steam and electric power and the large-scale plants needed to exploit them are not compatible with family

enterprise, illiteracy, or slavery—all of which prevailed in earlier times over much of even the developed world, and had to be replaced by more appropriate institutions and social views. Nor is modern technology compatible with the rural mode of life, the large and extended family pattern, and veneration of undisturbed nature" (p. 313).

Although there is no general agreement as to how the terms *institutions, culture,* and *society* are to be used, I find it useful to draw a distinction between the institutions that structure a society and the socially acquired skills and habits which constitute the culture of a group of individuals (see *Anatomy of Historical Knowledge,* pp. 11–12). As the quotation from Kuznets suggests, the question of mutual compatibility applies both to institutions and to aspects of culture, as well as to the relations between them. It is to be noted that, contrary to some uses, *culture* and *society* are not to be indentified: within a society there often are many cultural subgroups, and various aspects of culture, such as language, technology, or art forms, may spread from society to society, even though the societies having these cultural elements in common remain distinct.

6. While this is consistent with a Freudian interpretation of what constitute the basic needs of individuals, it need not be interpreted in Freudian terms: it could be true even if the needs of individuals are far more varied than Freud took them to be. Furthermore, the concept of "repression," in Freud's sense of that term, need not here be brought into play.

7. For a defense of this thesis, see my *Anatomy of Historical Knowledge,* ch. 4.

8. For a fuller discussion of the retrospective fallacy, see my *History, Man, and Reason,* pp. 134–36.

9. Precisely the same situation obtains in natural history: ecological explanations need to appeal to geographical as well as biological factors, and neither of these is to be explained in terms of the other. Furthermore, as Peirce insisted and as developments in evolutionary theory have shown, a statistical interpretation of chance is an essential element in a Darwinian theory of the origin of new varieties and species.

10. See, for example, the theories of Helvétius and of T. H. Green as discussed above, in Chapters 2 and 5, respectively.

11. McDougall's instinctivist social psychology represents one example of such a theory, and it was on the basis of a parallel assumption that Malinowski attempted to explain the basic structures of society (see Chapter 3, above).

12. B. F. Skinner's behaviorism is, at present, the best-known example of such a theory, but there have been others, such as the attempt to explain all behavior in terms of the concept of "tension reduction."

13. Henry Sidgwick, *Methods of Ethics,* 4th ed. (London: Macmillan, 1890), pp. 49–50 and 136. Cf. Francis Hutcheson's earlier discussion of this point in his posthumous *System of Moral Philosophy* (London: Millar, 1755), bk. 1, ch. 3, sec. 2.

14. For this distinction, see *Encyclopedia of Philosophy,* ed. Paul Edwards (New York: Macmillan and Free Press, 1967), 2:367.

15. Mill insisted that we do not always act for future pleasures or the

avoidance of future pains; rather, we always act in accordance with the degree of *pleasantness or unpleasantness of a present idea.* On this aspect of Mill's psychology, see my discussions in *History, Man, and Reason,* p. 195 (including n. 10), and in "On Interpreting Mill's *Utilitarianism,*" in *Philosophy, History and the Sciences,* pp. 261–63.

16. See *Descent of Man,* ch. 4.

17. It is also worth noting that this conditioned response did not continue indefinitely, but after a time had to be reactivated by having food accompany the sound of the bell.

18. For a defense of the traditional view, see my *Phenomenology of Moral Experience,* pp. 245–57, where I discuss "the principle of the primacy of the facts" in moral judgment.

19. With reference to Hume's theory, see Chapters 1 and 2, above.

# Index

Designed by Martha Farlow.

Composed by the Composing Room of Michigan, Inc., in Trump Medieval.

Printed by BookCrafters, Inc., on 50-lb. Glatfelter Booktext Natural and bound in Holliston Roxite A cloth.